AF538966

Jainism : Philosophy and Culture

Jainism : Philosophy and Culture

Edited by

RATAN SINGH

GLOBAL PUBLICATIONS
NEW DELHI-110 002 (INDIA)

GLOBAL PUBLICATIONS
4378/4B, G-4 JMD House
Murari Lal Street, Ansari Road
Daryaganj, New Delhi - 110 002
Phone : 23278062 (Off.)
e-mail : omega_publications@yahoo.com

Head Office :
79/23, Laxmi Garden
Near Satya Jyoti School,
Gurgaon (Haryana)
Mob : 9213562438

Jainism : Philosophy and Culture

First Published : 2011

ISBN : 978-93-80833-20-0

PRINTED IN INDIA

Published by Ishwari Prasad Garg for Global Publications, New Delhi-110002 and Printed at Suman Printers, Delhi

Preface

Jainism encourages spiritual development through cultivation of one's own personal wisdom and reliance on self-control (*vrata*). Right perception, Right knowledge and Right conduct (triple gems of Jainism) provide the path for attaining liberation (moksha) from the cycles of birth and death (samsara). Moksha is attained by liberation from all karma. Those who have attained moksha are called *siddha* (liberated souls), and those who are attached to the world through their karma are called *samsarin* (mundane souls). Every soul has to follow the path, as explained by the Jinas and revived by Tirthankaras, to attain the complete liberation.

Jains hold that the Universe and its laws of nature are eternal, without beginning or end. However, the universe constantly undergoes cyclical changes. The universe is occupied by both living beings ("Jiva") and non-living objects ("Ajîva"). The samsarin (worldly or mundane) soul incarnates in various life forms during its journey over time. Human, sub-human (animal, insect, plant, etc.), super-human (heavenly being), and hell-being are the four macro forms of the samsari souls. All worldly relations of one's soul with other souls and non-living objects and the thoughts, expressions and actions give rise to accumulation of karma in the past and present. And these in turn feedback to determine our current circumstances that are both rewarding and punishing. Jain scholars have explained in depth on techniques that will clear the past karmas accumulated as well as stopping the influx of fresh karmas.

The major topics dealt in this book are : *Jainism - Basic Facts; Ahimsa in Jainism; Vegetarianism and Jain Theory; Anekantavada; Jain Cosmology; Types of Karma; Causes of Karma; Jain Rituals and Festivals; Jain Meditation; Jain Philosophy; Buddhism, Jainism and Other Religion; Christianity and Islam; Legal Status of Jainism; etc.*

No doubt, these will serve the purpose of trainees and trainers, professional and policy planners in the field. Since the sources of information are all secondary, we express our gratitude to the scholars whose works are cited or substantially made use of. We are thankful to all those who rendered ready help and cooperation while working on this project.

We express our gratitude to various scholars, teachers and friends for their assistance and guidance. Finally, we thank our publishers for bringing out this book in very limited time.

—Editor

Contents

1
Jainism — Basic Facts

Jainism is an ancient religion of India that prescribes a path of non-violence towards all living beings. Its philosophy and practice rely mainly on self-effort to progress the soul up the spiritual ladder to divine consciousness. Any soul that has conquered its own inner enemies and achieved the state of supreme being is called 'Jina' (Conqueror or Victor).

Jainism is also referred to as *Shraman (self-reliant) Dharma* or the religion of Nirgantha (who does not have attachments and aversions).

Jainism was revived by a lineage of 24 enlightened ascetic leaders called Tirthankaras culminating with Parshva (9th century BC) and Mahavira (6th century BC). In the modern world, it is a small but influential religious minority with as many as 4.2 million followers in India, and successful growing immigrant communities in North America, Western Europe, the Far East, Australia and elsewhere.

Jains successfully sustained this ancient religion to this era and have significantly influenced and contributed to ethical, political and economic spheres in India. Jains have an ancient tradition of scholarship and have the highest degree of literacy in India; Jain libraries are the oldest in the country. Tamil Jains and Kannada/Tulu Jains who are native to their region residing in places Tamil Nadu, Karnataka and some parts of Kerala respectively early since 1st century BC are distinguishable in some of their routines and practices from North Indian Jains, but the core philosophies and belief systems are the same for both cultures.

Core Beliefs

- Every living being has a soul.
- Every soul is potentially divine, with innate qualities of infinite knowledge, perception, power, and bliss (masked by its karmas).
- Therefore, regard every living being as yourself, harming no one and be kind to all living beings.
- When a soul is freed from karmas, it becomes free and attains divine consciousness, experiencing infinite knowledge, perception, power, and bliss.
- Every soul is born as a celestial, human, sub-human or hellish being according to its own karmas.
- Every soul is the architect of its own life, here or hereafter.
- Right Faith, Right Knowledge and Right Conduct (triple gems of Jainism) provide the way to this realization. There is no supreme divine creator, owner, preserver or destroyer. The universe is self-regulated and every soul has the potential to achieve divine consciousness (siddha) through its own efforts.
- Non-violence (to be in soul consciousness rather than body consciousness) is the foundation of right view, the condition of right Knowledge and the kernel of right Conduct. It leads to a state of being unattached to worldly things and being nonjudgmental and non-violent; this includes compassion and forgiveness in thoughts, words and actions toward all living beings and respecting views of others (non-absolutism).
- Navakar Mantra is the fundamental prayer in Jainism and can be recited at any time of the day. Praying by reciting this mantra, the devotee bows with respect to liberated souls still in human form (Arihantas),

fully liberated souls (Siddhas), spiritual leaders (Acharyas), teachers (Upadyayas) and all the monks(sarva sadhus). By saluting them as namo namaha, Jains receive inspiration from them to follow their path to achieve true bliss and total freedom from the karmas binding their souls. In this main prayer, Jains do not ask for any favours or material benefits. This mantra serves as a simple gesture of deep respect towards beings who are more spiritually advanced. The mantra also reminds followers of the ultimate goal of reaching nirvana or moksha.

- Jainism stresses on the importance of controlling the senses including the mind, as they can drag one far away from true nature of the soul.
- Enjoy the company of the holy and better qualified, be merciful to those afflicted souls and tolerate the perversely inclined.
- Limit possessions and lead a pure life that is useful to yourself and others. Owning an object by itself is not possessiveness; however attachment to an object is. Non-possessiveness is the balancing of needs and desires while staying detached from our possessions.
- Four things are difficult for a soul to attain: 1. human birth, 2. knowledge of the laws governing the souls, 3. absolute conviction in the philosophy of non-violence and 4. practicing it in every day life activities.
- It is important not to waste human life in evil ways. Rather, strive to rise on the ladder of spiritual evolution.
- Jains worship the icons of Jinas, Arihants and Tirthankars, who have conquered the inner passions and attained divine consciousness, and study the scriptures of these liberated beings.

- The goal of Jainism is liberation of the soul from the negative effects of unenlightened thoughts, speech and action. This goal is achieved through clearance of karmic obstructions by following the triple gems of Jainism.

Principles and Other Beliefs

Sculpture representing two founders of Jainism: left, Rishabha first of the 24 tirthankara, a legendary personality, unconfirmed history; right Mahavir, the last of those 24, who consolidated and reformed the religious and philosophical system. Position of the characters is typical in Jain iconography. Body idealized, almost devoid of detail reveals the effect of yoga exercises, immobility and rigidity suggests his "revocation of flesh" (Kayotsarga) the materiality

Jainism regards every living soul as potentially divine. The goal of Jainism is to realize the soul's true nature. When the soul sheds its karmic bonds completely, it attains divine consciousness. Jainism prescribes a path of non-violence to progress the soul to this ultimate goal.

Jains believe that to attain enlightenment and ultimately liberation, one must practice the following ethical principles (vows) in thought, speech and action. The degree to which these principles are practiced is different for householder and monks. Thus:

- **Non-violence** (Ahimsa) - to cause no harm to living beings. This is the fundamental vow from which all other vows stem. It involves minimizing intentional and unintentional harm to any other living creature. "Non-violence", is sometimes interpreted as not killing, but the concept goes far beyond that. It includes not harming or insulting other living beings, either directly, or indirectly through others. There can be even no room for thought to injure others, and no speech that influences others to inflict harm. It also includes respecting the views of others (non-absolutism and acceptance of multiple views).

- **Truthfulness** (Satya) - to always speak the truth in a harmless manner. A person who speaks the truth becomes trustworthy like a mother, venerable like a preceptor and dear to everyone like a kinsman. Given that non-violence has priority, all other principles yield to it, whenever there is a conflict. For example, if speaking truth will lead to violence, it is perfectly ethical to be silent. Thiruvalluvar in his Tamil classic Thirukural devotes an entire chapter clarifying the definition of 'Truth'.

- **Non-stealing** (Asteya) - to not take anything that is not willingly given. Asteya, "non-stealing", is the strict adherence to one's own possessions, without desire to take another's. One should remain satisfied by whatever is earned through honest labour. Any attempt to squeeze others and/or exploit the weak is considered theft. Some of the guidelines for this principle are:

  (i) Always give people fair value for labour or product.

  (ii) Never take things which are not offered.

  (ii) Never take things that are placed, dropped or forgotten by others

  (iv) Never purchase cheaper things if the price is the result of improper method (e.g. pyramid scheme, illegal business, stolen goods, etc.)

- **Celibacy** (Brahmacarya) - to control the senses including mind from indulgence. Brahmacarya, "monastic celibacy", is the complete abstinence from sex, which is only incumbent upon monastics.

Householders practice monogamy as a way to uphold brahmacarya in spirit.

- **Non-possession** or **Non-materialism** (Aparigraha) - to detach from people, places, and material things. It should be noted ownership of an object itself is not possessiveness; however attachment to an object is possessiveness. Aparigraha, "non-possession", is the renunciation of property and wealth, before initiation into monkhood, without entertaining thoughts of the things renounced. This is done so one understands how to detach oneself from things and possessions, including home and family, so one may reach *moksa*. For householders, non-possession is owning without attachment, because the notion of possession is illusory. The reality of life is that change is constant; thus, objects owned by someone today will be property of someone else in future days. The householder is encouraged to discharge his or her duties to related people and objects as a trustee, without excessive attachment.

Jainism encourages spiritual development through cultivation of one's own personal wisdom and reliance on self-control (*vrata*). Right perception, Right knowledge and Right conduct (triple gems of Jainism) provide the path for attaining liberation (moksha) from the cycles of birth and death (samsara). Moksha is attained by liberation from all karma. Those who have attained moksha are called *siddha* (liberated souls), and those who are attached to the world through their karma are called *samsarin* (mundane souls). Every soul has to follow the path, as explained by the Jinas and revived by Tirthankaras, to attain the complete liberation.

Jains hold that the Universe and its laws of nature are eternal, without beginning or end. However, the universe constantly undergoes cyclical changes. The universe is occupied by both living beings ("Jîva") and non-living objects ("Ajîva"). The samsarin (worldly or mundane) soul incarnates in various life forms during its journey over time. Human, sub-human (animal, insect, plant, etc.), super-human (heavenly being), and hell-being are the four macro forms of the samsari souls. All worldly relations of one's soul with other souls and non-living objects and the thoughts, expressions and actions give rise to accumulation of karma in the past and present. And these in turn feedback to determine our current circumstances that are both rewarding and punishing. Jain scholars have explained in depth on techniques that will clear the past karmas accumulated as well as stopping the influx of fresh karmas.

The main Jain prayer (*navkar Mantra*) therefore salutes the five special categories of souls that have attained divine consciousness or are on their way to achieving it, so as to emulate them and follow their path to salvation.

Another major characteristic of Jain belief is the emphasis on the consequences of not only physical but also mental behaviours.

The principle of non-violence seeks to minimize karmas which may limit the capabilities of the soul. Jainism views every soul as worthy of respect because it has the potential to become Siddha (Param-atma - "highest soul"). Because all living beings possess a soul, great care and awareness is essential in one's actions. Jainism emphasizes the equality of all life, advocating harmlessness towards all, whether the creatures are great or small. This policy extends even to microscopic organisms. Jainism acknowledges that every person has different capabilities and capacities to practice and therefore accepts different level of compliance for ascetics and householders. The "great vows" (mahavrata) are prescribed for monks and "limited vows" (anuvrata) are prescribed for householders.

Emphasis on Non-Violence

Jains hold that this temporal world inflicts much misery and sorrow. In order to attain ever lasting bliss, one must transcend the cycle of transmigration (births and deaths). Most of the souls remain eternally trapped in seemingly never-ending repetitive cycle. The only way to break out of this cycle is to stop the influx of karma through rational perception, rational knowledge and rational conduct.

Jains believe that every human is responsible for his/her actions and all living beings have an eternal soul, *jîva*. All living beings are equal because they all possess the potential of being liberated and attaining moksha. Jains insist that we live, think and act respectfully so as to live in harmony with all forms of life. Compassion for all life, both human and non-human, is central to Jainism. Human life is valued as a unique, as it is the only life form that can attain ultimate liberation. Even heavenly beings have to go through the human life to achieve this goal.

History suggests that various strains of Hinduism became vegetarian due to strong Jain influences.. Jains run animal shelters all over India. For example, Delhi has a bird hospital run by Jains. Jainism's stance on nonviolence goes far beyond vegetarianism. Jains refuse food obtained with unnecessary cruelty. Many practice a lifestyle similar to veganism, due to the violence of modern dairy farms, and others exclude root vegetables from their diets to preserve the lives of these plants, since they are often uprooted during the harvest. Potatoes, garlic and onions in particular are avoided by Jains. Traditionally oriented Jains do not eat, drink, or travel after sunset, and prefer to drink water that is boiled and then cooled to room temperature. The purpose of these practices is to minimise the harm that may otherwise be caused to living organisms inadvertently.

Anekantavada (multiple points of view), is a foundation of Jain philosophy. Jain scholars view both physical objects and abstract ideas from different perspectives systematically. This is the application of non-violence in the sphere of thought. It is a jain philosophical standpoint just as there is the Advaitic standpoint of Sankara and the standpoint of the Middle Path of the Buddhists. This search to view things from different angles, leads to understanding and toleration of different and even conflicting views. When this happens prejuidices subside and tendency to accommodate increases. The theory of Anekanta is therefore unique experiment of non-violence at the root..

A derivation of this principle is the doctrine of Syadvada that highlights every model is relative to its view point. It is a matter of our daily experience that the same object which gives pleasure to us under certain circumstances becomes boring under different situations. Nonetheless relative truth is undoubtedly useful as it is a stepping stone to the ultimate realization and understaning of reality. The theory of Syadvada is based on the premise that every proposition is only relatively true. It all depends on the particular aspect from which we approach that proposition. Jains therefore developed logic that encompasses sevenfold predication so as to assist in the construction of proper judgment about any proposition.

Jains are usually very welcoming and friendly toward other faiths and often help with interfaith functions. Several non-Jain temples in India are administered by Jains. A palpable presence in Indian culture, Jains have contributed to Indian philosophy, art, architecture, science, and to Mohandas Gandhi's politics, which led to the mainly non-violent movement for Indian independence.. Though Mohandas Gandhi states clearly in his Autobiography that his mother was a Vaishnava, Jain monks visited his home regularly. He spent considerable time under the tutelage of Jain monks, learning the philosophies of non-violence and doing good always.

Tirthankaras

Jains believe that knowledge of the true living (*dharma*) has declined and revived cyclically throughout history. Those who rediscover and preach dharma are called *Tirthankara*. The literal meaning of *Tirthankar* is 'ford-builder'. Jains compare the process of becoming a pure soul to crossing a swift river, an endeavour requiring patience and care. A ford-builder has already crossed the river and can therefore guide others.

The purpose of life is to undo the negative effects of karma through mental and physical purification. This process leads to liberation accompanied by a great natural inner peace. A soul is called a 'victor' (in Sanskrit/Pali language, *Jina*) because one has achieved liberation by one's own efforts. A *Jain* is a follower of *Jinas* ("conquerors"). Jinas are spiritually advanced human beings who rediscovered the *dharma*, become fully liberated from the bondages of karma by conquering attachments and aversions, and teach the spiritual path to benefit all living beings. Jains follow the teachings of 24 special jinas who are known as *Tirthankars* ("those who have shown the way to salvation from the river of births and deaths"). Jaina tradition identifies Rishabh (also known as Adhinath) as the First Tirthankar of this declining (avasarpini) time cycle (kalachakra). The 24th, and last *Tirthankar* is Mahavir, lived from 599 to 527 BC. The 23rd Tirthankar, Parsva, lived from 872 to 772 BC. The last two Tirthankaras: Parsva and Mahavira are historical figures whose existence is recorded

The 24 Tirthankaras in chronological order are: Adinath (Rishabhnath), Ajitnath, Sambhavanath, Abhinandan Swami, Sumatinath, Padmaprabhu, Suparshvanath, Chandraprabhu, Pushpadanta (Suvidhinath), Sheetalnath, Shreyansanath, Vasupujya Swami, Vimalnath, Anantnath, Dharmanath,

Shantinath, Kunthunath, Aranath, Mallinath, Munisuvrata Swami, Nami Natha, Neminath, Parshvanath and Mahavir (Vardhamana).

Identified as divine, these individuals are called by title in Hindi *bhagavan* (e.g., Bhagavan Rishabha, Bhagavan Parshva, etc.). Tirthankar are not regarded as deities (heavenly powerful souls that are a few steps ahead of us) in the pantheistic or polytheistic sense, but rather as pure souls that have awakened the divine spiritual qualities which lie dormant within each of us.

It should be noted that only select few souls that reach Arihant status become Thirthankars, who take unique leadership role in assisting the other souls to move up on the spiritual path. Apart from Thirthankars, Jains worship special Arihants such as Gommateshwara or Bahubali. According to Jain Scriptures, Bahubali (also known as Gommateshvara) was the second of the one hundred sons of the first Tirthankara, Lord Rishabha and king of Podanpur. A statue of Lord Bahubali is located at Shravanabelagola in the Hassan district of Karnataka State. Shravanabelagola is a sacred place of pilgrimage for Jains with a splendid statue of monolithic stone on top of a hill. When standing at the statue's feet looking up, one sees the inspiring vision of the saint against the vastness of the sky. The figure is lofty like the sky, and the serenity of the face is unique and incomparable in its beauty. This statue of Gommateshwara Bahubali is carved from a single large stone which is fifty-seven feet high. The giant image was carved in 981 A.D., by order of Chavundaraya, the minister of the Ganga King Rachamalla. Bahubali is another name for Gommateshwara.

Creation and Cosmology

According to Jain beliefs, the universe was never created, nor will it ever cease to exist. Therefore, it is *shaswat* (infinite).

It has no beginning or end, but time is cyclical with progressive and regressive spirituality phases.

Jainism divide time into *Utsarpinis* (Progressive Time Cycle) and *Avsarpinis* (Regressive Time Cycle). An *Utsarpini* and an *Avsarpini* constitute one Time Cycle (*Kalchakra*). Every *Utsarpini* and *Avsarpini* is divided into six unequal periods known as *Aras*. During the *Utsarpini* half cycle, humanity develops from its worst to its best: ethics, progress, happiness, strength, health, and religion each start the cycle at their worst, before eventually completing the cycle at their best and starting the process again. During the *Avsarpini* half-cycle, these notions deteriorate from the best to the worst. Jains believe we are currently in the fifth *Ara* of the *Avsarpini* phase.

During the first and last two *Aras*, the knowledge and practice of dharma lapse among humanity and then reappear through the teachings of enlightened humans, those who have reached liberation from their karma, during the third and fourth Aras. Traditionally, in our universe and in this time cycle, Rishabh is regarded as the first to realize the truth. Mahavira (Vardhamana) was the last (24th) Tirthankara to attain enlightenment (599-527 BC).

According to Jainism, the universe consists of infinite amount of *Jiva* (life force or souls), and infinite amount of Ajiva (lifeless objects). The shape of the Universe as described in Jainism is shown alongside. Please note that unlike the current convention of using North direction as the top of map, this uses South as the top. The pure souls (who reached Siddha status) reside at the very south end of the Universe.

The *Deva Loka* (Heavens) are at the symbolic "chest" of Creation, where all *devas* (souls enjoying the positive karmic effects) reside. Similarly, beneath the "waist" are the *Narka Loka* (Hell). There are seven *Narka Lokas*, each for a varying degree suffering a soul has to go through to face the consequences of its negative karmic effects. From the first to the seventh hell, the degree of suffering increases and light reaching it decreases (with no light in the seventh hell). Human, animal, insect, plant and microscopic life forms reside on the middle.

Jain Monks and Nuns

In India there are several Jain Monks, in categories like Acharya, Upadhyaya and Muni. Trainee ascetics are known as Ailaka and Ksullaka in the Digambar tradition.

There are two categories of ascetics, *Sadhu* (monk) and *Sadhvi* (nun). They practice the five *Mahavratas*, three *Guptis* and five *Samitis*:

Five major vows (Mahavrata)

- **Non-violence** (Ahimsa): Non-violence in thought, word and deed so as not to cause harm to any living beings
- **Truthfulness** (Satya): Truth which is (hita) beneficial, (mita) succinct and (priya) pleasing. In other words, to speak the harmless truth
- **Non-stealing** (Astey): Not to take anything that has not been given to them willingly by the owner
- **Chastity** (Brahmacarya): Absolute purity of mind and body without indulging in sensual pleasure
- **Non-possession** (Aparigraha): Exercise no attachment or aversion to all people, places and material objects around.

Three Restraints (Gupti)

- Control of the mind (Managupti)
- Control of speech (Vacanagupti)
- Control of body (Kayagupti)

Five Carefulness (Samiti)

- Carefulness while walking (Irya Samiti)
- Carefulness while communicating (Bhasha Samiti)
- Carefulness while eating (Eshana Samiti)
- Carefulness while handling their fly-whisks, water gourds, etc. (Adana Nikshepana Samiti)
- Carefulness while disposing of bodily waste matter (Pratishthapana Samiti)

Male Digambara monks do not wear any clothes and are nude. They practice non-attachment to the body and hence, wear no clothes. Shvetambara monks and nuns wear white clothes. Shvetambaras believe that monks and nuns may wear simple un-stitched white clothes as long as they are not attached to them. Jain monks and nuns travel on foot. They do not use mechanical transport.

Digambar followers take up to eleven *Pratimaye* (oath). The Male Digambar monk eat standing at one place in their palms without using any utensil. They eat only once a day.

Jain Festivities

Jain festivals are characterised by both internal and external celebrations. The internal celebration is through praying and expressing devotion to Jinas, practicing meditation, spiritual studies, and renunciation.

- Paryushan is an important festival among the Jain festivals. It happens during late August / September commencing on the twelfth day of the fortnight of the wanning moon cycle and ending in the fourteenth of the fortnight of the waxing moon cycle. This is generally a rainy season in Northern parts of India. During this 18 day period Jain scholars and monks visit temples and explain the Jain philosophy. Jains during this period practice external austerities such as fasting, limiting their normal activities so as to reduce the harm to worms and insects that thrive during this season. At the conclusion of the festivities, a lookback is encouraged, and Pratikraman is done for repentance of faults and forgiveness is given and asked for from all.

- Diwali is celebrated on the new moon day of Kartik, usually in late October or early November on the Gregorian calendar. On the night of that day, Mahavir, the last Thirthankar attained Nirvana or deliverance and attained liberation from the bondage of all karmas. During the night of Diwali, holy hymns are recited and meditation is done on Mahavir. And on the very second day of Diwali they celebrate their New Year.
- Mahavir Jayanti, The birthday of Mahavir, the last Thirthankar is celebrated on the thirteenth day of the fortnight of the waxing moon, in the month of Chaitra. This day occurs in late March or early April on the Gregorian calendar. Lectures are held to preach the path of virtue. People meditate and offer prayers.
- Ashadh Chaturdasi, The sacred commencement of Chaturmas takes place on the 14th day of the fortnight of the waxing moon of Ashad. The Jain monks and nuns remain where they happen to be for four months until the 14th day of Kartik Shukla. During these four months the monks give daily discourses, undertake relgious ceremonies, etc.
- Apart from Mahavir Jayanti and Diwali, South Indian Tamil Jains of Digambara sect also celebrate Tamil New Year, Pongal (harvest festival), Avani Avittam similar to Tamil Hindus.

- Shrutha panchami or Gyan Panchami is on the fifth day of the fortnight of the waxing moon of Kartik (the fifth day after Diwali). This day is devoted for pure knowledge. On this day books preserved in the religious libraries are cleaned and studied.

Karma Theory

Karma in Jainism conveys a totally different meaning than commonly understood in the Hindu philosophy and western civilization. It is not the so called inaccessible force that controls the fate of living beings in inexplicable ways. It does not mean "deed", "work", nor invisible, mystical force (*adrsta*), but a complex of very fine matter, imperceptible to the senses, which interacts with the soul, causing great changes. Karma, then, is something material (*karmapaudgalam*), which produces certain conditions, like a medical pill has many effects. As Robert Zydendos observed, karma in Jainism is a system of laws, but natural rather than moral laws. In Jainism, actions that carry moral significance are considered to cause consequences in just the same way as physical actions that do not carry any moral significance. When one holds an apple in one's hand and then let go of the apple, the apple will fall: this is only natural. There is no judge, and no moral judgment involved, since this is a mechanical consequence of the physical action.

Customs and Practices

The hand with a wheel on the palm symbolizes the Jain Vow of Ahimsa, meaning non-violence. The word in the middle is "Ahimsa." The wheel represents the dharmacakra, to halt the cycle of reincarnation through the pursuit of truth.

Jain monks and nuns practice strict asceticism and strive to make their current birth their last, thus ending their cycle of transmigration. The laity, who pursue less rigorous practices, strive to attain rational perception and to do as much good as possible and get closer to the goal of attaining freedom from the cycle of transmigration. Following strict ethics, the laity usually choose professions that revere and protect life and totally avoid violent livelihoods.

Jains practice *Samayika,* which is a Sanskrit word meaning *equanimity* and derived from *samaya* (the soul). The goal of *samayika* is to attain equanimity. *Samayika* is begun by achieving a balance in time. If this current moment is defined as a moving line between the past and the future, *samayika* happens by being fully aware, alert and conscious in that moving time line when one experiences *atma,* one's true nature, common to all life forms. *Samayika* is especially significant during *Paryushana,* a special period during the monsoon, and is practiced during the *Samvatsari Pratikramana* ritual.

Jains believe that *Devas* (gods or celestial beings) cannot help *jiva* to obtain liberation, which must be achieved by individuals through their own efforts. In fact, devas themselves cannot achieve liberation until they reincarnate as humans and undertake the difficult act of removing karma. Their efforts to attain the exalted state of *siddha,* the permanent liberation of *jiva* from all involvement in worldly existence, must be their own.

The strict Jain ethical code for monks/nuns is:

1. *Ahimsa* (Non-violence)
2. *Satya* (truth)
3. *Achaurya* or *Asteya* (non-stealing)
4. *Brahmacharya* (Celibacy)
5. *Aparigraha* (Non-attachment to materialistic things)

Common men and women also have the five vows of non-violence, truth, non-stealing, celibacy and non-possession.

It is not possible to observe these vows completely in day-to-day life and therefore followed to a limited extent. As these vows are limited in their scope, they are called 'Anuvratas'. Apart from these, additionally there are seven vows designed to assist the householders in their spiritual journey.

Nonviolence includes vegetarianism. Jains are expected to be non-violent in thought, word, and deed, both toward humans and toward all other living beings, including their own selves. Jain monks and nuns walk barefoot and sweep the ground in front of them to avoid killing insects or other tiny beings. Even though all life is considered sacred by the Jains, human life is deemed the highest form of life. For this reason, it is considered vital never to harm or upset any person.

For laypersons, *brahmacharya* means either confining sex to marriage or complete celibacy. For monks and nuns, it means complete celibacy.

While performing holy deeds, Svetambara Jains wear cloths, *muhapatti,* over their mouths and noses to avoid saliva falling on texts or revered images. It is not the case, as is sometimes believed, that this is to avoid accidentally inhaling insects. Many healthy concepts are entwined. For example, Jains drink only boiled water. In ancient times, a person might get ill by drinking unboiled water, which could prevent equanimity, and illness may engender intolerance.

True spirituality, according to enlightened Jains, starts when one attains *Samyak darshana,* or true perception. Such souls are on the path to moksha, striving to remain in the nature of the soul. This is characterized by knowing and observing only all worldly affairs, without *raag* (attachment) and *dwesh* (repulsion), a state of pure knowledge and bliss. Attachment to worldly life collects new karma, and traps one in birth, death, and suffering. Worldly life has a dual nature (for example, love and hate, suffering and pleasure, etc.), for the perception of one state cannot exist without the contrasting perception of the other.

Jain Dharma shares some beliefs with Hinduism. Both believe in karma and reincarnation. However, the Jain version of the Ramayana and Mahabharata is different from Hindu beliefs, for example. Generally, Hindus believe that Rama was a reincarnation of God, whereas Jains believe he attained moksha (liberation)

Along with the Five Vows, Jains avoid harboring ill will and practice forgiveness. They believe that *atma* (soul) can lead one to becoming *parmatma* (liberated soul) and this must come from one's inner self. Jains refrain from all violence (Ahimsa) and recommend that sinful activities be avoided.

Mahatma Gandhi was deeply influenced (particularly through the guidance of Shrimad Rajchandra) by Jain tenets such as peaceful, protective living and honesty, and made them an integral part of his own philosophy. Jainism has a distinct idea underlying Tirthankar worship. The physical form is not worshiped, but their Gunas (virtues, qualities) are praised. Tirthankaras remain role-models, and sects such as the Sthanakavasi stringently reject statue worship.

Jain Fasting

Fasting is a tool for doing *Tapa* and to attach to your inner-being. It is a part of Jain festivals. It is three types based on the level of austerity; *Uttam, Madhyam* and *Jaghanya*; first being the most stringent:

1. Uttam: Renounce all worldly things including food & water on the day of fasting and eat only once on the eve & next day of fasting.
2. Madhyam: water is taken on the day of fast, but not the food.
3. Jaghanya: Eat only particular time on the day.

During fasting a person immerses himself in religious activities (worshiping, serving the saints & be in their proximity, reading scriptures, *Tapa*, and donate to the right candidates - *Supatra*). But before starting the fast Jains take a small vow known as *pachkaan*. A person taking the vow is bound to it and breaking it is considered to be a bad practice.

Most Jains fast at special times, like during festivals (known as *Parva. Paryushana and Ashthanhika* are the main *Parvas* which occurs 3 times in a year), and on holy days (eighth & fourteenth days of the moon cycle). Paryushana is the most prominent festival, lasting eight days for Svetambara Jains and ten days for Digambars, during the monsoon. The monsoon is considered the best time of fasting due to lenient weather. However, a Jain may fast at any time, especially if he/she feels some mistake(negative karma generally known as *paap* has been committed. Variations in fasts encourage Jains to do whatever they can to maintain self control.

A unique ritual in this religion involves a holy fasting until death; it is called *sallekhana*. Through this one achieves a death with dignity and dispassion as well as no more negative karma. When a person is aware of approaching death, and feels that s/he has completed all duties, s/he willingly ceases to eat or drink gradually. This form of dying is also called *Santhara / Samaadhi*. It can be as long as 12 years with gradual reduction in food intake.

Considered extremely spiritual and creditable, with all awareness of the transitory nature of human experience, it has recently led to a controversy. In Rajasthan, a lawyer petitioned the High Court of Rajasthan to declare *santhara* illegal. Jains see *santhara* as spiritual detachment, a declaration that a person has finished with this world and now chooses to leave. This choice however requires a great deal of spiritual accomplishment and maturity as a pre-requisite.

TYPES OF FASTING

1. Aathai: A person practicing this form of fasting, will not eat any thing for eight days. During this period, they live only by drinking previously boiled water (8 hours ago at the maximum). They drink water after going to temple or after prayer that is done after 11'o clock and before sunset. Normally on 8th day of fasting, the success is celebrated by the community by organising a procession to the temple. On the 9th day, the person will stop fasting. The relatives and friends will come and help the person to break the fast.

2. Masskhaman: A person practicing this form of fasting, will not eat any thing for thirty days. During this period, they live by drinking previously boiled water. Normally on 30th day of fasting their successful completion is celebrated.

3. Aorie: In this practice, for 9 days food taken without any one of important additive that provide taste such as Ghee (clarified butter), Spices, Salt, etc.

4. Varshitap: This is difficult form of fasting and demands a high level of skill and discipline. Lord Mahavir did not eat or drink water for 400 days. It is possible for people to try a variation of Varshitap by eating every alternate days, in general. They can eat only twice in every alternate days, but in between during some special calendar events, they may have to fast longer periods.

Jain Worship and Rituals

Every day most Jains bow and say their universal prayer, the "Namokara Mantra", a.k.a. the Navkar Mantra, Parmesthi Mantra, Panch Namaskar Mantra. Jains have built temples, or *Basadi* or *Derasar*, where idols of tirthankaras are revered.

Rituals may be elaborate because symbolic objects are offered and Tirthankaras praised in song. But some sects refuse to enter temples or revere images. All Jains accept that images of Tirthankaras are merely symbolic reminders of their paths to attain moksha. Jains are clear that the Jinas reside in moksha and are completely detached from the world.

Jain rituals include:

- *Panch-kalyanak Pratishtha,* Installation with five auspicious events.
- *Pratikramana,* Repentance of sins.
- *Samayika,* Meditation
- Guru Vandana, *Chaitya Vandana,* and other sutras to honor ascetics.

Over time, some sections of Jains also pray deities, which are yakshas and yakshinis.

Jain Cuisine

Jains practice a unique concept of restricted vegetarianism. They do not consume root vegetables such as potatoes, garlic, onions, carrots, radishes, cassava, sweet potatoes, turnips, etc. However, they consume rhizomes such as dried turmeric and dried ginger. The reason behind this restricted diet is that vegetables grown underground or *kundmul* are believed to contain far more bacteria, and thus life, than other vegetables. Brinjals are also not consumed by some Jains owing to the large number of seeds in the vegetable, as a seed is taken to be a form of life. Strict Jains do not consume food which has been left overnight, such as yogurt which may have been set overnight, and have their meals before sunset because large amounts of bacteria grow overnight when there is no ultraviolet light from the sun to kill them. Most Jain recipes substitute potato with Plantain.

Geographical Spread and Influence

Jainism has been a major cultural, philosophical, social and political force since the dawn of civilization in Asia, and its ancient influence has been noted in other religions, including Buddhism and Hinduism.

Arvind Sharma notes: "Contribution of Jainism to Indian heritage is more significant than what might be expected from its numerical strength. One is tempted to say that in this respect, Jainism has been for Indian civilisation, what Judaism has been for western civilisation."

This pervasive influence of Jain culture and philosophy in ancient Bihar may have given rise to Buddhism. The Buddhists have always maintained that during the time of Buddha and Mahavira (who, according to the Pali canon, were contemporaries), Jainism was already an ancient, deeply entrenched faith and culture there. (For connections between Buddhism and Jainism see Buddhism and Jainism). Over several thousand years, Jain influence on Hindu philosophy and religion has been considerable, while Hindu influence on Jain rituals may be observed in certain Jain sects. Certain Vedic Hindu holy books contain beautiful narrations about various Jain Tirthankaras (e.g., Lord Rushabdev). There have been no wars fought in the name of Jainism.

For instance, the concept of *puja* is Jain. The Vedic Religion prescribed *yajnas* and *havanas* for pleasing the gods. *Puja* is a specifically Jain concept, arising from the Dravidian words, "pu" (flower) and "ja" (offering).

With 10 to 12 million followers, Jainism is among the smallest of the major world religions, but in India its influence is much greater than these numbers would suggest. Jains live throughout India. Maharashtra, Rajasthan and Gujarat have the largest Jain populations among Indian states. Karnataka, Bundelkhand and Madhya Pradesh have relatively large Jain populations. There is a large following in Punjab, especially in Ludhiana and Patiala, and there used to be many Jains in Lahore (Punjab's historic capital) and other cities before the Partition of 1947, after which many fled to India. There are many Jain communities in different parts of India and around the world. They may speak local languages or follow different rituals but essentially follow the same principles.

Jains has a significance presence in the Southern Indian State of Karnataka from a long time. The holy Moodabidre,famously renouned as 'Southern Kashi' has 1000 pillar temple. Shravanabelagola has world famous monolithic statue of **Lord Bahubali**. Similar Monolithic statues of Lord Bahubali can be also seen in Venur, Dharmasthala,Karkala and Mysoreas well. In all of the above mentioned places, holy festival of **Mahamastakabhisheka** will be held every 12 years once where in the statue of the lord will be worshiped and bathed in Holy water, Milk, Turmeric and other natural herbs which has its own significant importance.

Outside India, the United States, United Kingdom, Canada and East Africa (Kenya, Tanzania and Uganda) have large Jain communities. The first Jain temple to be built outside India was constructed and consecrated in the 1960s in Mombasa, Kenya, although Jainism in the West mostly came about after the Oshwal and Jain diaspora spread to the West in the late 1970s and 1980s. Jainism is presently a strong faith in the United States and several dozen Jain temples have been built there. American Jainism accommodates all the sects. Smaller Jain communities exist in Nepal, South Africa, Japan, Singapore, Malaysia, Australia, Fiji, and Suriname. In Belgium the very successful Indian diamond community, almost all of whom are Jain, are also establishing a temple to strengthen Jain values in and across Western Europe.

Denominations

Jain *sangha* is divided into two major sects, Digambar and Svetambar, about 200 years after Mahâvîra's nirvana.

Some historians believe there was no clear division until the 5th century. S. Gopalan asserts that, "it seems certain that even at the time of Mahâvîra the two sects were in existence, though he was able to maintain at least a semblance of unity between them. The final 'parting of ways' came much later." According to the Svetambara version of the split between the two sects, the chief Jain monk, Acharya Bhadrabahu, foresaw a 12-year famine and led about 12,000 Digambar followers to southern India. Twelve years later they returned to found the Svetambara sect, and in 453 the Valabhi council edited and compiled the traditional Svetambara scriptures.

With one major exception, the differences between the two sects are minor and relatively obscure. The one major difference between the sects is that Digambars believe that women cannot attain moksha in the same birth, while Svetambars believe that women may attain liberation and that Mallinath, a Tirthankar, was a woman. This difference is rooted in the requirement in Digambar asceticism for nudity in order to attain moksha. Digambar Jain monks do not wear clothes because they believe clothes, like other possessions, increase dependency and desire for material things, and desire for anything ultimately leads to sorrow. Svetambar Jain monks, on the other hand, wear white, seamless clothes for practical reasons, and believe there is nothing in Jain scripture that condemns wearing clothes. Sadhvis (nuns) of both sects wear white. In Sanskrit, *ambar* refers to a covering generally, or a garment in particular. *Dig*, an older form of *disha*, refers to the cardinal directions. *Digambar* therefore means "covered by the four directions", or "sky-clad". *Svet* means white and Svetambars wear white garments. As nudity is impractical for women, it follows that without it they cannot attain moksha. This is based on the belief that women cannot reach perfect purity (yathakhyata), "Their lack of clothes can, therefore, be a hindrance to their leading a holy life". The earliest record of this belief is contained in the Prakrit Suttapahuda of the

Digambara mendicant Kundakunda (c. second century A.D.). This of course has severe consequences for women and effectively polarises the two sects in this regard.

Digambars believe that Mahavir remained unmarried, whereas Svetambars believe Mahavir did marry a woman who bore him a daughter. The two sects also differ on the origin of Mata Trishala, Mahavira's mother.

Digambars believe that only the first five lines are formally part of the Namokara Mantra (the main Jain prayer), whereas Svetambaras believe all nine form the mantra. Other differences are minor and not based on major points of doctrine.

Excavations at Mathura revealed many Jain statues from the Kushana period. Tirthankaras, represented without clothes, and monks with cloth wrapped around the left arm are identified as Ardhaphalaka and mentioned in some texts. The Yapaniya sect, believed to have originated from the Ardhaphalaka, follows Digambara nudity, along with several Svetambara beliefs.

Svetambaras are further divided into sub-sects, such as Sthanakavasi, Terapanthi and Deravasi. Some are *murtipujak* (revering statues) while non-Murtipujak Jains refuse statues or images. Svetambar follow the 12 *agam* literature (voice of omniscient).

Most simply call themselves Jains and follow general traditions rather than specific sectarian practices. In 1974 a committee with representatives from every sect compiled a new text called the Samana Suttam.

JAIN SYMBOLISM

The *swastika* is among the holiest of Jain symbols. Worshippers use rice grains to create a *swastika* around the temple altar.

The holiest symbol is a simple swastika. A Jain swastika is normally associated with the three dots on the top accompanied with a crest and a dot. Another important symbol incorporates a wheel on the palm of a hand, symbolizing *Ahimsa*. Other major Jain symbols include:

- 24 *Lanchhanas* (symbols) of the Tirthankaras
- *Triratna* and *Shrivatsa* symbols
- A Tirthankar's or Chakravarti's mother dreams
- *Dharmacakra* and *Siddha-chakra*
- Eight auspicious symbols (The *Asta Mangalas*). Their names are (in series of pictures)
    1. *Swastika* -Signifies peace and well-being
    2. *Shrivatsa* -A mark manifested on the centre of the Jina's chest, signifying a pure soul.
    3. *Nandyavartya* -Large swastika with nine corners
    4. *Vardhamanaka* -A shallow earthen dish used for lamps, suggests an increase in wealth, fame and merit due to a Jina's grace.
    5. *Bhadrasana* -Throne, considered auspicious because it is sanctified by the blessed Jina's feet.
    6. *Kalasha* -Pot filled with pure water signifying wisdom and completeness
    7. *Minayugala* -A fish couple. It signifies Cupid's banners coming to worship the Jina after defeating the God of Love
    8. *Darpana* -The mirror reflects one's true self because of its clarity

Culture

Jain Contributions to Indian Culture

While Jains represent less than 1% of the Indian population, their contributions to culture and society in

India are considerable. Jainism had a major influence in developing a system of philosophy and ethics that had a major impact on all aspects of Indian culture in all ages. Scholarly research and evidences have shown that philosophical concepts considered typically Indian – Karma, Ahimsa, Moksa, reincarnation and like - either originate in the sramana school of thought or were propagated and developed by Jaina teachers.

Jains have also wielded great influence on the culture and language of the south Indian state Karnataka and Gujarat most significantly.In the early period and beginning of the medieval period, between the 9th and 13th centuries, Kannada writers were predominantly of the Jain and Veerashaiva faiths. Jains were the earliest known cultivators of Kannada literature, which they dominated until the 12th century. Jain authors wrote about Jain Tirthankars and other aspects of the Jain religion. Pampa, also known as Adikavi Pampa, is one of the greatest Kannada poets of all time. He was born either in Annigeri or Banavasi, in modern Karnataka state, and was the court poet of Chalukya King Arikesari, a Rashtrakuta feudatory. The works of Jain writers Adikavi Pampa, Sri Ponna and Ranna, collectively called the "three gems of Kannada literature", heralded the age of classical Kannada in the 10th century. The earliest known Gujarati text, Bharat-Bahubali Ras, was written by a Jain monk. Some important people in Gujarat's Jain history were Acharya Hemacandra Suri and his pupil, the Chalukya ruler Kumarapala.

Jains are among the wealthiest Indians. They run numerous schools, colleges and hospitals and are important patrons of the Somapuras, the traditional temple architects in Gujarat. Jains have greatly influenced Gujarati cuisine. Gujarat is predominantly vegetarian (see Jain vegetarianism), and its food is mild as onions and garlic are omitted. Though the Jains form only 0.42% of the population of India, their contribution to the exchequer by way of income tax is an astounding 24% of the total tax collected.

Jains encourage their monks to do research and obtain higher education. Jain monks and nuns, particularly in Rajasthan, have published numerous research monographs. This is unique among Indian religious groups and parallels Christian clergy. The 2001 census states that Jains are India's most literate community and that India's oldest libraries at Patan and Jaisalmer are preserved by Jain institutions.

Jain Literature

Jains have contributed to India's classical and popular literature. For example, almost all early Kannada literature and many Tamil works were written by Jains.

- Some of the oldest known books in Hindi and Gujarati were written by Jain scholars. The first autobiography in Hindi, Ardha-Kathanaka was written by a Jain, Banarasidasa, an ardent follower of Acarya Kundakunda who lived in Agra.
- Many Tamil classics are written by Jains or with Jain beliefs and values as the core subject.
- Practically all the known texts in the Apabhramsha language are Jain works.

The oldest Jain literature is in Shauraseni and Ardha-Magadhi Prakrit (Agamas, Agama-Tulya, Siddhanta texts, etc.). Many classical texts are in Sanskrit (Tatvartha Sutra, Puranas, Kosh, Sravakacara, mathematics, Nighantus etc.). "Abhidhana Rajendra Kosha" written by Acharya Rajendrasuri, is only one available Jain encyclopedia or Jain dictionary to understand the Jain Prakrit, Sanskrit, and Ardha-Magadhi and other Jain languages, words, their use and references with in oldest Jain literature. Later Jain literature was written in Apabhramsha (Kahas, rasas, and grammars),

Hindi (Chhahadhala, Mokshamarga Prakashaka, and others), Tamil (Jivakacintamani, Valayapathi, Naaladiyaar and others), and Kannada (Vaddaradhane and various other texts). Jain versions of Ramayana and Mahabharata are found in Sanskrit, Prakrit, Apabhramsha and Kannada.

Jainism and Other Religions

Jains are not a part of the Vedic Religion (Hinduism). Ancient India had two philosophical streams of thought: The Shramana philosophical schools, represented by **Jainism** movement, and the Brahmana/Vedic/Puranic schools represented by Vedanta, Vaishnava and other movements. Both streams have existed side by side for few thousands of years, influencing each other.

The Hindu scholar, Lokmanya Tilak credited Jainism with influencing Hinduism and thus leading to the cessation of animal sacrifice in Vedic rituals. Bal Gangadhar Tilak has described Jainism as the originator of Ahimsa and wrote in a letter printed in Bombay Samachar, Mumbai:10 December 1904: "In ancient times, innumerable animals were butchered in sacrifices. Evidence in support of this is found in various poetic compositions such as the Meghaduta.

Swami Vivekananda also credited Jainism as influencing force behind the Indian culture and said:

> "What could have saved Indian society from the ponderous burden of omnifarious ritualistic ceremonialism, with its animal and other sacrifices, which all but crushed the very life of it, except the Jain revolution which took its strong stand exclusively on chaste morals and philosophical truths? Jains were the first great ascetics and they did some great work. "Don't injure any and do good to all that you can, and that is all the morality and ethics, and that is all the work there is, and the rest is all nonsense." And then they went to work

and elaborated this one principle all through, and it is a most wonderful ideal: how all that we call ethics they simply bring out from that one great principle of non-injury and doing good."

- Relationship between Jainism and Hinduism - According to the Encyclopædia Britannica Article on Hinduism,"...With Jainism which always remained an independent Indian religion. Hinduism has some common concepts and practices, that nowadays some Hindus tend to consider Jainism as Hindu sect.

- Independent Religion - From the Encyclopædia Britannica Article on Jainism: "...Along with Hinduism and Buddhism, it is one of the three most ancient Indian religious traditions still in existence. ...While often employing concepts shared with Hinduism and Buddhism, the result of a common cultural and linguistic background, the Jain tradition must be regarded as an independent phenomenon. It is an integral part of South Asian religious belief and practice, but it is not a Hindu sect or Buddhist heresy, as earlier scholars believed." The author Koenraad Elst in his book, *Who is a Hindu?*, summarises on the similarities between Jains and the mainstream Hindu society.

- Monier Williams, in his article of Jainism, mentions that Jains outdo every other Indian sect in carrying the prohibition of violence to the most extent.

Languages Used in Jain Literature

Jain literature exists in Prakrit, Sanskrit, Tamil, Apabhramsha, Rajasthani, Hindi, Marathi, Gujarati, Kutchi, Kannada, Tulu, Telugu, Dhundhari (Old Marwari), English, German, French, Spanish, Italian, Portuguese, Urdu and Russian.

Constitutional Status of Jainism in India

In 2005 the Supreme Court declined to issue a writ of Mandamus towards granting Jains the status of a religious minority throughout India. The Court noted that Jains have been declared a minority in five states already, and left it to the rest of the States to decide on the minority status of Jain religion.

In 2006 the Supreme Court in a judgment pertaining to a state, opined that "Jain Religion is indisputably not a part of the Hindu Religion". (para 25, Committee of Management Kanya Junior High School Bal Vidya Mandir, Etah, Uttar Pradesh v. Sachiv, U.P. Basic Shiksha Parishad, Allahabad, U.P. and Ors., Per Dalveer Bhandari J., Civil Appeal No. 9595 of 2003, decided On: 21.08.2006, Supreme Court of India)

●●

2

Ahimsa in Jainism

Ahimsâ in Jainism is a fundamental principle forming the cornerstone of its ethics and doctrine. The term "ahimsa" means "non-violence", "non-injury" or absence of desire to harm any life forms. Vegetarianism and other non-violent practices and rituals of Jains flow from the principle of Ahimsâ. According to Adian Rankin, the concept of Ahimsâ is so much intertwined with Jainism that it conjures up images of ascetics who cover their mouths and sweep the ground before them with small brushes to avoid injuring the most minuscule forms of life and Jain-owned animal sanctuaries where even the sickest, most deformed birds and beasts are protected and cherished. These overt manifestations of an ancient faith challenge the comfortable - and near-universal - assumption of human precedence over other creatures.

The Jain concept of Ahimsâ is quite different from the concept of non-violence found in other philosophies. In other religious traditions, violence is usually associated with causing harm to others. On the other hand, in Jainism, violence refers primarily to injuring one's own self – behaviour which inhibits the souls own ability to attain moksa or liberation. At the same time it also means violence to others because it is this tendency to harm others that ultimately harms ones own soul. Furthermore, the Jains have extended the concept of Ahimsâ not only to humans but to all animals, plants, micro-organisms and all beings having life or life potential. All life is sacred and everyone has a right to live fearlessly to its maximum potential. The living beings do not have any fear from those who have taken the vow of Ahimsâ. According to Jainism, protection of life, also known as *abhayadânam,* is the supreme charity that a person can make.

Ahimsâ does not merely indicate absence of physical violence, but also indicates absence of desire to indulge in any sort of violence. This Jain ideal of Ahimsâ profoundly influenced Mahatma Gandhi, through his friendship with the Jain scholar Shrimad Rajchandra that it formed a basis of his satyagraha (truth struggle) against colonial rule and caused him to rethink many aspects of contemporary Hindu practices. While Jainism is not a proselytizing religion and as such has no organised system of advocating its doctrine, Jains have been forefront in strongly advocating vegetarianism and non-violence through ages. Ahimsâ being central to the Jain philosophy, Jain Âcâryas have produced, through ages, quite elaborate and detailed doctrinal materials concerning its various aspects.

The Vow of Ascetics

The Jain monks and the nuns undertake five major vows known as Mahâvratas at the time of their ordination to monkhood, out of which Ahimsâ is the first and foremost. Jain monks and nuns must rank among the most "non-violent" people in the world. A Jain ascetic is expected to uphold the vow of Ahimsâ to the highest standard, even at the cost of his own life. The other four major vows – truthfulness, non-stealing, non-possession and celibacy – are in fact extension of the first vow of complete non-violence. According to Am[tacandra Sûri:

Ascetic Practices for Adherence of Ahimsâ

The ascetic practices of total renunciation of worldly affairs and possessions, refusal to stay in a single place for a long time, continuous practice of austerities like fasting etc. are geared towards observance of ahimsâ. The Jain mendicants abide by a rigorous set of rules of conduct, where they must eat, sleep and even walk with full diligence and with an awareness that even walking kills several hundreds of minute beings. They generally brush the ground clear of insects before they tread; some wear a small mask to avoid taking in tiny insects; some monks do not wear even clothes and eat food only when it is not prepared for themselves. The observation of three guptis or the controls of mind, speech and body and five samiti or regulation of walking, speaking, begging of food, keeping items and disposal of items are designed to help the monks in observing the vow of ahimsâ faultlessly. In fact entire day of a Jain monk is spent in ensuring that he observes his vow of ahimsâ through mind, body and speech faultlessly. This seemingly extreme behaviour of the monks comes from a sense that every action, no matter however subtle, has a karmic effect which can bind soul and inhibit liberation, especially those that result in *himsâ.*

The Vow of the Laity

A Jain layman, on account of his household and occupational compulsions, is unable to adhere to the five major vows of ascetic. Hence he observes anuvrata or minor vows which although are similar to the major vows of the ascetics are observed with a lesser severity. It is difficult to avoid some violence by a lay person to single-sensed immobile beings in the process of occupation, cooking, self defense etc. That is why he vows not to kill without a necessary purpose and determined intention, a moving sentient being, when it is innocent. Tying up, injuring, mutilating, burdening with heavy load and depriving from food and drinks any animal or human being with a mind polluted by anger and other passions are the five aticâra or transgressions of the vow of Ahimsâ. However, it is to be understood that ultimately, there is limited spiritual progress and no emancipation unless the major vows are adhered to.

Laity Practices for Adherence of Ahimsa

Jainism is perhaps the only religion in the world that requires all its adherents to follow a strict vegetarian diet. Vegetarian food that also involves more harm to the living beings such as roots, bulbs, multi seeded vegetables etc are avoided by strict Jains. The importance of Ahimsâ manifests in many other ways in the daily life of Jains. For a layperson it means participating in business that results in least amount of violence to living beings. No furs, plumes or silk are worn. Use of leather is kept to a minimum and must in any event be from naturally dead animals. Food is usually eaten during the day unless unavoidable, since there is too much danger of injuring insects in cooking at night. The Jain will not use an open light nor leave a container of liquid uncovered lest a stray insect be destroyed; even with this precaution, liquids are always strained before use. Through the ages Jains have sought to avoid occupations that unavoidably entail injury, and this accounts for the disproportionate number who have entered banking, commerce and other mercantile trades.

Jain Concept of Ahimsâ

While Jainism enjoins observance of total non-violence by the ascetics, it is often argued that the man is constantly obliged to engage in destructive activities of eating, drinking, breathing and surviving in order to support his body. According to Jainism, life is omnipresent with infinite beings including microorganisms pervading each and every part of universe. Hence it may still be possible to avoid killing of gross animals, but it is impossible to avoid killing of subtle microorganisms in air and water, plant life and various types of insects that may be crushed by walking. It would thus appear that the continual likelihood of destroying living organisms would create an inexcusable burden on the ascetics trying to follow the Jain path of total renunciation and non-violence.

However, the Jain conception of Ahimsâ is quite different than what is commonly understood by violence. The violence is defined more by the motives and the consequences to the self rather than by the act itself. Furthermore, according to Jain Scriptures, destruction of less developed organism brings about lesser karmas than destruction of developed animals and karmas generated in observance of religious duties faultlessly disappears almost immediately. Hence, it is possible to observe complete non-violence with right knowledge, even when some outward violence occurs to living beings in the course of performing religious duties by observing carefulness and pure mental disposition without any attachment.

Hierarchy of Living beings on basis of Senses

Jainism divides living beings on the basis of sensory organs (indriya) and vitalities or life force (prana) existing in such beings. Accordingly, higher the number of senses and vitalities a being has, the more is its capacity to suffer and feel pain. Hence according to Jainism, violence to higher sensed beings like man, cow, tiger and like who have five senses and capacity to think and feel pain attracts more karma than any violence to lesser sensed beings like insects, or single sensed beings like microbes and plants. Hence Jainism enjoins its adherents to completely avoid violence to higher sensed beings and as far as possible minimize violence to single sensed beings.

Mental States and Intention

Paul Dundas quotes Âcârya Jinabhadra (seventh century), who shows that the omnipresence of life-forms in the universe need not totally inhibit normal behaviour of the ascetics:

> "It is the intention that ultimately matters. From the real point of view, a man does not become a killer only because he has killed or because the world is crowded

with souls, or remain innocent only because he has not killed physically. Even if a person does not actually kill, he becomes a killer if he has the intention to kill; while a doctor has to cause pain but is still non-violent and innocent because his intention is pure, for it is the intention which is the deciding factor, not the external act which is inconclusive."

Thus pure intention along with carefulness was considered necessary to practice Ahimsâ as Jains admitted that even if intention may be pure, careless activities often resulted in violence unknowingly.

Carefulness

According to Jainism, a monk who is careless in his activities is guilty of violence irrespective of whether a living being remains alive or dies; on the other hand, the person who is ever vigilant and careful in observing the samitis experiences no karmic bondage simply because some violence may have taken place in connection with his activities. Carefulness came to be seen as a defense for the monks against violence in Jainism. One of the most famous passages in the *Uttradhayana Sûtra* describes Mahâvîra continually exhorting his chief disciple Gautama "to be careful all the while" lest the opportunity to destroy all the karmas and achieve perfection in this lifetime may be lost forever on account of carelessness. Tattvârthasûtra defines himsâ or violence simply as "removal of life by careless activity of mind, body and speech." Thus action in Jainism came to be regarded as truly violent only when accompanied by carlessness.

Significance of True Knowledge

The Jains also considered right knowledge as a prerequisite for practicing Ahimsâ. It is necessary to know what is living and what is non-living to practice Ahimsâ faultlessly. A person who is confused between Living and non-living can never observe non-violence. *Daœavaikâlika Sûtra* declared:

> "First knowledge, then compassion. Thus does one remain in full control. How can an ignorant person be compassionate, when he cannot distinguish between the good and the evil?" – DS iv

> It further declares –

> " Knowledge of living and non-living alone will enable one to become compassionate towards all living creatures. Knowing this all aspirants, proceed from knowledge to eternal virtues. What can an ignorant do ? How does he know what is noble and what is evil?"

The knowledge is also considered necessary to destroy Karmas. Saman SuttaA declared -

> "The ignorant cannot destroy their Karmas by their actions while the wise can do it by their inaction i.e. by controlling their activities because they are free from greed and lustful passions and do not commit any sin as they remain contented." (165)

Anekantavada - The Non-Violence of Mind

Anekantavada is the principle of relativity of truth or the doctrine of multiple aspects. Jains hold that truth is multifaceted and has multiple sides that cannot be completely comprehended by anyone. Anekantavada describes the world as a multifaceted, ever-changing reality with an infinity of viewpoints relative to the time, place, nature and state of one who is the viewer and that which is viewed. What is true from one point of view is open to question from another. Absolute truth cannot be grasped from any particular viewpoint alone, because absolute truth is the sum total of all different viewpoints that make up the universe. Because it is rooted in these doctrines, Jainism cannot exclusively uphold the views of any individual, community, nation, or species. It recognises inherently that other views are valid for other peoples, and for other life-forms. This perception leads to the doctrine of syadvada or sevenfold predication stating the truth from different viewpoints. Anekantvada is the doctrine and Syadvada is its expression. According to Jaina philosophers all important philosophical statements should be expressed in this sevenfold way in order to remove the danger of dogmatism (ekanta) in philosophy.

The concept of syadvada allows the Jains to accept the truth in other philosophies from their perspective and thus inculcating a tolerance for other viewpoints. Anekantvada is non-absolutist and stands firmly against all dogmatisms, even including any assertion that only Jainism is the right religious path. It is thus an intellectual Ahimsa or Ahimsa of mind. In Anekantvada, there is no "battle of ideas", because this is considered to be a form of intellectual himsa or damage, leading quite logically to physical violence and war. In today's world, the limitations of the adversarial, "either with us or against us " form of argument are increasingly apparent leading to political, religious and social conflicts. Even the mounting ecological crisis is linked to adversarialism, because it arises from a false division between humanity and "the rest" of nature.

Various Aspects and Consequences of Violence

Âcârya Amtacandra has described as to how the consequences of violence (karmas attracted) differ from person to persons for similar and different types of acts:

- A small violence may bring serious consequences to one person, while to another person grievous violence may bring about lesser consequences. For instance, a person hunting and killing only one small animal suffers severe consequences while a person who is building a temple or hospital, suffers milder the karmic consequences even though such a building results in killing of many animals.

- One who actually does not commit violence may be responsible for himsâ while one who actually commits violence is not responsible for himsâ. For instance, a burglar who fails in his robbery is still a felon but a diligent surgeon who is trying to save a patient is not responsible for violence even if a patient dies during the surgery.
- Even when violence is jointly committed by two persons, the same act may result in severe consequence for one person and mild consequence for another person. This may happen in case where one person is the leader and planner of violence who binds severe karmas, while another who is simply a follower binds much lesser karmas.
- Persons who have not committed violence may become responsible for violence committed by others. This may happen when a violence which is carried out by someone is approved and instigated by someone else.
- Ahimsâ often gives result of himsâ to one and himsâ may sometimes give result of Ahimsâ to another. For instance, one person saves another from oppression by use of violence and hence enjoys consequences of Ahimsâ although resorting to violence, while another does not act to save someone wishing that the other person is not saved and thus suffers the consequences of violence although he may have not actually done anything.

Jaina Conception of Himsâ

While the Jain ascetics observe absolute non-violence, so far as a Jain householder is concerned, the violence is divided as follows :-

1. **Sankalpinî himsâ or intentional violence** – Intentional violence knowingly done is the worst form

of violence and is a transgression of the laypersons vow of violence. Examples of sankalpinî himsâ are killing for hunting, amusement or decoration, or butchering for food or sacrifice or killing or hurting out of enimity, malice or mischief. sankalpinî himsâ has to be totally renounced by a householder.

2. **Â[ambhinî (Graharambhi) himsâ or domestic or household violence** – This violence is unavoidable committed in the course of preparing food, household cleanliness, washing, construction of houses, wells etc.

3. **Virodhinî himsâ or Self defence** - Virodhini himsâ is committed for self-defence of self, property, family or country against violent attackers, robbers, or dacoits. A householder tries to avoid himsâ at all cost, but in such cases it may be unavoidable and hence should be non-vindictive and kept to barest minimum.

4. **Udyoginî himsâ or Occupational Violence** – This violence is connected to occupational undertakings like agriculture, building and operating industries etc.

While sankalpinî himsâ has to be avoided at all costs, the other three types of himsâ although unavoidable in some cases, should not exceed the strict requirements of fulfilling the duties of a householder. Furthermore, they should not be influenced by passions like anger, greed, pride and deceit or they take the character of sanpalkinî himsâ.

Ways of Committing Violence

It would be wrong, however, to conclude that ahimsâ only prohibited physical violence. An early Jain text says:

> "With the three means of punishment – thoughts, words, deeds – ye shall not injure living beings."

In fact, violence can be committed by combination of the following four factors :

1. The instrumentality of our actions. We can commit violence by either through
   - (a) body i.e. physical action,
   - (b) speech i.e. verbal action, or
   - (c) mind i.e. mental actions
2. The process of committing violence. This includes whether we
   - (a) only decide or plan to act,
   - (b) make preparations for the act e.g. like collecting necessary materials or weapons, or
   - (c) actually begin the action
3. The modality of our action, including if we
   - (a) we ourselves commit violence,
   - (b) we instigate others to carry out the violence, or
   - (c) we give our silent approval for the violence
4. The motivation for action. This includes which of the following negative emotions that the violence is motivated by.
   - (a) Anger
   - (b) Greed
   - (c) Pride
   - (d) Manipulation or deceit

Thus violence is committed by a combination of any one element of the above four factors. Due to this, there are 108 ways with which the violence can be committed.

The Rationale of Non Violence

According to Jainism, the purpose of non-violence is not simply because it is a commandment of a God or any other supreme being. Its purpose is also not simply because its observance is conductive to general welfare of the state or the community. While it is true that in Jainism, the moral and religious injunctions were laid down as law by Arhats who have achieved perfection through their supreme moral efforts, their adherence is just not to please a God, but the life of the Arhats has demonstrated that such commandments were conductive to Arhat's own welfare, helping him to reach spiritual victory. Just as Arhats achieved spiritual victory by observing non-violence, so can anyone who follows this path.

Another aspect that provides a rationale to the avoidance of himsâ is that, any acts of himsâ results in himsâ to self. Any act of violence though outwardly is seen to harm others, harms the soul of the person indulging in the act. Thus by an act of violence, a soul may or may not injure the material vitalities known as dravya prana of someone else, but always causes injury to its own bhâva prana or the psychic vitalities by binding the soul with karmas. It would be entirely wrong to see Ahimsâ in Jainism in any sentimental light. The Jain doctrine of non-injury is based on rational consciousness, not emotional compassion; on responsibility to self, not on a social fellow feeling. The motive of Ahimsâ is totally self-centered and for the benefit of the individual. And yet, though the emphasis is on personal liberation, the Jain ethics makes that goal attainable only through consideration for others.

Furthermore, according to the Jain karmic theory, each and every soul, including self, has reincarnated as an animal, plant or microorganism innumerable number of times besides re-incarnated as humans. The concept of Ahimsâ is more meaningful when understood in conjunction with the concept of karmas. As the doctrine of transmigration of souls includes rebirth in animal as well as human form, it creates a humanitarian sentiment of kinship amongst all life forms. The motto of Jainism - *Parasparopagraho jîvânâm,* translated as: "all life is inter-related and it is the duty of souls to assist each other"- also provides a rational approach of Jains towards Ahimsâ.

In conclusion, the insistence of Ahimsâ is not so much about non-injury to others as it is about non-injury and spiritual welfare of the self. The ultimate rationale of Ahimsâ is fundamentally is about karmic results of the himsâ on self rather than the concern about the well being of other beings for its own sake.

Fruits of Non-Violence and Violence

According to the Jain scriptures, the result of the observance of Ahimsâ is good health, a strong body, and a strong constitution in the future life. There would be happiness, comforts, long life, a good name, handsome features, and an enjoyable youth.

The results of killing would be the opposite of these things, such as lameness, incurable disease, separation from friends and relatives, sorrow, short life, and after that, an incarnation in a low state (animal or hell). According to Hemacandra, diseases like leprosy and loss of limbs are the consequences of inflicting violence.

Misconceptions on Non-Violence

The Jain Scriptures discuss the misconceptions that are harboured in case of Ahimsâ. They often opposed the Vedic beliefs in sacrifices and other practices that justified violence in various ways. Âcârya Am[tacandra's Purusârthasiddhyupâya and Âcârya Hemacandra's

Yogaúâstra discusses these wrong beliefs at length to alert the Jain laity on such wrong beliefs. Following are such misconceptions that a Jain layman was advised to avoid.

Animal Sacrifices

Vedics believed that animals were created for yajna (sacrifice) and hence it was not considered a slaughter, as it elevated not only the person making the sacrifice, but also the animals. This belief was denounced by Hemacandra that those who mercilessly kill the animals under the pretext of offering the oblations to gods or for the sake of sacrifices are condemned to most terrifying existence in hells. Am[tacandra also condemned this practice by stating that it is a misconception to hold that Gods are pleased at sacrifices of living beings and there is no wrong in committing himsâ for the sake of religion.

Worshipping Violent Gods

Jain Âcâryas like Hemacandra, Somadeva, Jinasena also decried the worship of violent vedic Gods who demanded sacrifices of animals and glorified the killing of enemies. Âcârya Hemacandra says –

> "It is a matter of great grief that the gods who wield weapons such as bow and arrows, mace, disc, trident etc. are worshipped as true gods."

Oblations to Forefathers

Hemacandra discusses the Vedic beliefs of offering oblations to dead ancestors to please and satisfy their souls by sacrificing various animals. This was decried by Hemacandra as thus –

> The Vedic practice of offering sacrifices of animals to dead ancestors was also condemned by Jain Âcâryas.

Glory of Death on the Battlefield

The Hindu belief that the death in battlefield resulted in rebirth in heavens has been recorded in Mahabharata where Krsna tells Arjuna :

> "Slain you will attain heavens, conquering you will enjoy earth;
>
> Therefore rise, O Arjuna, resolved to do battle"
>
> -Bhagavad Gita ii 37

However according to Jainas death accompanied by hatred and violence can never lead to heavens. According to a story in Bhagavati Sûtra, all the 840,000 soldiers who perished in a war between Konika, the Magadhan emperor and other kings, were either reborn in hell or as animals. Only one person who maintained equanimity in the midst of death in battlefield was reborn in heaven.

Other Wrong Beliefs

Additionally Am[tacandra discusses the following wrong beliefs:

1. Animals should not be killed for guests or persons deserving respect as often advocated in certain scriptures.
2. It is also a wrong belief that wild animals that kill many other animals should be killed. This is often justified in the name of hunting of ferocious animals like tigers for sport.
3. Another wrong belief forwarded to justify killing of ferocious animals is that, these kill many lives and accumulate grave sins and hence killing them is an act of mercy. According to Jainism, killing can never be an act of mercy.

4. It is also a misconception to believe that it is advisable to kill those who are suffering so that they may get relief from agony. These sorts of arguments are forwarded to justify killing of those animals that may have become old or injured and hence have become commercially useless.

5. Other wrong beliefs are killing those who are in state of happiness or those who are in meditation under wrong belief that the mental state at the time of death will be perpetuated in future lives.

6. It is also a wrong belief that killing of self and others is justified as the soul that is imprisoned in the body will be permanent released and achieve salvation.

Non-Violence and Vegetarianism

Origins and Evolution of Ahimsa

Ahimsâ, an important tenet of all the religions originating in India, is now considered as an article of faith by the adherents of the Indian religions. However, not much is known about the historical origins of ahimsâ and as to how it became widespread and got deeply entrenched in the Indian philosophy. Scholars speculate that the doctrine of ahimsâ was probably first developed amongst the native non-Aryan people in around third millennium BCE and was adopted by the brahamanas during the later Upanishadic period under the influence of sramanas. The Vedas, the manusmriti, the Dharmasutra and Mahabharata contain many references on killing and slaughter of animals for sacrifices, oblations to dead ancestors, and as well as for various other occasions. However, as the doctrine of karma gained acceptance in the Hindu belief, the tenet of ahimsâ also gained prominence. Later Hindu scriptures condemn the slaughter of animals, upholding ahimsa as one of the highest ideal. Bal Gangadhar Tilak has credited Jainism with cessation of slaughter of animals in the brahamanical religion. Not surprisingly, some scholars have traced the origin of ahimsâ to Jainas and their precursor, the sramanas. According to Thomas McEvilley, a noted Indologist, certain seals of Indus Valley civilization depict a meditative figure surrounded by a multitude of wild animals, providing evidence of proto yoga tradition in India akin to Jainism. This particular image might suggest that all the animals depicted are sacred to this particular practitioner. Consequently, these animals would be protected from harm. This might be the first historical evidence of the practice of ahimsâ.

●●

3
Vegetarianism and Jain Theory

Jain vegetarianism is the diet of the Jains, the followers of Jainism. It is the most radical form of religiously-motivated diet regulation in the Indian subcontinent.

Like in Hinduism and Buddhism, Jain objections to the eating of meat and fish are based on the principle of nonviolence (ahimsa, literally "non-injuring"). Every act by which a person directly or indirectly supports killing or injury is seen as violence (*himsa*), which creates harmful karma. The aim of ahimsa is to prevent the accumulation of such karma. The extent to which this intention is put into effect varies greatly among Hindus, Buddhists and Jains. Jains consider nonviolence to be the most essential religious duty for everyone (*ahinsâ paramo dharmah,* a statement often inscribed on Jain temples). It is an indispensable condition for liberation from the cycle of reincarnation, which is the ultimate goal of all Jain activities. Jains share this goal with Hindus and Buddhists, but their approach is particularly rigorous and comprehensive. Their scrupulous and thorough way of applying nonviolence to everyday activities, and especially to food, shapes their entire lives and is the most significant hallmark of Jain identity. A side effect of this strict discipline is the exercise of asceticism, which is strongly encouraged in Jainism for lay people as well as for monks and nuns.

- For Jains, lacto-vegetarianism (generally known simply as vegetarianism in India) is mandatory. Food which contains even small particles of the bodies of dead animals or eggs is absolutely unacceptable. Some Jain scholars and activists support veganism, as the production of dairy products involves significant violence (*himsa*) against cows.

- Jains go out of their way so as not to hurt even small insects and other tiny animals, because they are convinced that harm caused by carelessness is as reprehensible as harm caused by deliberate action. Hence they take great pains to make sure that no minuscule animals are injured by the preparation of their meals and in the process of eating and drinking.

- Traditionally Jains have been prohibited from drinking unfiltered water. In the past, when wells or baolis were used for the water source, the cloth used for filtering used to be reversed and some filtered water was poured over it to return the organisms to the original body of water. This practice termed as 'jivani' or 'bilchhavani', is no longer possible because of the use of pipes for water supply.

  Jains today may also filter faucet water in the traditional fashion, and a few Jains continue to follow the filtering process even with commercial mineral or bottled drinking water.

- Jains make considerable efforts not to injure plants in everyday life as far as possible. They admit that plants must be destroyed for the sake of food, but they only accept such violence inasmuch as it is indispensable for human survival, and there are special instructions for preventing unnecessary violence against plants. Jains don't eat root vegetables such as potatoes, onions, roots and tubers, because tiny life forms are injured when the plant is pulled up and because the bulb is seen as a living being, as it is able to sprout.

Also, consumption of most root vegetables involves uprooting & killing the entire plant. Whereas consumption of most terrestrial vegetables doesn't kill the plant (it lives on after plucking the vegetables or it was seasonally supposed to wither away anyway).

- Food items that have started to decay are prohibited.
- Honey is forbidden, as its collection would amount to violence against the bees.
- Traditionally cooking or eating at night was discouraged because insects are attracted to the lamps or fire at night. Strict Jains take the vow (called anastamita or anthau) of not eating after sunset.
- During some specific fasting periods in the Jain religious 'Panchang' calendar, Jains refrain from consuming any green coloured vegetables (which have chlorophyll pigment) such as okra, leafy vegetables, etc.
- Strict Jains do not consume food which has been fermented overnight, as it would be considered 'stale'. Hence, they may not consume yogurt or dhokla & idli batter unless they've been freshly set on the same day.

Influence on Vegetarian Cuisines in India

The vegetarian cuisines of some of the regions has been strongly influenced by Jainism. These include

- Gujarati Jain cuisine
- Marwari Jain cuisine of Rajasthan
- Bundelkhandi Jain cuisine of central India
- Agrawal Jain cuisine of Delhi/UP

In India, vegetarian food is regarded to be appropriate for everyone for all occasions. This makes vegetarian restaurants quite popular. Many of the vegetarian restaurants and Mishtanna (sweet)shops (for example the legendary Ghantewala sweets in Delhi or Jamna Mithya in Sagar) in India are run by Jains.

Some restaurants in India serve strict **Jain** version of vegetarian dishes that leave out carrots, potatoes, onions and garlic. A few airlines also serve Jain vegetarian dishes upon prior request.

The Japanese Shojin Ryori is similar to Jain cuisine in leaving out onions and garlic. The term *satvika* often implies Indian cuisine without onions and garlic, the strict Jain cuisine also excludes other root vegetables like potatoes.

Some Rajasthani dishes such as gatte ki sabzi (or gatte ki kadhi) and papd ki sabzi were invented for Jain festivals during which the orthodox may avoid eating green vegetables.

Historical Background

When Mahavira revived and reorganized the Jain movement in the 6th or 5th century BCE, ahimsa was already an established, strictly observed rule. Parshva, a famous Jain leader (Tirthankar) whom modern Western historians consider to be a historical figure, lived in about the 8th century BCE and founded a community to which Mahavira's parents belonged. Parshva's followers vowed to observe ahimsa; this obligation was part of their "Fourfold Restraint" (*caujjama dhamma*). Mahavira adopted it into his code of conduct.

In the times of Mahavira and in the following centuries, Jains criticised Buddhists and followers of the Vedic religion or Hindus for negligence and inconsistency in the implementation of ahimsa. In particular, they strongly objected to the Vedic tradition of animal sacrifice with subsequent meat eating and to the hunting.

The early Buddhism discouraged eating animals that were slaughtered for the purpose of eating. The Buddha declared that

> ... meat should not be eaten under three circumstances: when it is seen or heard or suspected (that a living being has been purposely slaughtered for the eater); these, Jivaka, are the three circumstances in which meat should not be eaten, Jivaka! I declare there are three circumstances in which meat can be eaten: when it is not seen or heard or suspected (that a living being has been purposely slaughtered for the eater); Jivaka, I say these are the three circumstances in which meat can be eaten.
>
> —**Jivaka Sutta**, MN 55

In the Tamil classic Tirukkural, Valluvar, who is regarded to be a Jain by some scholars, criticizes the Buddhists for accepting the same of meat:

> 256 If the world did not purchase and consume meat, no one would slaughter and offer meat for sale

Many of the Brahmins in India, for example Kashmiri Pandit, Bengali Brahmin, Saraswat Brahmin have traditionally eaten meat. However in regions with strong Jain influence such as Rajasthan and Gujarat, or strong Jain influence in the past such as Tamil Nadu, the Brahmins are strictly vegetarian. Bal Gangadhar Tilak has described Jainism as the originator of Ahimsa. He wrote in a letter:

> "In ancient times, innumerable animals were butchered in sacrifices. Evidence in support of this is found in various poetic compositions such as the Meghaduta. But the credit for the disappearance of this terrible massacre from the Brahminical religion goes to Jainism."

Some Western authors have interpreted the texts in different way to show that ancient Jain ascetics accepted meat as alms if the animal had not been specifically killed for them. If this is correct then they applied the same standard as early Buddhists. Some passages in two of the earliest Svetambara Jain texts, the *Acaranga Sutra* and the *Dasaveyaliya,* have been interpreted as regulations for specific types of meat and bones which were considered to be acceptable alms. This can also be interpreted at references to fruits and seeds. Another Svetambara text, the *Viyahapannatti,* tells a story where Mahavira himself eats the "Kukutmansa" which may be interpreted as meat of a cock. Kutkutmansa is also interpreted as a fleshy fruit of a plant. Medieval Jain commentators of these passages interpreted them in the literal meaning (meat eating), but also mentioned the opinion that the offensive words had different meanings, some of which did not refer to animals, and hence the contents were compatible with vegetarianism. Jains point out the absurdity of such interpretations which are totally inconsistent with the ancient texts and practices. Jains, who are strict vegetarians, do not accept the interpretations of Western scholars.

KARMA IN JAINISM

In **Jainism, karma** is the basic principle within an overarching psycho-cosmology. In the Jain cosmology, human moral actions form the basis of the transmigration of the soul (*jîva*). The soul is constrained to a cycle of rebirth, trapped within the temporal world (*samsâra*), until it finally achieves liberation (*moksa*). Liberation is achieved by following a path of purification.

In Jain philosophy, karma not only encompasses the causality of transmigration, but is also conceived of as an extremely subtle matter, which infiltrates the soul—obscuring its natural, transparent and pure qualities. Karma is thought of as a kind of pollution, that taints the soul with various colours (*leúyâ*). Based on its karma, a soul undergoes transmigration and reincarnates in various states of existence—like heavens or hells, or as humans or animals.

Jains cite inequalities, sufferings, and pain as evidence for the existence of karma. Jain texts have classified the various types of karma according to their effects on the potency of the soul. The Jain theory seeks to explain the karmic process by specifying the various causes of karmic influx (*âsrava*) and bondage (*bandha*), placing equal emphasis on deeds themselves, and the intentions behind those deeds. The Jain karmic theory attaches great responsibility to individual actions, and eliminates any reliance on some supposed existence of divine grace or retribution. The Jain doctrine also holds that it is possible for us to both modify our karma, and to obtain release from it, through the austerities and purity of conduct.

Several scholars date the origin of the doctrine of karma prior to the migration of the Indo-Aryan peoples. They see its current form as a result of development in the teachings of the Œramanas, and later assimilation into brahmanical Hinduism, by the time of the Upanisads. The Jain concept of karma has been subject to criticism from rival Indian philosophies—like Vedanta Hinduism, Buddhism, and Sâmkhya.

Philosophical Overview

According to Jains, all souls are intrinsically pure in their inherent and ideal state, possessing the qualities of infinite knowledge, infinite perception, infinite bliss and infinite energy. However, in contemporary experience, these qualities are found to be defiled and obstructed, on account of the association of these souls with karma. The soul has been associated with karma in this way throughout an eternity of beginningless time. This bondage of the soul is explained in the Jain texts by analogy with gold ore, which—in its natural state—is always found unrefined of admixture with impurities. Similarly, the ideally pure state of the soul has always been overlaid with the impurities of karma. This analogy with gold ore is also taken one step further: the purification of the soul can be achieved if the proper methods of refining are applied. Over the centuries, Jain monks have developed a large and sophisticated corpus of literature describing the nature of the soul, various aspects of the working of karma, and the ways and means of attaining *moksa*.

Self Regulating Mechanism

According to Indologist Robert J. Zydenbos, karma is a system of natural laws, where actions that carry moral significance are considered to cause certain consequences in the same way as physical actions. When one holds an apple and then lets it go, the apple will fall. There is no judge, and no moral judgment involved, since this is a mechanical consequence of the physical action. In the same manner, consequences occur naturally when one utters a lie, steals something, commits senseless violence or leads a life of debauchery. Rather than assume that these consequences—the moral rewards and retributions—are a work of some divine judge, Jains believe that there is an innate moral order in the cosmos, self-regulating through the workings of the law of karma. Morality and ethics are important in Jainism not because of a God, but because a life led in agreement with moral and ethical principles (*mahavrata*) is considered beneficial: it leads to a decrease—and finally to the total loss of—karma, which in turns leads to everlasting happiness. The Jain conception of karma takes away the responsibility for salvation from God and bestows it on man himself. In the words of the Jain scholar, J. L. Jaini:

> Jainism, more than any other creed, gives absolute religious independence and freedom to man. Nothing can intervene between the actions which we do and the fruits thereof. Once done, they become our masters and must fructify. As my independence is great, so my responsibility is co-extensive with it. I can live as I like; but my voice is irrevocable, and I cannot escape the consequences of it. No God, his Prophet or his deputy

or beloved can interfere with human life. The soul, and it alone is responsible for all it does.

Material Theory

Jainism speaks of karmic "dirt", as karma is thought to be manifest as very subtle and microscopically imperceptible particles pervading the entire universe. They are so small that one space-point—the smallest possible extent of space—contains an infinite number of karmic particles (or quantity of karmic dirt). It is these karmic particles that adhere to the soul and affect its natural potency. This material karma is called *dravya karma;* and the resultant emotions—pleasure, pain, love, hatred, and so on—experienced by the soul are called *bhava karma,* psychic karma. The relationship between the material and psychic karma is that of cause and effect. The material karma gives rise to the feelings and emotions in worldly souls, which—in turn—give rise to psychic karma, causing emotional modifications within the soul. These emotions, yet again, result in influx and bondage of fresh material karma. Jains hold that the karmic matter is actually an agent that enables the consciousness to act within the material context of this universe. They are the material carrier of a soul's desire to physically experience this world. When attracted to the consciousness, they are stored in an interactive karmic field called *kârmana úarîra,* which emanates from the soul. Thus, karma is a subtle matter surrounding the consciousness of a soul. When these two components—consciousness and ripened karma—interact, the soul experiences life as known in the present material universe.

Predominance of Karma

According to Jainism, karmic consequences are unerringly certain and inescapable. No divine grace can save a person from experiencing them. Only the practice of austerities and self-control can modify or alleviate the consequences of karma. Even then, in some cases, there is no option but to accept karma with equanimity. The second-century Jain text, Bhagavatî Ârâdhanâ (verse no. 1616) sums up the predominance of karma in Jain doctrine: "There is nothing mightier in the world than karma; karma tramples down all powers, as an elephant a clump of lotuses." This predominance of karma is a theme often explored by Jain ascetics in the literature they have produced, throughout all centuries. Paul Dundas notes that the ascetics often used cautionary tales to underline the full karmic implications of morally incorrect modes of life, or excessively intense emotional relationships. However, he notes that such narratives were often softened by concluding statements about the transforming effects of the protagonists' pious actions, and their eventual attainment of liberation.

The biographies of the exploits of legendary persons like Rama (Râma) and Krishna (K[sna), in the Jain versions of the Ramayana and Mahabharata, also have karma as one of the major themes. The major events, characters and circumstances are explained by reference to their past lives, with examples of specific actions of particular intensity in one life determining events in the next. Jain texts narrate how even Mâhavîra, the 24th *tîrthankara* (ford-maker), had to bear the brunt of his previous karma before attaining *kevala jñâna* (enlightenment). He attained it only after bearing twelve years of severe austerity with detachment. The Âcâranga Sûtra speaks of how Mâhavîra bore his karma with complete equanimity, as follows.

He was struck with a stick, the fist, a lance, hit with a fruit, a clod, a potsherd. Beating him again and again many cried. When he once sat without moving his body many cut his flesh, tore his hair under pain, or covered him with dust. Throwing him up they let him fall, or disturbed him in his religious postures; abandoning the care of his body, the Venerable One humbled himself and bore pain, free from desires. As a hero at the head of the battle is surrounded by all sides, so was there Mâhavîra.

Karma forms a central and fundamental part of Jain faith, being intricately connected to other of its philosophical concepts like transmigration, reincarnation, liberation, non-violence (*ahimsâ*) and non-attachment, among others. Actions are seen to have consequences: some immediate, some delayed, even into future incarnations. So the doctrine of karma is not considered simply in relation to one life-time, but also in relation to both future incarnations and past lives. *Uttarâdhyayana-sûtra* 3.3–4 states: "The *jîva* or the soul is sometimes born in the world of gods, sometimes in hell. Sometimes it acquires the body of a demon; all this happens on account of its karma. This *jîva* sometimes takes birth as a worm, as an insect or as an ant." The text further states (32.7): "Karma is the root of birth and death. The souls bound by karma go round and round in the cycle of existence."

Actions and emotions in the current lifetime affect future incarnations depending on the nature of the particular karma. For example, a good and virtuous life indicates a latent desire to experience good and virtuous themes of life. Therefore, such a person attracts karma that ensures that his future births will allow him to experience and manifest his virtues and good feelings unhindered. In this case, he may take birth in heaven or in a prosperous and virtuous human family. On the other hand, a person who has indulged in immoral deeds, or with a cruel disposition, indicates a latent desire to experience cruel themes of life. As a natural consequence, he will attract karma which will ensure that he is reincarnated in hell, or in lower life forms, to enable his soul to experience the cruel themes of life.

There is no retribution, judgment or reward involved but a natural consequences of the choices in life made either knowingly or unknowingly. Hence, whatever suffering or pleasure that a soul may be experiencing in its present life is on account of choices that it has made in the past. As a result of this doctrine, Jainism attributes supreme importance to pure thinking and moral behaviour. Apart from Buddhism, Jainism may be the only religion that does not invoke the fear of God as a reason for moral behaviour.

Four States of Existence

The Jain texts postulate four *gatis,* that is states-of-existence or birth-categories, within which the soul transmigrates. The four *gatis* are: *deva* (demi-gods), *manusya* (humans), *nâraki* (hell beings) and *tiryañca* (animals, plants and micro-organisms). The four *gatis* have four corresponding realms or habitation levels in the vertically tiered Jain universe: demi-gods occupy the higher levels where the heavens are situated; humans, plants and animals occupy the middle levels; and hellish beings occupy the lower levels where seven hells are situated.

Single-sensed souls, however, called *nigoda,* and element-bodied souls pervade all tiers of this universe. *Nigodas* are souls at the bottom end of the existential hierarchy. They are so tiny and undifferentiated, that they lack even individual bodies, living in colonies. According to Jain texts, this infinity of *nigodas* can also be found in plant tissues, root vegetables and animal bodies. Depending on its karma, a soul transmigrates and reincarnates within the scope of this cosmology of destinies. The four main destinies are further divided into sub-categories and still smaller sub–sub categories. In all, Jain texts speak of a cycle of 8.4 million birth destinies in which souls find themselves again and again as they cycle within *samsara.*

In Jainism, God has no role to play in an individual's destiny; one's personal destiny is not seen as a consequence of any system of reward or punishment, but rather as a result of its own personal karma. A text from a volume of the ancient Jain canon, *Bhagvati sûtra* 8.9.9, links specific states of existence to specific karmas. Violent deeds, killing of creatures having five sense organs, eating fish, and so on, lead to rebirth in hell. Deception, fraud and falsehood leads to rebirth in the animal and vegetable world. Kindness, compassion and humble character result in human birth; while austerities and the making and keeping of vows leads to rebirth in heaven.

Each soul is thus responsible for its own predicament, as well as its own salvation. Accumulated karma represent a sum total of all unfulfilled desires, attachments and aspirations of a soul. It enables the soul to experience the various themes of the lives that it desires to experience. Hence a soul may transmigrate from one life form to another for countless of years, taking with it the karma that it has earned, until it finds conditions that bring about the required fruits. In certain philosophies, heavens and hells are often viewed as places for eternal salvation or eternal damnation for good and bad deeds. But according to Jainism, such places, including the earth are simply the places which allow the soul to experience its unfulfilled karma.

Lesya – Colouring of the Soul

According to the Jain theory of karma, the karmic matter imparts a colour (*leúyâ*) to the soul, depending on the mental activities behind an action. The coloring of the soul is explained through the analogy of crystal, that acquires the color of the matter associated with it. In the same way, the soul also reflects the qualities of taste, smell and touch of associated karmic matter, although it is usually the colour that is referred to when discussing the *leúyâs*. *Uttarâdhyayana-sûtra* 34.3 speaks of six main categories of *leúyâ* represented by six colours: black, blue, grey, yellow, red and white. The black, blue and grey are inauspicious *leúyâ*, leading to the soul being born into misfortunes. The yellow, red and white are auspicious *leúyâs*, that lead to the soul being born into good fortune. *Uttarâdhyayana-sûtra* describes the mental disposition of persons having black and white *leúyâs*:

> A man who acts on the impulse of the five sins, does not possess the three *guptis*, has not ceased to injure the six

> (kinds of living beings), commits cruel acts, is wicked and violent, is afraid of no consequences, is mischievous and does not subdue his senses – a man of such habits develops the black *leúyâ.*
>
> — *Uttarâdhyayana-sûtra,* 34.21:22

> A man who abstains from constant thinking about his misery and about sinful deeds, but engages in meditation on the law and truth only, whose mind is at ease, who controls himself, who practises the *samitis* and *guptis,* whether he be still subject to passion or free from passion, is calm, and subdues his senses—a man of such habits develops the white *leúyâ.*
>
> — *Uttarâdhyayana-sûtra,* 34.31:32

The Jain texts further illustrate the effects of *leúyâs* on the mental dispositions of a soul, using an example of the reactions of six travellers on seeing a fruit-bearing tree. They see a tree laden with fruit and begin to think of getting those fruits: one of them suggests uprooting the entire tree and eating the fruit; the second one suggests cutting the trunk of the tree; the third one suggests simply cutting the branches; the fourth one suggests cutting the twigs and sparing the branches and the tree; the fifth one suggests plucking only the fruits; the sixth one suggests picking up only the fruits that have fallen down.

The thoughts, words and bodily activities of each of these six travellers are different based on their mental dispositions and are respectively illustrative of the six *leúyâs.* At one extreme, the person with the black *leúyâ,* having evil disposition, thinks of uprooting the whole tree even though he wants to eat only one fruit. At the other extreme, the person with the white *leúyâ,* having a pure disposition, thinks of picking up the fallen fruit, in order to spare the tree.

Role of Deeds and Intent

The role of intent is one of the most important and definitive elements of the karma theory, in all its traditions. In Jainism, intent is important but not an essential precondition of sin or wrong conduct. Evil intent forms only one of the modes of committing sin. Any action committed, knowingly or *unknowingly,* has karmic repercussions. In certain philosophies, like Buddhism, a person is guilty of violence only if he had an intention to commit violence. On the other hand, according to Jains, if an act produces violence, then the person is guilty of it, whether or not he had an intention to commit it.

John Koller explains the role of intent in Jainism with the example of a monk, who unknowingly offered poisoned food to his brethren. According to the Jain view, the monk is guilty of a violent act if the other monks die because they eat the poisoned food; but according to the Buddhist view he would not be guilty. The crucial difference between the two views is that the Buddhist view excuses the act, categorising it as non-intentional, since he was not aware that the food was poisoned; whereas the Jain view holds the monk to have been responsible, due to his ignorance and carelessness. Jains argue that the monk's very ignorance and carelessness constitute an intent to do violence and hence entail his guilt. So the absence of intent does not absolve a person from the karmic *consequences* of guilt either, according to the Jain analysis.

Intent is a function of kasâya, which refers to negative emotions and negative qualities of mental (or deliberative) action. The presence of intent acts as an aggravating factor, increasing the vibrations of the soul, which results in the soul absorbing more karma. This is explained by *Tattvârthasûtra* 6.7: " intentional act produces a strong karmic bondage and unintentional produces weak, shortlived karmic bondage."

Similarly, the physical act is also not a necessary condition for karma to bind to the soul: the existence of intent alone is sufficient. This is explained by Kundakunda (1st Century CE) in *Samayasâra* 262–263: "The intent to kill, to steal, to be unchaste and to acquire property, whether these offences are actually carried or not, leads to bondage of evil karmas." Jainism thus places an equal emphasis on the physical act as well as intent for binding of karmas.

Origins and Influence

The doctrine of karma is central to all Indian religions, however, it is difficult to say just when and where in India the concept of karma originated. According to Glasenapp, the doctrine of karma must have existed at least a thousand years before the beginning of the Christian era. There is no clear consensus amongst scholars as to its origins, although it is believed by some that the concept of karma has a philosophical background that is non-Vedic and non-brahmanical origin. According to the scholars, the Jain conception of karma—as something material that encumbers the soul—is probably the oldest distinct element, common to all the karmic theories. It is probable that the concept of karma and reincarnation entered the mainstream brahaminical thought via the Sramana—literally "renouncer (of tradition)"—movement, to which Jainism and Buddhism belong. Historian G. C. Pande opines that early Upananisadic thinkers like Yâjñavalkya were acquainted with the Sramanic philosophy and tried to incorporate ideas of karma, *Samsâra* and *moksa* into the Vedic thought.

Jain and Buddhist scholar, Dr. Padmanabh Jaini observes: "Perhaps the entire concept that a person's situation and experiences are in fact the results of deeds committed in various lives may not be Aryan origin at all, but rather may have developed as a part of the indigenous Gangetic traditions from which the various Sramana movements arose. In any case we shall see, Jaina views on the process and possibilities of rebirth are distinctly non-Hindu; the social ramifications of these views, moreover, have been profound." The earliest works of the Jain canon, Acaranga Sutra and Sutrakritanga, contain a general outline of the doctrines of karma and reincarnation, with only minimal technical details and classification. Detailed codification of types of karma and their effects is not attested until the time of Umasvati in 2nd century CE.

With regards to the influence of the theory of karma on development of various religious and social practices in ancient India, Dr. Padmanabh Jaini states:

> The emphasis on reaping the fruits only of one's own karma was not restricted to the Jainas; both Hindus and Buddhist writers have produced doctrinal materials stressing the same point. Each of the latter traditions, however, developed practices in basic contradiction to such belief. In addition to *úrâddha* (the ritual Hindu offerings to the dead ancestors), we find among Hindus widespread adherence to the notion of divine intervention in one's fate, while (Mahayana) Buddhists eventually came to propound such theories like boon-granting Bodhisattvas, transfer of merit and like. Only Jainas have been absolutely unwilling to allow such ideas to penetrate their community, despite the fact that there must have been tremendous amount of social pressure on them to do so.

The Jain socio-religious practices like regular fasting, practicing severe austerities and penances, the ritual death of *sallekhanâ* and rejection of god as the creator and operator of the universe can all be linked to the Jain theory of karma. Jaini notes that the disagreement over the karmic theory of transmigration resulted in the social distinction between the Jains and their Hindu neighbours. Thus one of the most important Hindu ritual of *úrâddha* (offerings to ancestors) was not only rejected but strongly criticised by the Jains as superstition. Certain authors have also noted the strong influence of the concept of karma on the Jain ethics, especially the ethics of non-violence. It is suggested that, belief in the doctrine of rebirth may have led to the idea of the unity of all life and, consequently, to the ethical concept of non-violence in ancient India. Once the doctrine of transmigration of souls came to include rebirth on earth in animal as well as human form, depending upon one's karmas, it is quite probable that, it created a humanitarian sentiment of kinship amongst all life forms and thus contributed to the notion of *ahimsâ.*

The Process of Bondage and Release

The karmic process in Jainism is based on seven truths or fundamental principles (*tattva*) of Jainism which explain the human predicament. Out that the seven *tattvas,* the four—influx (*âsrava*), bondage (*bandha*), stoppage (*samvara*) and release (*nirjarâ*)—pertain to the karmic process.

Attraction and Binding

The karmic bondage occurs as a result of the following two processes: *âsrava* and *bandha*. *Âsravu* is the inflow of karma. The karmic influx occurs when the particles are attracted to the soul on account of *yoga*. *Yoga* is the vibrations of the soul due to activities of mind, speech and body. However, the *yoga* alone do not produce bondage. The karmas have effect only when they are bound to the consciousness. This binding of the karma to the consciousness is called *bandha.* Out of the many causes of bondage, emotions or passions are considered as the main cause of bondage. The karmas are literally bound on account of the stickiness of the soul due to existence of various passions or mental dispositions. The passions like anger, pride, deceit and greed are called sticky (*kasâyas*) because they act like glue in making karmic particles stick to the soul resulting in *bandha*. The karmic inflow on account of *yoga* driven by passions and emotions cause a long term inflow of karma prolonging the cycle of reincarnations. On the other hand, the karmic inflows on account of actions that are not driven by passions and emotions have only a transient, short-lived karmic effect. Hence the ancient Jain texts talk of subduing these negative emotions:

> When he wishes that which is good for him, he should get rid of the four faults—anger, pride, deceit and greed—which increase the evil. Anger and pride when not suppressed, and deceit and greed when arising: all these four black passions water the roots of re-birth.
>
> —*Daúavaikâlika sûtra, 8:36–39*

Causes of Attraction and Bondage

The Jain theory of karma proposes that karma particles are attracted and then bound to the consciousness of souls by a combination of four factors pertaining to actions: instrumentality, process, modality and motivation.

- The **instrumentality** of an action refers to whether the instrument of the action was: the body, as in physical actions; one's speech, as in speech acts; or the mind, as in thoughtful deliberation.

- The **modality** of an action refers to different modes in which one can participate in an action, for example: being the one who carries out the act itself; being one who instigates another to perform the act; or being one who gives permission, approval or endorsement of an act.

- The **process** of an action refers to the temporal sequence in which it occurs: the decision to act, plans to facilitate the act, making preparations necessary for the act, and ultimately the carrying through of the act itself.

- The **motivation** for an action refers to the internal passions or negative emotions that prompt the act, including: anger, greed, pride, deceit and so on.

All actions have the above four factor present in them. When different permutations of the sub-elements of the four factors are calculated, the Jain teachers speak of 108 ways in which the karmic matter can be attracted to the soul. Even giving silent assent or endorsement to acts of violence from far away has karmic consequences for the soul. Hence, the scriptures advise carefulness in actions, awareness of the world, and purity in thoughts as means to avoid the burden of karma.

According to *Tattvârthasûtra*, the causes of *bandha* or the karmic bondage—in the order they are required to be eliminate by a soul for spiritual progress—are:

- *Mithyâtva* (Irrationality and a deluded world view) – The deluded world view is the misunderstanding as to how this world really functions on account of one-sided perspectives, perverse viewpoints, irrational scepticism, pointless generalisations and ignorance.

- *Pramâda* (carelessness and laxity of conduct) – This third cause of bondage consists of absentmindedness, lack of enthusiasm towards acquiring merit and spiritual growth, and improper actions of mind, body and speech without any regard to oneself or others.

- *Avirati* (non-restraint or a vowless life) – The second cause of bondage, *avirati* is the inability to refrain voluntarily from the evil actions, that harms oneself and others. The state of *avirati* can only be overcome by observing the minor vows of a layman.

- *Kasâya* (passions or negative emotions) – The four passions—anger, pride, deceit and greed—are the primary reason for the attachment of the karmas to the soul. They keep the soul immersed in the darkness of delusion leading to deluded conduct and unending cycles of reincarnations.

- *Yoga* (activities of mind, speech and body) – The threefold activities of mind, body and speech attract and bind the karmas when such actions are influenced by passions.

Each cause presupposes the existence of the next cause, but the next cause does not necessarily pre-suppose the existence of the previous cause. A soul is able to advance on the spiritual ladder called *gunasthâna*, only when it is able to eliminate the above causes of bondage one by one.

Experiencing the Effects

The nature of experience of the effects of the karma depends on the following four factors:

- ***Prikriti*** (nature or type of karma) – According to Jain texts, there are eight main types of karma which categorized into the 'harming' and the 'non-harming'; each divided into four types. The harming karmas (*ghâtiyâ karmas*) directly affect the soul powers by impeding its perception, knowledge and energy, and also brings about delusion. These harming karmas are: *darúanâvarana* (perception-obscuring karma), *jñânavârana* (knowledge-obscuring karma), *antarâya* (obstacle-creating karma) and *mohanîya* (deluding karma). The non-harming category (*aghâtiyâ karmas*) is responsible for the reborn soul's physical and mental circumstances, longevity, spiritual potential and experience of pleasant and unpleasant sensations. These non-harming karmas are: *nâmu* (body determining karma), *âyu* (lifespan-determining karma), *gotra* (status-determining karma) and *vedanîya* (feeling-producing karma), respectively. Different types of karmas thus affect the soul in different ways as per their nature.

- ***Anubhava*** (intensity of karmas) – The degree of the experience of the karmas, that is, mild or intense, depends on the *anubhava* quality or the intensity of the bondage. It determines the power of karmas and its effect on the soul. *Anubhava* depends on the intensity of the passions at the time of binding the karmas. More intense the emotions—like anger, greed etc.—at the time of binding the karma, the more intense will be its experience at the time of maturity.
- ***Stithi*** (the duration of the karmic bond) – The karmic bond remains latent and bound to the consciousness up to the time it is activated. Although latent karma does not affect the soul directly, its existence limits the spiritual growth of the soul. Jain texts provide minimum and the maximum duration for which such karma is bound before it matures.
- ***Pradesha*** (The quantity of the karmas) – It the quantity of karmic matter that is received and gets activated at the time of experience.

Both emotions and activity play a part in binding of karmas. Duration and intensity of the karmic bond are determined by emotions or "*kasâya*" and type and quantity of the karmas bound is depended on *yoga* or activity.

Maturity

The consequences of karma are inevitable. The consequences may take some time to take effect but the karma is never fruitless. To explain this, a Jain monk, Ratnaprabhacharya says: "The prosperity of a vicious man and misery of a virtuous man are respectively but the effects of good deeds and bad deeds done previously. The vice and virtue may have their effects in their next lives. In this way the law of causality is not infringed here."

The latent karma becomes active and bears fruit when the supportive conditions arise. A great part of attracted karma bears its consequences with minor fleeting effects, as generally most of our activities are influenced by mild negative emotions. However, those actions that are influenced by intense negative emotions cause an equally strong karmic attachment which usually does not bear fruit immediately. It takes on an inactive state and waits for the supportive conditions—like proper time, place, and environment—to arise for it to manifest and produce effects. If the supportive conditions do not arise, the respective karmas will manifest at the end of maximum period for which it can remain bound to the soul. These supportive conditions for activation of latent karmas are determined by the nature of karmas, intensity of emotional engagement at the time of binding karmas and our actual relation to time, place, surroundings. There are certain laws of precedence among the karmas, according to which the fruition of some of the .karmas may be deferred but not absolutely barred.

Modifications

Although the Jains believe the karmic consequences as inevitable, Jain texts also hold that a soul has energy to transform and modify the effects of the karmas.. Karma undergoes following modifications:

1. *Udaya* (maturity) – It is the fruition of karmas as per its nature in the due course.
2. *Udîrana* (premature operation) – By this process, it is possible to make certain karmas operative before their predetermined time.
3. *Udvartanâ* (augmentation) – By this process, there is a subsequent increase in duration and intensity of

the karmas due to additional negative emotions and feelings.

4. *Apavartanâ* (diminution) – In this case, there is subsequent decrease in duration and intensity of the karmas due to positive emotions and feelings.
5. *Samkramana* (transformation) -- It is the mutation or conversion of one sub-type of karmas into another sub-type. However, this does not occur between different types. For example, *papa* (bad karma) can be converted into *punya* (good karma) as both sub-types belong to the same type of karma.
6. *Upaúamanâ* (state of subsidence) – During this state the operation of karma does not occur. The karma becomes operative only when the duration of subsidence ceases.
7. *Nidhatti* (prevention) – In this state, premature operation and transformation is not possible but augmentation and diminution of karmas is possible.
8. *Nikâcanâ* (invariance) – For some sub-types, no variations or modifications are possible — the consequences are the same as were established at the time of bonding.

The Jain karmic theory, thus speaks of great powers of soul to manipulate the karmas by its actions.

Release

Jains assert that emancipation is not possible as long as the soul is released from bondage of the karmas. This is possible by *samvara,* that is, stoppage of inflow of new karmas, and *nirjarâ,* that is, shedding of existing karmas through conscious efforts. *Samvara* or stoppage of karmic influx is achieved through practice of:

1. Three *guptis* or three controls of mind, speech and body,

2. Five *samitis* or observing carefulness in movement, speaking, eating, placing objects and disposing refuse.
3. Ten *dharmas* or observation of good acts like – forgiveness, humility, straightforwardness, contentment, truthfulness, self control, penance, renunciation, non-attachment and continence.
4. *Anupreksh̄as* or meditation on the truths of this universe.
5. *Parisahajaya*, that is, a man on moral path must develop a perfectly patient and unperturbed attitude in the midst of trying and difficult circumstances.
6. *Câritra*, that is, endeavour to remain in steady spiritual practices.

Nirjarâ or annihilation of the existing karmas is possible through *tapas*, that is, austerities and penances. *Tapas* can be either external or internal. Six forms of external *tapas* are—fasting, control of appetite, accepting food under certain conditions, renunciation of delicious food, sitting and sleeping in lonely place and renunciation of comforts. Six forms of internal *tapas* are—atonement, reverence, rendering of service to worthy ones, spiritual study, avoiding selfish feelings and meditation.

Rationale

Justice Tukol notes that the supreme importance of the doctrine of karma lies in providing a rational and satisfying explanation to the apparent unexplainable phenomenon of birth and death, of happiness and misery, of inequalities and of existence of different species of living beings. *Sûtrakrtânga*, one of the oldest canon of Jainism, states:

> Here in the east, west, north, and south many men have been born according to their merit, as inhabitants of this our world—some as Aryas, some as non-Aryas, some in

> noble families, some in low families, some as big men, some as small men, some of good complexion, some of bad complexion, some as handsome men, some as ugly men. And of these men one man is king.
>
> — *Sûtrakrtânga*, 2.1.13

Jains thus cite inequalities, sufferings, and pain as evidence for the existence of karma. The theory of karma is able to explain day-to-day observable phenomena such as inequality between the rich and the poor, luck, differences in lifespan, and the ability to enjoy life despite being immoral. According to Jains, such inequalities and oddities that exist even from the time of birth can be attributed to the deeds of the past lives and thus provide evidence to existence of karmas:

One is stout while another is lean; one is a master while another is a slave and similarly we find the high and the low, the mutilated and the lame, the blind and the deaf and many such oddities. The thrones of mighty monarchs are gone. The proud and the haughty have been humiliated in a moment and reduced to ashes. Even amongst the twins born of the same mother, we find one a dullard and another intelligent, one rich and another poor, one black and another white. What is all this due to? They could not have done any deeds while they were in their mother's womb. Then, why then should such oddities exist? We have then to infer that these disparities must be the result of their deeds in their past births though they are born together at one time. There are many oddities in this world and it will have to be admitted that behind all this some powerful force is at work whereby the world appears to be full of oddities. This force is called 'karma'. We are unable to perceive karma by our naked eyes, yet we are able to know it from its actions.

Scientific Interpretation

Jain philosopher-monks postulated the existence of karma as subtle and microscopic particles that cannot be perceived by senses, some two millennia before modern science proved the existence of atoms and subatomic particles. However, these and other elementary particles that have been either discovered or postulated cannot be equated with karmic particles. Some authors have sought to explain the concept of karmic particles in the context of modern science and physics. Hermann Kuhn points out that, although the idea of "karmic particles" is not yet proven, one only needs to recall that science found proof of the existence of molecules and atoms only the 19th and 20th century. Anyone who would have suggested that these "indivisible" particles were made up of even subtler units like quarks and leptons only a hundred years ago may have been dismissed, though such theories were in existence. With regards to interaction of consciousness and karmic matter, he further states that, it can be easily understood considering that ideas like the mind fundamentally affecting matter are now accepted in scientific circles. While admitting that though science has not discovered karmic matter yet, he is of opinion that it does not state anything against its existence. K. V. Mardia, in his book *The Scientific Foundations of Jainism,* has interpreted karma in terms of modern physics, suggesting that the particles are made of *karmons,* dynamic high energy particles which permeate the universe. However, most scientists do not consider karma and reincarnation to be within the bounds of science, as it is neither a testable nor a falsifiable theory.

Criticisms

The Jain theory of karma has been challenged since ancient times by Vedanta Hindu, Buddhist and Sâmkhya philosophies.

In particular, Vedanta Hindus considered the Jain position on the supremacy and potency of karma, specifically its insistence on non-intervention by any Supreme Being in regard to the fate of souls, as worthy of the label *nâstika* or atheistic. For example, in a commentary to Brahma Sutras (III, 2, 38, and 41)), Adi Sankara, argues that the original karmic actions themselves cannot bring about the proper results at some future time; neither can super sensuous, non-intelligent qualities like adrsta—an unseen force being the metaphysical link between work and its result—by themselves mediate the appropriate, justly deserved pleasure and pain. The fruits, according to him, then, must be administered through the action of a conscious agent, namely, a supreme being (Ishvara).

Strong emphasis on the doctrine of karma and intense asceticism was also criticised by the Buddhists, even though they also believe in karma. The ancient Buddhist scripture *Samyutta Nikâya* narrates the story of Asibandhakaputta, a headman who was originally a disciple of Mâhavîra. He debates with the Buddha, telling him that, according to Mâhavîra (Nigantha Nâtaputta), a man's fate or karma is decided by what he does habitually. The Buddha responds, considering this view to be inadequate, stating that even a habitual sinner spends more time "not doing the sin" and only some time actually "doing the sin."

In another Buddhist text *Majjhima Nikâya,* the Buddha criticizes Jain emphasis on the destruction of unobservable and unverifiable types of karma as a means to end suffering, rather than on eliminating evil mental states such as greed, hatred and delusion, which are observable and verifiable. In the Upâlisutta dialogue of this *Majjhima Nikâya* text, Buddha contends with a Jain monk who asserts that bodily actions are the most criminal, in comparison to the actions of speech and mind. Buddha criticises this view, saying that the actions of *mind* are most criminal, and not the actions of speech or body. Buddha also criticises the Jain ascetic practice of various austerities, claiming that he, Buddha, is happier when *not* practising the austerities.

While admitting the complexity and sophistication of the Jain doctrine, Padmanabh Jaini compares it with that of Hindu doctrine of rebirth and points out that the Jain seers are silent on the exact moment and mode of rebirth, that is, the re-entry of soul in womb after the death. The concept of *nitya-nigoda,* which states that there are certain categories of souls who have always been *nigodas,* is also criticised. According to Jainism, *nigodas* are lowest form of extremely microscopic beings having momentary life spans, living in colonies and pervading the entire universe. According to Dr. Jaini, the entire concept of *nitya-nigoda* undermines the concept of karma, as these beings clearly would not have had prior opportunity to perform any karmically meaningful actions.

Karma is also criticised on the grounds that it leads to the dampening of spirits with men suffering the ills of life because the course of one's life is determined by karma. It is often maintained that the impression of karma as the accumulation of a mountain of bad deeds looming over our heads without any recourse leads to fatalism. However, as Paul Dundas puts it, the Jain theory of karma does not imply lack of free will or operation of total deterministic control over destinies.

●●

4
Anekantavada

Anekantavada is one of the most important and fundamental doctrines of Jainism. It refers to the principles of pluralism and multiplicity of viewpoints, the notion that truth and reality are perceived differently from diverse points of view, and that no single point of view is the complete truth.

Jains contrast all attempts to proclaim absolute truth with *adhgajanyâyah,* which can be illustrated through the parable of the "blind men and an elephant". In this story, each blind man felt a different part of an elephant (trunk, leg, ear, etc.). All the men claimed to understand and explain the true appearance of the elephant, but could only partly succeed, due to their limited perspectives. This principle is more formally stated by observing that objects are infinite in their qualities and modes of existence, so they cannot be completely grasped in all aspects and manifestations by finite human perception. According to the Jains, only the *Kevalins*—the omniscient beings—can comprehend objects in all aspects and manifestations; others are only capable of partial knowledge. Consequently, no single, specific, human view can claim to represent absolute truth.

The origins of *anekântavâda* can be traced back to the teachings of Mâhavîra (599–527 BCE), the 24th Jain *Tîrthankara.* The dialectical concepts of *syâdvâda* (conditioned viewpoints) and *nayavâda* (partial viewpoints) arose from *anekântavâda,* providing it with more detailed logical structure and expression. The Sanskrit compound *an-eka-anta-vâda* literally means "doctrine of non-exclusivity or multiple view points(an- 'which is not', eka-' one', vada- 'viewpoint')"; it is translated into English as "scepticism" or "non-absolutism". *An-ekânta* "uncertainty, non-exclusivity" is the opposite of *ekânta* (*eka+anta*) "exclusiveness, absoluteness, necessity" (or also "monotheistic doctrine").

Anekântavâda encourages its adherents to consider the views and beliefs of their rivals and opposing parties. Proponents of *anekântavâda* apply this principle to religion and philosophy, reminding themselves that any religion or philosophy—even Jainism—which clings too dogmatically to its own tenets, is committing an error based on its limited point of view. The principle of *anekântavâda* also influenced Mohandas Karamchand Gandhi to adopt principles of religious tolerance, *ahimsâ* and *satyagraha*.

Philosophical Overview

The etymological root of *anekântavâda* lies in the compound of two Sanskrit words: *anekânta* ("manifoldness") and *vâda* ("school of thought"). The word *anekânta* is a compound of the Sanskrit negative prefix *an*, *ek* ("singularity"), and *anta* ("attribute"). Hence, *anekânta* means "not of solitary attribute". The Jain doctrine lays a strong emphasis on *samyaktva*, that is, rationality and logic. According to Jains, the ultimate principle should always be logical and no principle can be devoid of logic or reason. Thus, the Jain texts contain deliberative exhortations on every subject whether they are constructive or obstructive, inferential or analytical, enlightening or destructive.

Jain Doctrines of Relativity

Anekântavâda is onc of the three Jain doctrines of relativity used for logic and reasoning. The other two are:

- *syâdvâda*—the theory of conditioned predication and;
- *nayavâda*—the theory of partial standpoints.

These Jain philosophical concepts made important contributions to ancient Indian philosophy, especially in the areas of skepticism and relativity.

Syadvada

Syâdvâda is the theory of conditioned predication which provides an expression to *anekânta* by recommending that the epithet *Syâd* be prefixed to every phrase or expression. *Syâdvâda* is not only an extension of *anekânta* ontology, but a separate system of logic capable of standing on its own. The Sanskrit etymological root of the term *syâd* is "perhaps" or "maybe", but in the context of *syâdvâda*, it means "in some ways" or "from a perspective". As reality is complex, no single proposition can express the nature of reality fully. Thus the term "*syât*" should be prefixed before each proposition giving it a conditional point of view and thus removing any dogmatism in the statement. Since it ensures that each statement is expressed from seven different conditional and relative viewpoints or propositions, *syâdvâda* is known as *saptibhangînâya* or the theory of seven conditioned predications. These seven propositions, also known as *saptibhangî*, are:

1. *syâd-asti*—in some ways, it is,
2. *syâd-nâsti*—in some ways, it is not,
3. *syâd-asti-nâsti*—in some ways, it is, and it is not,
4. *syâd-asti-avaktavyah*—in some ways, it is, and it is indescribable,
5. *syâd-nâsti-avaktavyah*—in some ways, it is not, and it is indescribable,
6. *syâd-asti-nâsti-avaktavyah*—in some ways, it is, it is not, and it is indescribable,
7. *syâd-avaktavyah*—in some ways, it is indescribable.

Each of these seven propositions examines the complex and multifaceted nature of reality from a relative point of view of time, space, substance and mode. To ignore the complexity of reality is to commit the fallacy of dogmatism.

Nayavâda

Nayavâda is the theory of partial standpoints or viewpoints. *Nayavâda* is a compound of two Sanskrit words—*naya* ("partial viewpoint") and *vâda* ("school of thought or debate"). It is used to arrive at a certain inference from a point of view. An object has infinite aspects to it, but when we describe an object in practice, we speak of only relevant aspects and ignore irrelevant ones. This does not deny the other attributes, qualities, modes and other aspects; they are just irrelevant from a particular perspective. Authors like Natubhai Shah explain *nayavâda* with the example of a car; for instance, when we talk of a "blue BMW" we are simply considering the color and make of the car. However, our statement does not imply that the car is devoid of other attributes like engine type, cylinders, speed, price and the like. This particular viewpoint is called a *naya* or a partial viewpoint. As a type of critical philosophy, *nayavâda* holds that all philosophical disputes arise out of confusion of standpoints, and the standpoints we adopt are, although we may not realize it, "the outcome of purposes that we may pursue". While operating within the limits of language and seeing the complex nature of reality, Mâhavîra used the language of *nayas*. *Naya*, being a partial expression of truth, enables us to comprehend reality part by part.

Syncretisation of Changing and Unchanging Reality

The age of Mâhavîra and Buddha was an age of intense intellectual debates, especially on the nature of reality and self. Upanishadic thought postulated the absolute unchanging reality of *Brahman* and *atman* and claimed that change was mere illusion. The theory advanced by Buddhists denied the reality of permanence of conditioned phenomena, asserting only interdependence and impermanence. According to the

Vedânta (Upanishadic) conceptual scheme, the Buddhists were wrong in denying permanence and absolutism, and within the Buddhist conceptual scheme, the vedântins were wrong in denying the reality of impermanence. The two positions were contradictory and mutually exclusive from each others' point of view. The Jains managed a synthesis of the two uncompromising positions with *anekântavâda*. From the perspective of a higher, inclusive level made possible by the ontology and epistemology of *anekântavâda* and *syâdvâda*, Jains do not see such claims as contradictory or mutually exclusive; instead, they are seen as *ekantika* or only partially true. The Jain breadth of vision embraces the perspectives of both Vedânta which, according to Jainism, "recognizes substances but not process", and Buddhism, which "recognizes process but not substance". Jainism, on the other hand, pays equal attention to both substance *(dravya)* and process *(paryaya)*.

Mâhavîra's responses to various questions asked by his disciples and recorded in the Jain canon *Bhagvatisûtra* demonstrate recognition that there are complex and multiple aspects to truth and reality and a mutually exclusive approach cannot be taken to explain such reality:

> **Gautama**: Lord! Is the soul permanent or impermanent?
>
> **Mâhavîra**: The soul is permanent as well as impermanent. From the point of view of the substance it is eternal. From the point of view of its modes it undergoes birth, decay and destruction and hence impermanent.
>
> —*Bhagvatisûtra*, 7:58–59
>
> **Jayanti**: Lord! Of the states of slumber or awakening, which one is better?
>
> **Mâhavîra**: For some souls the state of slumber is better, for some souls the states of awakening. Slumber is better for those who are engaged in sinful activities and

awakening for those who are engaged in meritorious deeds.

—*Bhagvatisûtra*, 12:53–54

Thousands of questions were asked and Mâhavîra's responses suggested a complex and multifaceted reality with each answer qualified from a viewpoint. According to Jainism, even a *Tîrthankara,* who possesses and perceives infinite knowledge, cannot express reality completely because of the limitations of language, which is of human creation.

This philosophical syncretisation of paradox of change through *anekânta* has been acknowledged by modern scholars such as Arvind Sharma, who wrote:

Our experience of the world presents a profound paradox which we can ignore existentially, but not philosophically. This paradox is the paradox of change. Something – A changes and therefore it cannot be permanent. On the other hand, if A is not permanent, then what changes? In this debate between the 'permanence' and 'change', Hinduism seems more inclined to grasp the first horn of the dilemma and Buddhism the second. It is Jainism that has the philosophical courage to grasp both horns fearlessly and simultaneously, and the philosophical skill not to be gored by either.

However, *anekântavâda* is simply not about syncretisation or compromise between competing ideas, as it is about finding the hidden elements of shared truth between such ideas. *Anekântavâda* is not about denying the truth; rather truth is acknowledged as an ultimate spiritual goal. For ordinary humans, it is an elusive goal, but they are still obliged to work towards its attainment. *Anekântavâda* also does not mean compromising or diluting ones own values and principles. On the contrary, it allows us to understand and be tolerant of conflicting and opposing views, while respectfully maintaining the validity of ones own view-point. Hence,

John Koller calls *anekântavâda* as – "epistemological respect for view of others". *Anekântavâda,* thus, did not prevent the Jain thinkers from defending the truth and validity of their own doctrine while simultaneously respecting and understanding the rival doctrines. Anne Vallely notes that the epistemological respect for other view-points was put to practice when she was invited by Âcârya Tulsi, the head of Jain Terâpanthî order, to teach their Jain nuns, the tenets of Christianity. Commenting on their adherence to *ahimsâ* and *anekântavâda,* she says:

> The Jain *samanîs* of Ladnun uncompromisingly maintain *ahimsâ* to be an eternal and unchangeable moral law. Other views and beliefs that contradict this belief would certainly be challenged, and ultimately rejected. But what is significant, is that both the rejection and retention of views is tempered by the belief that our perception conveys only a partial reality, that reality itself is manifold, and that to that, assume one particular viewpoint is final, is to hold a limited picture of reality.

Anekântavâda is also different from moral relativism. It does not mean conceding that all arguments and all views are equal, but rather logic and evidence determine which views are true, in what respect and to what extent. While employing *anekântavâda,* the 17th century philosopher monk, Yaœovijaya Gani also cautions against *anâbhigrahika* (indiscriminate attachment to all views as being true), which is effectively a kind of misconceived relativism. Jains thus consider *anekântavâda* as a positive concept corresponding to religious pluralism that transcends monism and dualism, implying a sophisticated conception of a complex reality. It does not merely involve rejection of partisanship, but reflects a positive spirit of reconciliation of opposite views. However, it is argued that pluralism often degenerates to some form of moral relativism or religious exclusivism. According to Anne Vallely, *anekânta* is a way out of this epistemological quagmire, as it makes a genuinely pluralistic view possible without lapsing into extreme moral relativism or exclusivity.

Parable of the Blind Men and Elephant

The ancient Jain texts often explain the concepts of *anekântvâda* and *syâdvâda* with the parable of the blind men and an elephant (*Andhgajanyâyah*), which addresses the manifold nature of truth.

A group of blind men heard that a strange animal, called an elephant, had been brought to the town, but none of them were aware of its shape and form. Out of curiosity, they said: "We must inspect and know it by touch, of which we are capable". So, they sought it out, and when they found it they groped about it. In the case of the first person, whose hand landed on the trunk, said "This being is like a drain pipe". For another one whose hand reached its ear, it seemed like a kind of fan. As for another person, whose hand was upon its leg, said, "I perceive the shape of the elephant to be like a pillar". And in the case of the one who placed his hand upon its back said, "Indeed, this elephant is like a throne". Now, each of these presented a true aspect when he related what he had gained from experiencing the elephant. None of them had strayed from the true description of the elephant. Yet they fell short of fathoming the true appearance of the elephant.

Two of the many references to this parable are found in *Tattvarthaslokavatika* of Vidyanandi (9th century) and *Syâdvâdamanjari* of Âcârya Mallisena (13th century). Mallisena uses the parable to argue that immature people deny various aspects of truth; deluded by the aspects they *do* understand, they deny the aspects they *don't* understand. "Due to extreme delusion produced on account of a partial viewpoint, the immature deny one aspect and try to establish another. This is the maxim of the blind (men) and the elephant." Mallisena also cites the parable when noting the importance of considering all viewpoints in obtaining a full picture of reality. "It is impossible to properly understand an entity consisting of infinite properties without the method of modal description consisting of all viewpoints, since it will otherwise lead to a situation of seizing mere sprouts (i.e., a superficial, inadequate cognition), on the maxim of the blind (men) and the elephant."

History and Development

The principle of *anekântavâda* is the foundation of many Jain philosophical concepts. The development of *anekântavâda* also encouraged the development of the dialectics of *syâdvâda* (conditioned viewpoints), *saptibhangî* (the seven conditioned predication), and *nayavâda* (partial viewpoints).

Origins

The origins of *anekântavâda* lie in the teachings of Mâhavîra, who used it effectively to show the relativity of truth and reality. Taking a relativistic viewpoint, Mâhavîra is said to have explained the nature of the soul as both permanent, from the point of view of underlying substance, and temporary, from the point of view of its modes and modification. The importance and antiquity of *anekântavâda* are also demonstrated by the fact that it formed the subject matter of *Astinasti Pravâda*, the fourth part of the lost *Purva* that contained teachings of the *Tirthankaras* prior to Mâhavira. German Indologist Hermann Jacobi believes Mâhavîra effectively employed the dialectics of *anekântavâda* to refute the agnosticism of Sañjaya Belatthaputta. *Sutrakritanga*, the second oldest canon of Jainism, contains the first references to *syâdvâda* and *saptibhangî*. According to *Sûtrakritanga*, Mâhavîra advised his disciples to use *syâdvâda* to preach his teachings:

> A monk living single should not ridicule heretical doctrines, and should avoid hard words though they be true; he should not be vain, nor brag, but he should without embarrassment and passion preach the Law. A

monk should be modest, though he be of a fearless mind; he should expound the *syâdvâda*, he should use the two permitted kinds of speech, living among virtuous men, impartial and wise.

—*Sûtrakritânga*, 14:21-22

Early History

Sutrakritanga contains references to *Vibhagyavâda*, which, according to Jacobi, is the same as *syâdvâda* and *saptibhangî*. The early Jain canons and teachings contained multitudes of references to *anekântavâda* and *syâdvâda* in rudimentary form without giving it proper structure or establishing it as a separate doctrine. *Bhagvatisûtra* mentions only three primary predications of the *saptibhangînaya*. After Mâhavîra, Kundakunda (1st century CE) was the first author–saint to expound on the doctrine of *syâdvâda* and *saptibhangî* and give it a proper structure in his famous works *Pravacanasâra* and *Pancastikayasâra*. Kundakunda also used *nayas* to discuss the essence of the self in *Samayasâra*. Proper classification of the *nayas* was provided by the philosopher monk, Umâsvâti (2nd century CE) in *Tattvârthasûtra*. Samantabhadra (2nd century CE) and Siddhasena Divâkara (3rd century CE) further fine-tuned Jain epistemology and logic by expounding on the concepts of *anekântavâda* in proper form and structure.

Âcârya Siddhasena Divâkara expounded on the nature of truth in the court of King Vikramâditya:

Vikramâditya: What is 'truth'? That which is said repeatedly, that which is said loudly, that which is said with authority or that which is agreed by the majority?

Divâkara: None of the above. Every one has his own definition of 'truth' and that it is conditional.

Vikramâditya: How about traditions? They have been established by our ancestors and have passed the test of time?

Divâkara: Would the system established by ancestors hold true on examination? In case it does not, I am not here to justify it for the sake of saving the traditional grace of the dead, irrespective of the wrath I may have to face.

—Âcârya Siddhasena Divâkara, *Vardhamana Dvâtrimsikâ*, 6/2

In *Sanmatitarka*, Divâkara further adds:

"All doctrines are right in their own respective spheres—but if they encroach upon the province of other doctrines and try to refute their view, they are wrong. A man who holds the view of the cumulative character of truth never says that a particular view is right or that a particular view is wrong."

Age of Logic

The period beginning with the start of common era, up to the modern period is often referred to as the age of logic in the history of Jain philosophy. By the time of Akalanka (5th century CE), whose works are a landmark in Jain logic, *anekântavâda* was firmly entrenched in Jain texts, as is evident from the various teachings of the Jain scriptures.

Âcârya Haribhadra (8th century CE) was one of the leading proponents of *anekântavâda*. He was the first classical author to write a doxography, a compendium of a variety of intellectual views. This attempted to contextualise Jain thoughts within the broad framework, rather than espouse narrow partisan views. It interacted with the many possible intellectual orientations available to Indian thinkers around the 8th century.

Âcârya Amrtacandra starts his famous 10th century CE work *Purusathasiddhiupaya* with strong praise for *anekântavâda*: "I bow down to the principle of *anekânta*, the source and foundation of the highest scriptures, the dispeller of wrong one-sided notions, that which takes into account all aspects of truth, reconciling diverse and even contradictory traits of all objects or entity."

Âcârya Vidyânandi (11th century CE) provides the analogy of the ocean to explain the nature of truth in *Tattvarthaslokavârtikka*, 116: "Water from the ocean contained in a pot can neither be called an ocean nor a non-ocean, but simply a part of ocean. Similarly, a doctrine, though arising from absolute truth can neither be called a whole truth nor a non-truth."

Yaœovijaya Gani, a 17th century Jain monk, went beyond *anekântavâda* by advocating *madhâyastha*, meaning "standing in the middle" or "equidistance". This position allowed him to praise qualities in others even though the people were non-Jain and belonged to other faiths. There was a period of stagnation after Yasovijayaji, as there were no new contributions to the development of Jain philosophy.

Role in Ensuring the Survival of Jainism

Anekântavâda played a pivotal role in the growth as well as the survival of Jainism in ancient India, especially against onslaughts from Œaivas, Vaisnavas, Buddhists, Muslims, and Christians at various times. According to Hermann Jacobi, Mâhavîra used such concepts as *syâdvâda* and *saptbhangi* to silence some of his opponents. The discussions of the agnostics led by Sañjaya Belammhaputta had probably influenced many of their contemporaries and consequently *syâdvâda* may have seemed to them a way out of *ajñânavâda*. Jacobi further speculates that many of their followers would have gone over to Mâhavîra's creed, convinced of the truth of the *saptbhanginaya*. According to Professor Christopher Key Chapple, *anekântavâda* allowed Jains to survive during the most hostile and unfavourable moments in history. According to John Koller, professor of Asian studies, *anekântavâda* allowed

Jain thinkers to maintain the validity of their doctrine, while at the same time respectfully criticizing the views of their opponents.

Anekântavâda was often used by Jain monks to obtain royal patronage from Hindu Kings. Âcârya Hemacandra used *anekântavâda* to gain the confidence and respect of the Câlukya Emperor Jayasimha Siddharaja. According to the Jain text *Prabandhacantamani*, Emperor Siddharaja desired enlightenment and liberation and he questioned teachers from various traditions. He remained in a quandary when he discovered that they all promoted their own teachings while disparaging other teachings. Among the teachers he questioned was Hemacandra, who, rather than promote Jainism, told him a story with a different message. According to his story, a sick man was cured of his disease after eating all the herbs available, as he was not aware which herb was medicinal. The moral of the tale, according to Hemacandra, was that just as the man was restored by the herb, even though no one knew which particular herb did the trick, so in the *kaliyuga* ("age of vice") the wise should obtain salvation by supporting all religious traditions, even though no-one can say with absolute certainty which tradition it is that provides that salvation.

Influence

Jain religious tolerance fits well with the ecumenical disposition typical of Indian religions. It can be traced to the analogous Jain principles of *anekântavâda* and *ahimsâ*. The epistemology of *anekântavâda* and *syâdvâda* also had a profound impact on the development of ancient Indian logic and philosophy. In recent times, Jainism influenced Gandhi, who advocated *ahimsâ* and *satyagraha*.

Intellectual Ahimsâ and Religious Tolerance

The concepts of *anekântavâda* and *syâdvâda* allow Jains to accept the truth in other philosophies from their own perspective and thus inculcate tolerance for other viewpoints. *Anekântavâda* is non-absolutist and stands firmly against all dogmatisms, including any assertion that Jainism is the only correct religious path. It is thus an intellectual *ahimsâ*, or *ahimsâ* of the mind. Burch writes, "Jain logic is intellectual *ahimsâ*. Just as a right-acting person respects the life of all beings, so a right-thinking person acknowledges the validity of all judgments. This means recognizing all aspects of reality, not merely one or some aspects, as is done in non-Jain philosophies."

Mâhavîra encouraged his followers to study and understand rival traditions in his *Acaranga Sutra*: "Comprehend one philosophical view through the comprehensive study of another one."

In *anekântavâda*, there is no "battle of ideas", because this is considered to be a form of intellectual *himsa* or violence, leading quite logically to physical violence and war. In today's world, the limitations of the adversarial, "either with us or against us" form of argument are increasingly apparent by the fact that the argument leads to political, religious and social conflicts. *Sûtrakrtânga*, the second oldest canon of Jainism, provides a solution by stating: "Those who praise their own doctrines and ideology and disparage the doctrine of others distort the truth and will be confined to the cycle of birth and death."

Contemporary Role and Influence

Some modern authors believe that Jain philosophy in general and *anekântavâda* in particular can provide a solution to many problems facing the world. They claim that even the mounting ecological crisis is linked to adversarialism, because it arises from a false division between humanity and "the rest" of nature. Modern judicial systems, democracy, freedom of speech, and secularism all implicitly reflect an attitude of *anekântavâda*. Many authors, such as Kamla Jain, have claimed that the Jain tradition, with its emphasis on *ahimsâ* and *anekântavâda,* is capable of solving religious intolerance, terrorism, wars, the depletion of natural resources, environmental degradation and many other problems. Referring to the 9/11 tragedy, John Koller believes that violence in society mainly exists due to faulty epistemology and metaphysics as well as faulty ethics. A failure to respect the life and views of others, rooted in dogmatic and mistaken knowledge and refusal to acknowledge the legitimate claims of different perspectives, leads to violent and destructive behaviour. Koller suggests that *anekântavâda* has a larger role to play in the world peace. According to Koller, because *anekântavâda* is designed to avoid one-sided errors, reconcile contradictory viewpoints, and accept the multiplicity and relativity of truth, the Jain philosophy is in a unique position to support dialogue and negotiations amongst various nations and peoples.

Some Indologists like Professor John Cort have cautioned against giving undue importance to "intellectual *ahimsâ*" as the basis of *anekântavâda.* He points out that Jain monks have also used *anekântavâda* and *syâdvâda* as debating weapons to silence their critics and prove the validity of the Jain doctrine over others. According to Dundas, in Jain hands, this method of analysis became a fearsome weapon of philosophical polemic with which the doctrines of Hinduism and Buddhism could be pared down to their ideological bases of simple permanence and impermanence, respectively, and thus could be shown to be one-pointed and inadequate as the overall interpretations of reality which they purported to be. On the other hand, the many-sided approach was claimed by the Jains to be immune from criticism since it did not present itself as a philosophical or dogmatic view.

Influence on Mohandas Karamchand Gandhi

Since childhood, Mohandas Karamchand Gandhi was exposed to the actual practice of non-violence, non-possession and *anekântavâda* by his mother. According to biographers like Uma Majumdar, Rajmohan Gandhi, and Stephen Hay, these early childhood impressions and experiences contributed to the formation of Gandhi's character and his further moral and spiritual development. In his writings, Mahatma Gandhi attributed his seemingly contradictory positions over a period of time to the learning process, experiments with truth and his belief in *anekântavâda*. He proclaimed that the duty of every individual is to determine what is personally true and act on that relative perception of truth. According to Gandhi, a satyagrahi is duty bound to act according to his relative truth, but at the same time, he is also equally bound to learn from truth held by his opponent. In response to a friend's query on religious tolerance, he responded in the journal "Young India - 21 Jan 1926":

> I am an Advaitist and yet I can support Dvaitism (dualism). The world is changing every moment, and is therefore unreal, it has no permanent existence. But though it is constantly changing, it has a something about it which persists and it is therefore to that extent real. I have therefore no objection to calling it real and unreal, and thus being called an *Anekântavadi* or a *Syâdvadi*. But my *Syâdvâda* is not the *Syâdvâda* of the learned, it is peculiarly my own. I cannot engage in a debate with them. It has been my experience that I am always true from my point of view, and am often wrong from the point of view of my honest critics. I know that we are both right from our respective points of view. And this knowledge saves me from attributing motives to my opponents or critics. The seven blind men who gave seven different descriptions of the elephant were all right from their respective points of view, and wrong from the point of view of one another, and right and wrong from the point of view of the man who knew the elephant. I very much like this doctrine of the manyness

(sic) of reality. It is this doctrine that has taught me to judge a Musulman (sic) from his standpoint and a Christian from his. Formerly I used to resent the ignorance of my opponents. Today I can love them because I am gifted with the eye to see myself as others see me and vice versa. I want to take the whole world in the embrace of my love. My *Anekântavâda* is the result of the twin doctrine of Satyagraha and *ahimsâ*.

Criticism

The doctrines of *anekântavâda* and *syâdavâda* are often criticised on the grounds that they engender a degree of hesitancy and uncertainty, and may compound problems rather than solve them. It is also pointed out that Jain epistemology asserts its own doctrines, but at the cost of being unable to deny contradictory doctrines. Furthermore, it is also argued that this doctrine could be self-defeating. It is argued that if reality is so complex that no single doctrine can describe it adequately, then *anekântavâda* itself, being a single doctrine, must be inadequate. This criticism seems to have been anticipated by Âcârya Samantabhadra who said: "From the point of view of *pramana* (means of knowledge) it is *anekânta* (multi-sided), but from a point of view of *naya* (partial view) it is *ekanta* (one-sided)."

In defense of the doctrine, Jains point out that *anekântavâda* seeks to reconcile apparently opposing viewpoints rather than refuting them.

Anekântavâda received much criticism from the Vedantists, notably Adi Sankarâcârya (9th century C.E.). Sankara argued against some tenets of Jainism in his *bhasya* on *Brahmasutra* (2:2:33–36). His main arguments centre on *anekântavâda*:

> It is impossible that contradictory attributes such as being and non-being should at the same time belong to one and the same thing; just as observation teaches us

that a thing cannot be hot and cold at the same moment. The third alternative expressed in the words – they either are such or not such – results in cognition of indefinite nature, which is no more a source of true knowledge than doubt is. Thus the means of knowledge, the object of knowledge, the knowing subject, and the act of knowledge become all alike indefinite. How can his followers act on a doctrine, the matter of which is altogether indeterminate? The result of your efforts is perfect knowledge and is not perfect knowledge. Observation shows that, only when a course of action is known to have a definite result, people set about it without hesitation. Hence a man who proclaims a doctrine of altogether indefinite contents does not deserve to be listened anymore than a drunken or a mad man.

—Adi Sankarâcârya, *Brahmasutra,* 2.2:33–36

However, many believe that Sankara fails to address genuine *anekântavâda*. By identifying *syâdavâda* with *sansayavâda,* he instead addresses "agnosticism", which was argued by Sañjaya Belatthaputta. Many authors like Pandya believe that Sankara overlooked that, the affirmation of the existence of an object is in respect to the object itself, and its negation is in respect to what the object is not. Genuine *anekântavâda* thus considers positive and negative attributes of an object, at the same time, and without any contradictions.

Another Buddhist logician Dharmakirti ridiculed *anekântavâda* in *Pramânavarttikakârika*: "With the differentiation removed, all things have dual nature. Then, if somebody is implored to eat curd, then why he does not eat camel?" The insinuation is obvious; if curd exists from the nature of curd and does not exist from the nature of a camel, then one is justified in eating camel, as by eating camel, he is merely eating the negation of curd. Âcârya Akalanka, while agreeing that Dharmakirti may be right from one viewpoint, took it upon himself to issue a rejoinder:

> The person who criticises without understanding the prima facie view is acting like a jester and not a critic. The Buddha was born a deer and the deer was born as Buddha; but Buddha is adorable and deer is only a food. Similarly, due to the strength of an entity, with its differences and similarities specified, nobody would eat camel if implored to eat curd.

●●

5
Jain Cosmology

Jain cosmology is the description of the shape and functioning of the physical and metaphysical Universe (*loka*) and its constituents (such as living, matter, space, time etc.) according to Jainism, which includes the canonical Jain texts, commentaries and the writings of the Jain philosopher-monks. Jain cosmology considers the loka, or universe, as an uncreated entity, existing since infinity, having no beginning or an end. Jain texts describe the shape of the universe as similar to a man standing with legs apart and arm resting on his waist. This Universe, according to Jainism, is narrow at the top, broad at the middle and once again becomes broad at the bottom. Mahâpurâna of Âcârya Jinasena is famous for this quote:

> "Some foolish men declare that a creator made the world. The doctrine that the world was created is ill advised and should be rejected. If God created the world, where was he before the creation? If you say he was transcendent then and needed no support, where is he now? How could God have made this world without any raw material? If you say that he made this first, and then the world, you are faced with an endless regression."

The Concept of Reality – the Constituents of the Universe

This Universe is made up of what Jains call six dravya or reals or substances classified as follows –

- **Jîva *i.e.* Living Substances**

  Jîva i.e. Souls - Soul (Jîva) exists as a reality, having a separate existence from the body that houses it. It is characterised by chetana i.e. consciousness and upayoga i.e. knowledge and perception. Though the soul experiences both birth and death, it is neither really destroyed nor created. Decay and origin refer respectively to the disappearing of one state of soul and appearing of another state, these being merely the modes of the soul.

- **Ajîva *i.e.* or Non-Living Substances**
  - **Pudgala i.e. Matter** - Matter is classified as solid, liquid, gaseous, energy, fine Karmic materials and extra-fine matter i.e. ultimate particles. Paramânu or ultimate particle (atoms) is the basic building block of all matter. One of the qualities of the Paramânu and Pudgala is that of permanence and indestructibility. It combines and changes its modes but its basic qualities remain the same. According to Jainism, it cannot be created nor destroyed.
  - **Dharma-tattva i.e Principle of Motion** and
  - **Adharma-tattva i.e. Principle of Rest** - Dharmastikâya and Adharmastikâya are distinctly peculiar to Jaina system of thought depicting the principle of Motion and Rest. They are said to pervade the entire universe. Dharma and Adharma are by itself not motion or rest but mediate motion and rest in other bodies. Without Dharmastikâya motion is not possible and without Adharmastikâya rest is not possible in universe.
  - **Âkâúa i.e Space** - Space is a substance that accommodates the living souls, the matter, the principle of motion, the principle of rest and time. It is all-pervading, infinite and made of infinite space-points.

- **Kâla i.e. Time** - Kâla is a real entity according to Jainism and all activities, changes or modifications can be achieved only through the progress of time.

Time Cycle

According to Jainism, the time is beginningless and eternal. The Kâlacakra, the cosmic wheel of time rotates ceaseless. The wheel of time, is divided into two half-rotations - Utsarpinî or ascending time cycle and Avasarpinî, the descending time cycle, occurring continuously after each other. Utsarpinî is a period of progressive prosperity and happiness where the time spans and ages are at an increasing scale, while Avsarpinî is a period of increasing sorrow and immorality with decline in timespans of the epochs. Each of this half time cycle consisting of innumerable period of time is further sub-divided into six Aras or epochs of unequal periods. Currently, the time cycle is in avasarpinî or descending phase with the following epochs :

- **Susama-duhsamâ** - During the third ara of Susama-duhsamâ, the age limit of the people became one palyopama year. During this are people were on average 2 miles tall. They took their food on every second day. The earth and water as well as height and strength of the body went on decreasing and they became less than they were during the second ara. The first three ara the children were born as twins, one male and one female, who married each other and once again gave birth to twins. On account of happiness and pleasures, the religion, renunciation and austerities was not possible. At the end of the third ara, the wish-fulfilling trees stopped giving the desired fruits and the people started living in the societies. The first Tirthankara, Zsabhdeva was born at the end of this ara. He taught the people the skills of farming, commerce, defence, politics and arts and organised the people in societies. That is why he is known as the father of human civilisation.

- **Duhsama-susamâ** - During the fourth ara of Duhsama-susamâ, people lived for 705.6 Quintillion Years. During this are people were on average 1500 Meters tall. The fourth ara was the age of religion, where the renunciation, austerities and liberation was possible. The 63 Úalâkâpurusa's or the illustrious persons who promote the Jain religion regularly appear in this ara. The balance 23 Tîrthankars, including lord Mâhavîra appeared in this ara. This ara came to an end 3 years and 8 months after the nirvâna of Mâhavîra.
- **Duhsama** - As per Jain cosmology, currently we are in the 5th ara. As of 2010, exactly 2,537 years have elapsed and 18,463 years are still left. It is an age of sorrow and misery. The maximum age a person can live to in this ara is 130 years. The maximum height a person can be in this ara is six feet. No liberation is possible, although people practice religion in lax and diluted form. However, at the end of this ara, even the Jain religion will disappear, only to appear back with the advent of 1st Tirthankara in the next cycle.
- **Duhsama- duhsama**- The sixth Ara, Duhsama-duhsama will be the age if intense misery and sorrow, making it impossible to practice religion in any form. The age, height and strength of the human beings will decrease to a great extent. In this ara people will live for no more than 16-20 years. This trend will start reversing at the onset of utsarpinî kâl.

In utsarpinî, the order of the aras is reversed; starting from Duhsama- duhsamâ, it ends with Susama-susamâ and thus this never ending cycle continues. Each of these aras progress into the next phase seamlessly without any apocalyptic consequences. The increase or decrease in the happiness, life spans and length of people and general moral conduct of the society changes in a phased and graded manner as the time passes. No divine or supernatural beings are credited or responsible with these spontaneous temporal changes, either in a creative or overseeing role, rather the human beings and creatures are born under the impulse of their own karmas.

Jain Geography

The early Jains contemplated over the nature of the earth and universe and developed a detailed hypothesis on the various aspects of the astronomy and cosmology. According to the Jain texts, the universe is divided into 3 parts –

- **Urdhva Loka** – the realms of the gods or heavens
- **Madhya Loka** – the realms of the humans, animals and plants
- **Adho Loka** – the realms of the hellish beings or the infernal regions

The Jain texts on Geography

The Jain texts provide a detailed description on The following Upanga âgamas describe the Jain cosmology and geography in a great detail :—

1. Sûryaprajñapti – Treatise on Sun
2. Jambûdvîpaprajñapti - Treatise on the island of Roseapple tree; it contains a description of Jambûdvî and life biographies of Rsabha and King Bharata
3. Candraprajñapti - Treatise on moon

Additionally, the following texts describe the Jain cosmology and related topics in details:-

1. Trilokasâra – Essence of the three worlds (heavens, middle level, hells)

2. Trilokaprajñapti – Treatise on the three worlds
3. Trilokadipikâ – Illumination of the three worlds
4. Tattvârthasûtra – Description on nature of realities
5. Ksetrasamasa – Summary of Jain geography
6. Bruhatsamgrahni – Treatise on Jain cosmology and geography

Urdhva Loka, the Upper World

Udharva loka consists of 12 Dev Lok, 9 Greveyak and 5 Anutar Viman, which are the realms of the Vaimaniks or the astral gods who are non-liberated gods. Above the Anutar vimans, at the apex of the universe, is the Siddhasila, the realms of the infinite liberated gods also known as the Siddhas, the perfected omniscient and blissful beings, who are venerated by the Jains.

Below the siddhasila are the five Anutar Vimans named :

1. Vijay
2. Vijayant
3. Jayant
4. Aparajit
5. Savarthsiddha

Below the Anutar Vimas are the 9 Greveyaks whose names are :

1. Bhadre
2. Subhadre
3. Sujae
4. Sumanase
5. Priydansne
6. Sudansne
7. Aamohe
8. Supadibaddhe
9. Jasodhare.

Below the Greveyaks, are the 12 Devalokas whose names are :

1. Sudharma
2. Ishan
3. Sanatkumar
4. Mahendra
5. Brahmloka
6. Lantak
7. Mahashukra
8. Sahastrar
9. Aanat
10. Pranat
11. Aaran
12. Achyuta.

Vaimanik devas are divided into, two groups i.e. –

- The higher groups, dwelling in 9 Greveyak and 5 Anutar Viman. They are independent and dewelling in their own vehicles. The anuttara devas attain liberation within one or two lifetimes.
- The lower groups, organised like earthly kingdoms - rulers (Indra), organised like earthly kingdoms - rulers (Indras), counselors, guards, queens, followers, armies etc.

Madhya Loka, the Middle World

Madhya Loka, at the centre of the universe consists of 900 yojans above and 900 yojans below earth surface. It is inhabited by :

1. Jyotishka devas (luminous gods) - 790 to 900 yojans above earth

2. Human, Tiryanch (Animals, birds, plants) on the surface
3. Vyantar devas (Intermediary gods)- 100 yojan below the ground level

Madhyaloka consists of many continent-islands surrounded by oceans, first eight whose names are :-

Continent/ Island	*Ocean*
Jambûdvîpa	Lavanoda (Salt - ocean)
Ghatki Khand	Kaloda (Black sea)
Puskarvardvîpa	Puskaroda (Lotus Ocean)
Varunvardvîpa	Varunoda (Varun Ocean)
Kshirvardvîpa	Kshiroda (Ocean of milk)
Ghrutvardvîpa	Ghrutoda (Butter milk ocean)
Ikshuvardvîpa	Iksuvaroda (Sugar Ocean)
Nandishwardvîpa	Nandishwaroda

Mount Meru is at the centre of the world surrounded by Jambûdvîpa, in form of a circle forming a diameter of 100,000 yojans.

Jambûdvîpa continent has 6 mighty mountains, dividing the continent into 7 zones (Ksetra). The names of these zones are:

1. Bharat Kshetra
2. Mahavideh Kshetra
3. Airavat Kshetra
4. Ramyak
5. Hairanyvat Kshetra
6. Haimava Kshetra
7. Hari Kshetra

The three zones i.e. Bharat Kshetra, Mahavideh Kshetra and Airavat Kshetra are also known as Karma bhoomi because practice of austerities and liberation is possible and the Tirthankaras preach the Jain doctrine. The other four zones, Ramyak, Hairanyvat Kshetra, Haimava Kshetra and Hari Kshetra are known as akarmabhoomi or bhogbhumi as humans live a sinless life of pleasure and no religion or liberation is possible.

Adho Loka, the Lower World

The lower world consists of seven hells which is inhabited by Bhavanpati demigods and the hellish beings. Hellish beings reside in the following hells -

1. Ratna prabha-dharma.
2. Sharkara prabha-vansha.
3. Valuka prabha-megha.
4. Pank prabha-anjana.
5. Dhum prabha-arista.
6. Tamah prabha-maghavi.
7. Mahatamah prabha-maadhavi

Úalâkâpurusas- The Deeds of the 63 Illustrious Men

During the each motion of the half-cycle of the wheel of time, 63 Úalâkâpurusa or 63 illustrious men, consisting of the 24 Tîrthankaras and their contemporaries regularly appear. . The Jain universal or legendary history is basically a compilation of the deeds of these illustrious men. They are categorised as follows :-

- 24 Tîrthankaras – The 24 Tîrthankaras or the ford makers appear in succession to activate the true religion and establish the community of ascetics and laymen.
- 12 Chakravartîs – The Chakravartîs are the universal monarchs who rule over the six continents.

- 9 Baladevas and 9 Vâsudevas or Nârâyanas (heros) – Baladeva and Vàsudeva are half brothers who jointly rule over three continents.
- 9 Prativâsudevas (anti-heros) – They are anti-heros who are ultimately killed by the Vâsudevas.

KARMA IN JAINISM

In **Jainism, karma** is the basic principle within an overarching psycho-cosmology. In the Jain cosmology, human moral actions form the basis of the transmigration of the soul (*jîva*). The soul is constrained to a cycle of rebirth, trapped within the temporal world (*samsâra*), until it finally achieves liberation (*moksa*). Liberation is achieved by following a path of purification.

In Jain philosophy, karma not only encompasses the causality of transmigration, but is also conceived of as an extremely subtle matter, which infiltrates the soul—obscuring its natural, transparent and pure qualities. Karma is thought of as a kind of pollution, that taints the soul with various colours (*leúyâ*). Based on its karma, a soul undergoes transmigration and reincarnates in various states of existence—like heavens or hells, or as humans or animals.

Jains cite inequalities, sufferings, and pain as evidence for the existence of karma. Jain texts have classified the various types of karma according to their effects on the potency of the soul. The Jain theory seeks to explain the karmic process by specifying the various causes of karmic influx (*âsrava*) and bondage (*bandha*), placing equal emphasis on deeds themselves, and the intentions behind those deeds. The Jain karmic theory attaches great responsibility to individual actions, and eliminates any reliance on some supposed existence of divine grace or retribution. The Jain doctrine also holds that it is possible for us to both modify our karma, and to obtain release from it, through the austerities and purity of conduct.

Several scholars date the origin of the doctrine of karma prior to the migration of the Indo-Aryan peoples. They see its current form as a result of development in the teachings of the Œramanas, and later assimilation into brahmanical Hinduism, by the time of the Upanisads. The Jain concept of karma has been subject to criticism from rival Indian philosophies—like Vedanta Hinduism, Buddhism, and Sâmkhya.

Philosophical Overview

According to Jains, all souls are intrinsically pure in their inherent and ideal state, possessing the qualities of infinite knowledge, infinite perception, infinite bliss and infinite energy. However, in contemporary experience, these qualities are found to be defiled and obstructed, on account of the association of these souls with karma. The soul has been associated with karma in this way throughout an eternity of beginningless time. This bondage of the soul is explained in the Jain texts by analogy with gold ore, which—in its natural state—is always found unrefined of admixture with impurities. Similarly, the ideally pure state of the soul has always been overlaid with the impurities of karma. This analogy with gold ore is also taken one step further: the purification of the soul can be achieved if the proper methods of refining are applied. Over the centuries, Jain monks have developed a large and sophisticated corpus of literature describing the nature of the soul, various aspects of the working of karma, and the ways and means of attaining *moksa*.

Material Theory

Jainism speaks of karmic "dirt", as karma is thought to be manifest as very subtle and microscopically imperceptible particles pervading the entire universe. They are so small that one space-point—the smallest possible extent of space—contains an infinite number of karmic particles (or quantity of karmic dirt). It is these karmic particles that adhere to the soul and affect its natural potency. This material karma is called *dravya karma*; and the resultant emotions—pleasure, pain, love, hatred, and so on—experienced by the soul are called *bhava karma*, psychic karma. The relationship between the material and psychic karma is that of cause and effect. The material karma gives rise to the feelings and emotions in worldly souls, which—in turn—give rise to psychic karma, causing emotional modifications within the soul. These emotions, yet again, result in influx and bondage of fresh material karma. Jains hold that the karmic matter is actually an agent that enables the consciousness to act within the material context of this universe. They are the material carrier of a soul's desire to physically experience this world. When attracted to the consciousness, they are stored in an interactive karmic field called *kârmana úarîra*, which emanates from the soul. Thus, karma is a subtle matter surrounding the consciousness of a soul. When these two components—consciousness and ripened karma—interact, the soul experiences life as known in the present material universe.

Self Regulating Mechanism

According to Indologist Robert J. Zydenbos, karma is a system of natural laws, where actions that carry moral significance are considered to cause certain consequences in the same way as physical actions. When one holds an apple and then lets it go, the apple will fall. There is no judge, and no moral judgment involved, since this is a mechanical consequence of the physical action. In the same manner, consequences occur naturally when one utters a lie, steals something, commits senseless violence or leads a life of debauchery. Rather than assume that these consequences—the moral rewards and retributions—are a work of some divine judge, Jains believe that there is an innate moral order in the cosmos, self-regulating through the workings of the law of karma. Morality and ethics are important in Jainism not because of a God, but because a life led in agreement with moral and ethical principles (*mahavrata*) is considered beneficial: it leads to a decrease—and finally to the total loss of—karma, which in turns leads to everlasting happiness. The Jain conception of karma takes away the responsibility for salvation from God and bestows it on man himself. In the words of the Jain scholar, J. L. Jaini:

> Jainism, more than any other creed, gives absolute religious independence and freedom to man. Nothing can intervene between the actions which we do and the fruits thereof. Once done, they become our masters and must fructify. As my independence is great, so my responsibility is co-extensive with it. I can live as I like; but my voice is irrevocable, and I cannot escape the consequences of it. No God, his Prophet or his deputy or beloved can interfere with human life. The soul, and it alone is responsible for all it does.

Predominance of Karma

According to Jainism, karmic consequences are unerringly certain and inescapable. No divine grace can save a person from experiencing them. Only the practice of austerities and self-control can modify or alleviate the consequences of karma. Even then, in some cases, there is no option but to accept karma with equanimity. The second-century Jain text, Bhagavatî Ârâdhanâ (verse no. 1616) sums up the predominance of karma in Jain doctrine: "There is nothing mightier in the world than karma; karma tramples down all powers, as an elephant a clump of lotuses." This predominance of karma is a theme often explored by Jain ascetics in the literature they have produced, throughout all centuries. Paul Dundas notes that the ascetics often used cautionary tales to underline the full karmic implications of morally incorrect modes of life, or excessively intense emotional relationships. However, he notes that such narratives were often softened by concluding statements about the transforming effects of the protagonists' pious actions, and their eventual attainment of liberation.

The biographies of the exploits of legendary persons like Rama (Râma) and Krishna (Krsna), in the Jain versions of the Ramayana and Mahabharata, also have karma as one of the major themes. The major events, characters and circumstances are explained by reference to their past lives, with examples of specific actions of particular intensity in one life determining events in the next. Jain texts narrate how even Mâhavîra, the 24th *tîrthankara* (ford-maker), had to bear the brunt of his previous karma before attaining *kevala jñâna* (enlightenment). He attained it only after bearing twelve years of severe austerity with detachment. The Âcâranga Sûtra speaks of how Mâhavîra bore his karma with complete equanimity, as follows.

> He was struck with a stick, the fist, a lance, hit with a fruit, a clod, a potsherd. Beating him again and again many cried. When he once sat without moving his body many cut his flesh, tore his hair under pain, or covered him with dust. Throwing him up they let him fall, or disturbed him in his religious postures; abandoning the care of his body, the Venerable One humbled himself and bore pain, free from desires. As a hero at the head of the battle is surrounded by all sides, so was there Mâhavîra. Bearing all hardships, the Venerable One, undisturbed, proceeded on the road to *nirvâna*.
>
> —Âcâranga Sûtra 8–356:60

Reincarnation and Transmigration

Karma forms a central and fundamental part of Jain faith, being intricately connected to other of its philosophical concepts like transmigration, reincarnation, liberation, non-violence (*ahimsâ*) and non-attachment, among others. Actions are seen to have consequences: some immediate, some delayed, even into future incarnations. So the doctrine of karma is not considered simply in relation to one life-time, but also in relation to both future incarnations and past lives. *Uttarâdhyayana-sûtra* 3.3–4 states: "The *jîva* or the soul is sometimes born in the world of gods, sometimes in hell. Sometimes it acquires the body of a demon; all this happens on account of its karma. This *jîva* sometimes takes birth as a worm, as an insect or as an ant." The text further states (32.7): "Karma is the root of birth and death. The souls bound by karma go round and round in the cycle of existence."

Actions and emotions in the current lifetime affect future incarnations depending on the nature of the particular karma. For example, a good and virtuous life indicates a latent desire to experience good and virtuous themes of life. Therefore, such a person attracts karma that ensures that his future births will allow him to experience and manifest his virtues and good feelings unhindered. In this case, he may take birth in heaven or in a prosperous and virtuous human family. On the other hand, a person who has indulged in immoral deeds, or with a cruel disposition, indicates a latent desire to experience cruel themes of life. As a natural consequence, he will attract karma which will ensure that he is reincarnated in hell, or in lower life forms, to enable his soul to experience the cruel themes of life.

There is no retribution, judgment or reward involved but a natural consequences of the choices in life made either knowingly or unknowingly. Hence, whatever suffering or pleasure that a soul may be experiencing in its present life is on account of choices that it has made in the past. As a result of this doctrine, Jainism attributes supreme importance to pure thinking and moral behaviour. Apart from Buddhism, Jainism may be the only religion that does not invoke the fear of God as a reason for moral behaviour.

The Process of Bondage and Release

The karmic process in Jainism is based on seven truths or fundamental principles (*tattva*) of Jainism which explain the human predicament. Out that the seven *tattvas*, the four—influx (*âsrava*), bondage (*bandha*), stoppage (*samvara*) and release (*nirjarâ*)—pertain to the karmic process.

Attraction and Binding

The karmic bondage occurs as a result of the following two processes: *âsrava* and *bandha*. *Âsrava* is the inflow of karma. The karmic influx occurs when the particles are attracted to the soul on account of *yoga*. *Yoga* is the vibrations of the soul due to activities of mind, speech and body. However, the *yoga* alone do not produce bondage. The karmas have effect only when they are bound to the consciousness. This binding of the karma to the consciousness is called *bandha*. Out of the many causes of bondage, emotions or passions are considered as the main cause of bondage. The karmas are literally bound on account of the stickiness of the soul due to existence of various passions or mental dispositions. The passions like anger, pride, deceit and greed are called sticky (*kasâyas*) because they act like glue in making karmic particles stick to the soul resulting in *bandha*. The karmic inflow on account of *yoga* driven by passions and emotions cause a long term inflow of karma prolonging the cycle of reincarnations. On the other hand, the karmic inflows on account of actions that are not driven by passions and emotions have only a transient, short-lived karmic effect. Hence the ancient Jain texts talk of subduing these negative emotions:

> When he wishes that which is good for him, he should get rid of the four faults—anger, pride, deceit and greed—which increase the evil. Anger and pride when not suppressed, and deceit and greed when arising: all these four black passions water the roots of re-birth.
>
> —*Daúavaikâlika sûtra, 8:36–39*

Causes of Attraction and Bondage

The Jain theory of karma proposes that karma particles are attracted and then bound to the consciousness of souls by a combination of four factors pertaining to actions: instrumentality, process, modality and motivation.

- The **instrumentality** of an action refers to whether the instrument of the action was: the body, as in physical actions; one's speech, as in speech acts; or the mind, as in thoughtful deliberation.
- The **modality** of an action refers to different modes in which one can participate in an action, for example: being the one who carries out the act itself; being one who instigates another to perform the act; or being one who gives permission, approval or endorsement of an act.
- The **process** of an action refers to the temporal sequence in which it occurs: the decision to act, plans to facilitate the act, making preparations necessary for the act, and ultimately the carrying through of the act itself.
- The **motivation** for an action refers to the internal passions or negative emotions that prompt the act, including: anger, greed, pride, deceit and so on.

All actions have the above four factor present in them. When different permutations of the sub-elements of the four factors are calculated, the Jain teachers speak of 108 ways in which the karmic matter can be attracted to the soul. Even giving silent assent or endorsement to acts of violence from far away has karmic consequences for the soul. Hence, the scriptures advise carefulness in actions, awareness of the world, and purity in thoughts as means to avoid the burden of karma.

According to *Tattvârthasûtra*, the causes of *bandha* or the karmic bondage—in the order they are required to be eliminate by a soul for spiritual progress—are:

- *Mithyâtva* (Irrationality and a deluded world view)—The deluded world view is the misunderstanding as to how this world really functions on account of one-sided perspectives, perverse viewpoints, irrational scepticism, pointless generalisations and ignorance.

- *Pramâda* (carelessness and laxity of conduct) – This third cause of bondage consists of absentmindedness, lack of enthusiasm towards acquiring merit and spiritual growth, and improper actions of mind, body and speech without any regard to oneself or others.
- *Avirati* (non-restraint or a vowless life) – The second cause of bondage, *avirati* is the inability to refrain voluntarily from the evil actions, that harms oneself and others. The state of *avirati* can only be overcome by observing the minor vows of a layman.
- *Kasâya* (passions or negative emotions) – The four passions—anger, pride, deceit and greed—are the primary reason for the attachment of the karmas to the soul. They keep the soul immersed in the darkness of delusion leading to deluded conduct and unending cycles of reincarnations.
- *Yoga* (activities of mind, speech and body) – The threefold activities of mind, body and speech attract and bind the karmas when such actions are influenced by passions.

Each cause presupposes the existence of the next cause, but the next cause does not necessarily pre-suppose the existence of the previous cause. A soul is able to advance on the spiritual ladder called *gunasthâna*, only when it is able to eliminate the above causes of bondage one by one.

Experiencing the Effects

The nature of experience of the effects of the karma depends on the following four factors:

- ***Prikriti*** (nature or type of karma) – According to Jain texts, there are eight main types of karma which categorized into the 'harming' and the 'non-harming'; each divided into four types. The harming karmas (*ghâtiyâ karmas*) directly affect the soul powers by impeding its perception, knowledge and energy, and also brings about delusion. These harming karmas are: *darúanâvarana* (perception-obscuring karma), *jñânavârana* (knowledge-obscuring karma), *antarâya* (obstacle-creating karma) and *mohanîya* (deluding karma). The non-harming category (*aghâtiyâ karmas*) is responsible for the reborn soul's physical and mental circumstances, longevity, spiritual potential and experience of pleasant and unpleasant sensations. These non-harming karmas are: *nâma* (body-determining karma), *âyu* (lifespan-determining karma), *gotra* (status-determining karma) and *vedanîya* (feeling-producing karma), respectively. Different types of karmas thus affect the soul in different ways as per their nature.

- ***Anubhava*** (intensity of karmas) -- The degree of the experience of the karmas, that is, mild or intense, depends on the *anubhava* quality or the intensity of the bondage. It determines the power of karmas and its effect on the soul. *Anubhava* depends on the intensity of the passions at the time of binding the karmas More intense the emotions—like anger, greed etc.—at the time of binding the karma, the more intense will be its experience at the time of maturity.

- ***Stithi*** (the duration of the karmic bond) – The karmic bond remains latent and bound to the consciousness up to the time it is activated. Although latent karma does not affect the soul directly, its existence limits the spiritual growth of the soul. Jain texts provide minimum and the maximum duration for which such karma is bound before it matures.

- ***Pradesha*** (The quantity of the karmas) – It the quantity of karmic matter that is received and gets activated at the time of experience.

Both emotions and activity play a part in binding of karmas. Duration and intensity of the karmic bond are determined by emotions or *"kasâya"* and type and quantity of the karmas bound is depended on *yoga* or activity.

Maturity

The consequences of karma are inevitable. The consequences may take some time to take effect but the karma is never fruitless. To explain this, a Jain monk, Ratnaprabhacharya says: "The prosperity of a vicious man and misery of a virtuous man are respectively but the effects of good deeds and bad deeds done previously. The vice and virtue may have their effects in their next lives. In this way the law of causality is not infringed here."

The latent karma becomes active and bears fruit when the supportive conditions arise. A great part of attracted karma bears its consequences with minor fleeting effects, as generally most of our activities are influenced by mild negative emotions. However, those actions that are influenced by intense negative emotions cause an equally strong karmic attachment which usually does not bear fruit immediately. It takes on an inactive state and waits for the supportive conditions—like proper time, place, and environment—to arise for it to manifest and produce effects. If the supportive conditions do not arise, the respective karmas will manifest at the end of maximum period for which it can remain bound to the soul. These supportive conditions for activation of latent karmas are determined by the nature of karmas, intensity of emotional engagement at the time of binding karmas and our actual relation to time, place, surroundings. There are certain laws of precedence among the karmas, according to which the fruition of some of the karmas may be deferred but not absolutely barred.

Modifications

Although the Jains believe the karmic consequences as inevitable, Jain texts also hold that a soul has energy to transform and modify the effects of the karmas.. Karma undergoes following modifications:

1. *Udaya* (maturity) – It is the fruition of karmas as per its nature in the due course.
2. *Udîrana* (premature operation) – By this process, it is possible to make certain karmas operative before their predetermined time.
3. *Apavartanâ* (diminution) – In this case, there is subsequent decrease in duration and intensity of the karmas due to positive emotions and feelings.
4. *Udvartanâ* (augmentation) -- By this process, there is a subsequent increase in duration and intensity of the karmas due to additional negative emotions and feelings.
5. *Samkramasa* (transformation) – It is the mutation or conversion of one sub-type of karmas into another sub-type. However, this does not occur between different types. For example, *papa* (bad karma) can be converted into *punya* (good karma) as both sub-types belong to the same type of karma.
6. *Nidhatti* (prevention) – In this state, premature operation and transformation is not possible but augmentation and diminution of karmas is possible.
7. *Upaüamanä* (state of subsidence) – During this state the operation of karma does not occur. The karma becomes operative only when the duration of subsidence ceases.

8. *Nikâcanâ* (invariance) – For some sub-types, no variations or modifications are possible—the consequences are the same as were established at the time of bonding.

The Jain karmic theory, thus speaks of great powers of soul to manipulate the karmas by its actions.

Release

Jains assert that emancipation is not possible as long as the soul is released from bondage of the karmas. This is possible by *samvara*, that is, stoppage of inflow of new karmas, and *nirjarâ*, that is, shedding of existing karmas through conscious efforts. *Samvara* or stoppage of karmic influx is achieved through practice of:

1. Three *guptis* or three controls of mind, speech and body,

2. Five *samitis* or observing carefulness in movement, speaking, eating, placing objects and disposing refuse.

3. Ten *dharmas* or observation of good acts like – forgiveness, humility, straightforwardness, contentment, truthfulness, self control, penance, renunciation, non-attachment and continence.

4. *Anuprekshas* or meditation on the truths of this universe.

5. *Parisahajaya*, that is, a man on moral path must develop a perfectly patient and unperturbed attitude in the midst of trying and difficult circumstances.

6. *Câritra*, that is, endeavour to remain in steady spiritual practices.

Nirjarâ or annihilation of the existing karmas is possible through *tapas*, that is, austerities and penances. *Tapas* can be either external or internal. Six forms of external *tapas* are—fasting, control of appetite, accepting food under certain conditions, renunciation of delicious food, sitting and sleeping in lonely place and renunciation of comforts. Six forms of internal *tapas* are—atonement, reverence, rendering of service to worthy ones, spiritual study, avoiding selfish feelings and meditation.

Rationale

Justice Tukol notes that the supreme importance of the doctrine of karma lies in providing a rational and satisfying explanation to the apparent unexplainable phenomenon of birth and death, of happiness and misery, of inequalities and of existence of different species of living beings. *Sûtrak[tânga,* one of the oldest canon of Jainism, states:

> Here in the east, west, north, and south many men have been born according to their merit, as inhabitants of this our world—some as Aryas, some as non-Aryas, some in noble families, some in low families, some as big men, some as small men, some of good complexion, some of bad complexion, some as handsome men, some as ugly men. And of these men one man is king.
>
> — *Sûtrak[tânga,* 2.1.13

Jains thus cite inequalities, sufferings, and pain as evidence for the existence of karma. The theory of karma is able to explain day-to-day observable phenomena such as inequality between the rich and the poor, luck, differences in lifespan, and the ability to enjoy life despite being immoral. According to Jains, such inequalities and oddities that exist even from the time of birth can be attributed to the deeds of the past lives and thus provide evidence to existence of karmas:

One is stout while another is lean; one is a master while another is a slave and similarly we find the high and the low, the mutilated and the lame, the blind and the deaf and many such oddities. The thrones of mighty monarchs are gone. The proud and the haughty have been humiliated in a moment and reduced to ashes. Even amongst the twins born of the same mother, we find one a dullard and another intelligent, one rich and another poor, one black and another white. What is all this due to? They could not have done any deeds while they were in their mother's womb. Then, why then should such oddities exist? We have then to infer that these disparities must be the result of their deeds in their past births though they are born together at one time. There are many oddities in this world and it will have to be admitted that behind all this some powerful force is at work whereby the world appears to be full of oddities. This force is called 'karma'. We are unable to perceive karma by our naked eyes, yet we are able to know it from its actions.

Scientific Interpretation

Jain philosopher-monks postulated the existence of karma as subtle and microscopic particles that cannot be perceived by senses, some two millennia before modern science proved the existence of atoms and subatomic particles. However, these and other elementary particles that have been either discovered or postulated cannot be equated with karmic particles. Some authors have sought to explain the concept of karmic particles in the context of modern science and physics. Hermann Kuhn points out that, although the idea of "karmic particles" is not yet proven, one only needs to recall that science found proof of the existence of molecules and atoms only the 19th and 20th century. Anyone who would have suggested that these "indivisible" particles were made up of even subtler units like quarks and leptons only a hundred years ago may have been dismissed, though such theories were in existence. With regards to interaction of consciousness and karmic matter, he further states that, it can be easily understood considering that ideas like the mind fundamentally affecting matter are now accepted in scientific circles. While admitting that though science has not discovered karmic matter yet, he is of opinion that it does not state anything against its existence. K. V. Mardia, in his book *The Scientific Foundations of Jainism,* has interpreted karma in terms of modern physics, suggesting that the particles are made of *karmons,* dynamic high energy particles which permeate the universe. However, most scientists do not consider karma and reincarnation to be within the bounds of science, as it is neither a testable nor a falsifiable theory.

Criticisms

The Jain theory of karma has been challenged since ancient times by Vedanta Hindu, Buddhist and Sâmkhya philosophies.

In particular, Vedanta Hindus considered the Jain position on the supremacy and potency of karma, specifically its insistence on non-intervention by any Supreme Being in regard to the fate of souls, as worthy of the label *nâstika* or atheistic. For example, in a commentary to Brahma Sutras (III, 2, 38, and 41), Adi Sankara, argues that the original karmic actions themselves cannot bring about the proper results at some future time; neither can super sensuous, non-intelligent qualities like adrsta—an unseen force being the metaphysical link between work and its result—by themselves mediate the appropriate, justly deserved pleasure and pain. The fruits, according to him, then, must be administered through the action of a conscious agent, namely, a supreme being (Ishvara).

Strong emphasis on the doctrine of karma and intense asceticism was also criticised by the Buddhists, even though they also believe in karma. The ancient Buddhist scripture *Sasyutta Nikâya* narrates the story of Asibandhakaputta, a headman who was originally a disciple of Mâhavîra. He debates with the Buddha, telling him that, according to Mâhavîra, a man's fate or karma is decided by what he does habitually. The Buddha responds, considering this view to be inadequate, stating that even a habitual sinner spends more time "not doing the sin" and only some time actually "doing the sin."

In another Buddhist text *Majjhima Nikâya*, the Buddha criticizes Jain emphasis on the destruction of unobservable and unverifiable types of karma as a means to end suffering, rather than on eliminating evil mental states such as greed, hatred and delusion, which are observable and verifiable. In the Upâlisutta dialogue of this *Majjhima Nikâya* text, Buddha contends with a Jain monk who asserts that bodily actions are the most criminal, in comparison to the actions of speech and mind. Buddha criticises this view, saying that the actions of *mind* are most criminal, and not the actions of speech or body. Buddha also criticises the Jain ascetic practice of various austerities, claiming that he, Buddha, is happier when *not* practising the austerities.

While admitting the complexity and sophistication of the Jain doctrine, Padmanabh Jaini compares it with that of Hindu doctrine of rebirth and points out that the Jain seers are silent on the exact moment and mode of rebirth, that is, the re-entry of soul in womb after the death. The concept of *nitya-nigoda*, which states that there are certain categories of souls who have always been *nigodas*, is also criticised. According to Jainism, *nigodas* are lowest form of extremely microscopic beings having momentary life spans, living in colonies and pervading the entire universe. According to Dr. Jaini, the entire concept of *nitya-nigoda* undermines the concept of karma, as these beings clearly would not have had prior opportunity to perform any karmically meaningful actions.

Karma is also criticised on the grounds that it leads to the dampening of spirits with men suffering the ills of life because the course of one's life is determined by karma. It is often maintained that the impression of karma as the accumulation of a mountain of bad deeds looming over our heads without any recourse leads to fatalism. However, as Paul Dundas puts it, the Jain theory of karma does not imply lack of free will or operation of total deterministic control over destinies. Furthermore, the doctrine of karma does not promote fatalism amongst its believers on account of belief in personal responsibility of actions and that austerities could expatiate the evil karmas and it was possible to attain salvation by emulating the life of the Jinas.

●●

6
Types of Karma

According to Jain karma theory, there are eight main **types of karma** (*Prikriti*) which are categorized into the 'harming' and the 'non-harming'; each divided into four types. The harming karmas (*ghâtiyâ karmas*) directly affect the soul powers by impeding it's perception, knowledge and energy, and also brings about delusion. These harming karmas are: *darúanâvarasa* (perception obscuring karma), *jñânavârasa* (knowledge obscuring karma), *antarâya* (obstacles creating karma) and *mohanîya* (deluding karma). The non-harming category (*aghâtiyâ karmas*) is responsible for the reborn soul's physical and mental circumstances, longevity, spiritual potential and experience of pleasant and unpleasant sensations. These non-harming karmas are: *nâma* (body determining karma), *âyu* (life span determining karma), *gotra* (status determining karma) and *vedanîya* (feeling producing karma) respectively. Different types of karmas thus affect the soul in different ways as per their nature. Each of these types has various sub-types. *Tattvârthasûtra* generally speaks of 148 sub-types of karmas in all. These are: 5 of *jñânavarasa,* 9 of *darœanavarasa,* 2 of *vedanîya,* 28 of *mohanîya* 4 of *âyuska,* 93 of *nâma,* 2 of *gotra,* and 5 of *antarâya.*

Ghatiya Karmas

Ghâtiyâ karmas (harming karmas) directly affect the attributes of the soul. These are :

1. Knowledge-obscuring karma (*Jñânâvarasîya karma*) – These karmas obscure the knowledge attribute of the soul.

2. Perception-obscuring karma (*Darúanâvarasîya karma*) – These karmas diminish the powers of Perception of a soul.

3. Deluding karma (*Mohanîya karma*) – These karmas are an instrumental cause of destruction the soul's right belief and right conduct. Of all karmas, deluding karma is the most difficult to overcome. Once this is eradicated, liberation is ensured within a few lifetimes.

4. Obstructing karma (*Antarâya karma*) – The fruition of these karmas creates obstructions to giving donations, obtaining gains, and enjoying things.

When *ghâtiyâ karmas* are totally destroyed, the soul attains *kevala Jnana* or omniscience. Liberation is guaranteed for such souls in the same lifetime as soon the aghâtiyâ karmas are exhausted in the due course.

Jnanavaraniya Karma

Jñânâvarasîya karma or the knowledge-obscuring karma are of five types:

1. *mati jnanavarana-karma* which causes the obscuration of the knowledge, transmitted through the senses,

2. *sruta jnanavarana-karma* which produces the obscuration of knowledge acquired by interpreting signs (i.e.words, writings, gestures),

3. *avadhi jnanavarana-karma* which hinders transcendental knowledge of material things,

4. *manahparyaya jnanavarana-karma* which hinders transcendental knowledge of the thoughts of others,

5. *kevala jnanavarana-karma* which obscures the omniscience inherent in the jiva by natural disposition.

Of these, the last mentioned karman hinders omniscience altogether; the four others do not result in complete destruction of the corresponding faculties of knowledge, but often produce only greater or less disturbances.

Darsanavarana Karma

Darsanavarana karma or the perception-obscuring karma are of four types:

1. *caksur darsanavarana-karma* which produces the obscuration of the darsana conditional upon the eye,
2. *acaksur darsanavarana-karma* which causes the obscuration of the undifferentiated cognition, conditional upon the other senses and the organ of thinking,
3. *avadhi darsanavarana-karma* which causes the obscuration of the transcendental undifferentiated cognition of material things,
4. *kevala darsanavarana-karma* which hinder the absolute undifferentiated cognition (the counterpart of the omniscience).

The last mentioned karma hinders completely; the three others produce under certain circumstances only a disturbance of the respective cognition faculties.

In addition to these four darsanavarana karmas there are five others which produce physio-psychological conditions in which the sense organs are not active, and which, therefore, exclude all possibility of perception. These are the five nidra karmas, (sleep karmas), namely:

1. *nidra-karma* which produces a light, pleasant slumber, out of which the sleeper is already aroused by the clicking of finger nails.

2. *nidranidra-karma* which produces a deep slumber, out of which the sleeper can only be awakened by being shaken violently,
3. *pracala-karma* which sitting or standing upright
4. *pracalapracala-karma* which produces an exceedingly intensive sleep, that overcomes a person while walking,
5. *styanagrddhi (styanarddhi) karma* which causes somnambulism, acting an unconscious state.

Mohaniya Karman

Mohaniya is derived from *Moha* which means attachment. *Mohaniya* karma (deluding karma) is the most dangerous, out of all the eight karmas because 'moha' (attachment) is the root cause of all Kasayas (passions). It is also most difficult karma to to destroy. If mohaniya karma is destroyed fully, the self becomes free from all Kasayas and liberation is assured. Two main categories of Mohaniya karman are—darsana mohaniya and caritra mohaniya karma. With their subtypes there are 28 sub-types of mohaniya karman.

Darsana Mohaniya Karman

The *darsana mohaniya-karma* causes a disturbance of the knowledge of the religious truth inherent in the jiva by natural disposition. These are further divided into three tyes according as to whether the disturbance is an absolute or a partial one:

1. *mithyatva karma*: This causes complete unbelief or heterodoxy. If it realize itself, the jiva does not believe in the truths as proclaimed by Mahavira; he believes false prophets to be saints and enjoins false doctrines.
2. *samyagmithyatva (misra) karma*: This produces a mixed belief, i.e., if it operates the soul waves to and for

betwixt true and false; it is indifferent to the religion of the Jina and has no predilection for, nor hatred against it.

3. *samyaktva karma*: This induces the correct belief. This samyaktva is, however, not the correct faith in its completeness, but only in a preliminary degree; it is a so called mithyatva, from which the mithyatva quality has been abstracted a mithyatva free from poison.

Caritra Mohaniya Karman

The *caritra mohaniya-karma* disturbs the right conduct possessed innately by the jiva; it hinders the soul from acting according to the religious prescriptions. The disturbance of the conduct is produced through the sixteen passions *(kasaya)*, the six emotions with are categorised as non-passions *(nokasaya)* and the three sexes *(veda)*.

The four main passions are *krodha* (anger), *maya* (deceitfulness), *mana* (pride) and *lobha* (greed). The karmas are literally bound on account of the stickiness of the soul due to existence of various passions or mental dispositions Each of these is separated into 4 sub divisions, according to the intensity of their manifestation. The first one is *anantanubandhin* (of life long duration) which completely hinders belief and conduct. The second one is *apratyakhyanavarana* (hindering and non-renunciation) It makes impossible every reninciation, but allows the existence of true belief and lasts for one year. The third one of still milder intensity is *pratyakhyanavarana* (hindering with renunciation). It hinders the beginning of complete self discipline, but does not prevent the existence of true belief and partial self discipline (desavirati). Its effect lasts for 4 months. The last one is samjvalana (flaming up). It allows complete self discipline, yet works against the attainment of complete right conduct (yathakhyata caritra). It lasts a fortnight.

The nokasayas or the six non-passions are: *hasya* (laughing, joking or making fun of), *rati* (prejudicial liking or impartiality), *arati* (improper conduct) *soka* (sorrow), *bhaya* (fear), and *jugupsa* (disgust). All these six emotions are *caritra mohaniyas*, because the soul which is subjected to them, is hindered through them in the practice of right conduct.

The vedas or the sex passion hinders the jiva from obeying the laws and from practicing self discipline. It is of three fold variety, according to the three species of sexes:

- *Purusa veda* (the male sex and corresponding sex passion) - Through this, in the man the desire for union with a female is produced. Also man has at first an exceedingly strong desire, which disappears as soon as his lust is satisfied.
- *stri veda* (the female sex and corresponding sex passion) – Through this, in a woman the desire for union with a man is excited. Also the desire in the woman is weak so long as she is untouched, but grows into immensity through the enjoyment of intercourse.
- *napumsaka veda* (the third sex and corresponding sex passion) – Effects the third sex belong all those beings who have no sexual organs. The sexual desire is with them exceedingly strong because it is directed towards men and women. It is to be compared to the burning of a town, which lasts long and finds no satisfaction.

Antaraya Karma

The *antaraya-karma* hinders the energy (*virya*) of the *jiva* in a five fold manner:

1. *Dana antaraya-karma* hinders dispensing alms. When it operates a person who knows the merit in giving and who has something to give away, is not capable to give it, although there is someone worthy of the gift.

2. *Labha antaraya-karma* hinders receiving. When it operates, a person is not capable of receiving a present, although a friendly giver and a suitable present are present.

3. *Bhoga antaraya-karma* hinders the enjoyment of something which can only be taken once (such as eating drinking).

4. *Upabhoga antaraya-karma* hinders the enjoyment of something which can be repeatedly used (such as a dwelling, clothing, women).

5. *virya antaraya-karma* hinders the will power. When it operates, even a strong, full grown man is incapable of bending a blade of grass.

Aghatiya Karmas

These do not affect the soul directly; rather, they have an effect on the body that houses the soul. These are:

1. Lifespan-determining karma (*Âyu karma*) – These karmas determine the subsequent states of existence and lifespan therein after death. The soul gets locked either into animal (tiryañca), infernal (nâraki), human (manusya), or celestial (deva) bodies for its next birth.

2. Body-determining karma (*Nâma karma*) – These karmas determine the type of body occupied by the soul.

3. Status-determining karma (*Gotra karma*) - The fruition of these karmas gives one high status or low status in society.

4. Feeling-producing karma (*Vedanîya karma*) - These karmas become an instrumental cause of the interruption of the soul's uninterrupted happiness. As a result of this, the soul remains agitated.

As soon as the Aghâtiyâ karmas gets exhausted soul attains *moksa* (liberation).

Ayu Karma

The *ayus-karma* confers on a being a certain quantum of life in one of the four states of existence. Therefore there are four types of *ayu karmas*: *deva ayu* (the celestial lifespan), *manusya ayus* (the human lifespan), *tiryancha ayu* (the animal lifespan), and *naraka ayu* (the infernal lifespan). The *ayu-karma* bestows a certain quantity of life, but not a definite number of years of life. For, as with a sponge, the quantity of water that it absorbs is determined, but not the time it takes to leave it, so also the quantum of life is determined, but not the time occupied in its consumption. The word ayu would, therefore, be approximately interpreted by "quantity of life" or "quantity of vitality"). The ayu of the new existence is always bound during the life immediately preceding it, especially in the 3rd, 9th, or 27th part or within the last 48 minutes of life.

Nama Karma

The *nama-karma* causes the individual diversities of the jivas. It is divided into 93 *uttara prakrtis* (sub-types), which are mostly quoted in a definitely fixed succession in 4 groups (*pinda prakrtis, pratyeka prakrtis, trasadasaka, sthavara dasaka*). They are the following:

- Four states of existence:
  - *Deva gati nama-karma* bestows the celestial state of existence,
  - *manusya gati nama-karma* bestows the human state of existence,
  - *tiryag gati nama-karma* bestows the animal state of existence, and
  - *naraka gati nama-karma* which bestows the infernal state of existence.

- Five classes of beings:
  - *Ekendriya jati nama karma* causes birth as a being with one sense.
  - *Dvindriya jati nama karma* causes birth as a being with two senses.
  - *Trindriya jati nama karma* causes birth as a being with three senses.
  - *Caturindriya jati nama karma* causes birth as being with four senses
  - *Pancendriya jati nama karma* causes birth as a being with five senses.
- Five types of bodies:
  - *Audarika sarira nama karma* gives a gross physical body peculiar to animals and men.
  - *Vaikriya sarira nama karma* gives the transformational body which consists of fine matter that changes in form and dimension. This body exists by nature in gods, infernal beings and certain animals; men can attain it through higher perfection.
  - *Aharaka sarira nama karma* gives the translocation body. This body consists of good and pure substance and is without active and passive resistance. It is created for a short time by an *apramatta samyata ascetic* (ascetic with some carelessness) , in order to seek for information concerning intricate dogmatic questions from an arhat who is in another part of the world, while his own physical body remains in its original place.
  - *Taijasa sarira nama karma* gives the fiery body. This body consists of fire pudgalas and serves for the digestion of swallowed food. It can also be used by ascetics to burn other beings or things.

- *Karmana sarira nama karma* gives the karman body which is possessed by all worldly souls. This body is the receptacle for karman matter. It changes every moment, because new karman is continually assimilated by the soul and the already existing one consumed. Accompanied by it, the jiva at death leaves his other bodies and betakes himself to the place of his new birth, where the karman body then forms the basis of the newly produced other bodies. This body is destroyed only when all the karma are destroyed.

Of these 5 bodies each succeeding one is finer than the one preceding it, but contains more material points than it; it is therefore denser. Every worldly soul (that is, soul not yet liberated) is always connected with a fiery and a karman body, but can, in addition, still possess one or two other bodies. At any given point of time four bodies can co-exist with a soul. For example, humans normally have three bodies simultaneously—*audarika sarira* (normal visible gross physical body), *taijasa sarira* (fiery body), and *karmana sarira* (karmic body). Some higher spiritual ascetics may possess *vaikriya sarira* (transformational body).

- Corresponting to these five bodies there are thirteen more karmas to make the bodies operative. There are three types of *angopanga nama karma* for body parts—*audarika angopanga nama-karma, vaikriya angopanga nama-karma and aharaka angopanga nama-karma.* Fiery and the karman body are subtle and have no body parts. Each body requires specific binding to operate that is enabled by its respective karma. Hence there are five types of bandhana or bindings for these body parts—*audarıka bandana nama-karma, vaikriya bandana nama-karma, aharaka bandana nama-karma, taijasa bandana nama-karma* and *karmana bandana nama karma* which procures the binding of physical, transformational, translocational, fiery and karmic body respectively. At the same time, combination of molecules (*samghatanas*) is required for binding of bodies, which are—*audarika samghatana nama-karma, vaikriya samghatana nama-karma adharaka samghatana nama-karma, taijasa samghatana nama-karma*, and *karmana samghatana nama-karma.*

- Six Karmas related to joints:
  - o *Vajra rsabha naraca samhanana nama-karma* gives an excellent joining. The two bones are hooked into one another, through the joining, a nail (*vajra*) is hammered and the whole joint is surrounded by a bandage.
  - o *Rsabha naraca samhanana nama-karma* gives a joining not so firm as the preceding one, because the nail is missing.
  - o *Naraca samhanan nama-karma* gives a joining which is still weaker, because the bandage is missing.
  - o *Ardha naraca samhanana nama-karma* gives a joining which is on one side like the preceding one, while on the other the bones are simply pressed together and nailed.
  - o *Kilika samhanana nama-karma* gives a weak joining, by which the bones are merely pressed together and nailed.
  - o *Sevarta (chedaprstha) samhanana nama-karma* gives quite a weak joining, by which the ends of the bones only touch one another. The humans in this era as per Jain cosmology have this type of joint structure.

The *samhananas* play a great role in Jain doctrine. Only the first four make a meditation possible and only the best structure, the 1st joining of the joints, permits the highest kind of concentration which precedes salvation.

- The six samsthana nama-karmas related to body symmetry are:
  - o *Samacaturasra samsthana nama-karma,* which causes the entire body to be symmetrically built.
  - o *Nyagrodhaparimandala samsthana nama-karma,* which causes the upper part of the body to be symmetrical, but not the lower.
  - o *Sadi samsthana nama-karma,* which makes the body below the navel symmetrical and above it unsymmetrical.
  - o *Kubja samsthana nama-karma* makes the body hunchbacked, i.e. hands, feet, head and neck symmetrical, breast and belly unsymmetrical.
  - o *Vamana samsthana nama-karma* dwarf like, i.e. breast and belly symmetrical, hands, feet etc. unsymmetrical.
  - o *Hunda samsthana nama-karma* makes the entire body unsymmetrical.

The conception of symmetry is explained in the following way: One imagines a man sitting in the paryanka posture, i.e. crossing the legs and placing the hands over the navel. If one imagines that the two knees are joined by a line, and from the right shoulder to the left knee, and from the left shoulder to the right knee, and from the forehead to the hands, a straight line is drawn, one gets four lines. If these are equal to one another, symmetry is apparent; if they are not so, one of the other 5 *samsthanas* results. Gods have only the first symmetry, infernal beings and jivas who have been produced through coagulation only the 6th figure; in the case of animals and men (also of kevalins) all six *samsthanas* are to be found.

- The following karmas provide different types colours to the bodies: *krsna varna nama-karma* (black), *nila varna nama-karma* (dark, blue green, like an emerald), *lohita varna nama-karma* (colour which is red, like vermillion), *haridra varna nama-karma* (yellow, like turmeric) and *sita varna nama* (white, like a shell). Other colors, such as brown etc., are produced by mixing. Black and green are considered as being pleasant, the others as unpleasant colors.

- The following karmas provide different types of odours to the bodies: *surabhi gandha nama-karma* produces pleasant odors (e.g., that of camphor) and *durabhi gandha nama-karma* produces unpleasant odors (e.g., that of garlic).

- The following karmas provide different abilities of tastes to the bodies: *tikta rasa nama-karma* gives a bitter taste (like that of the nimba fruit), *kasaya rasa nama-karma* gives an astringent taste (like that of bibhitaka), *amla rasa nama-karma* gives a sour taste (like that of tamarind) and *madhura rasa nama-karma* gives a sweet taste (like that of sugar). The salt taste is produced by a combination of the sweet taste with another. Bitter and biting tastes are considered unpleasant, the others pleasant.

- Eight karmas related to different type of touches are:
    - o *Guru sparsa nama-karma* which causes a thing to be heavy, likc an iron ball.
    - o *Laghu sparsa nama-karma* which causes a thing to be light, like particles in a sunbeam.
    - o *Mrdu sparsa nama-karma* causes a thing to be smooth, like a tinisa tendril.
    - o *Khara sparsa nama-karma* which causes a thing to be rough, like stone.

- o *Sita sparsa nama-karma* causes a thing to be cold, like snow.
- o *Usna sparsa nama-karma* causes a thing to be warm, like fire.
- o *Snigdha sparsa nama-karma* causes a thing to be adhesive, like oil.
- o *Ruksa sparsa nama-karma* cases a thing to be dry like ashes.

Heavy, hard, dry, cold are considered to be unpleasant touches, the others pleasant.

- The *anupurvi nama-karma* causes that the *jiva,* when one existence is finished, goes from the place of death in the proper direction to the place of his new birth. According to the 4 states of existence (celestial, human, animal, infernal) there are 4 anupurvi karmas, namely: *deva anupurvi nama karma, manusya anupurvi nama karma, tiryag anupurvi nama karma,* and *naraka anupurvi nama karma.*

- Karma that bestows different gaits to souls are: *prasasta vihayogati nama-karma* which causes a being to move in a pleasant manner, as e.g. oxen, elephants and geese do and *aprasasta vihayogati nama-karma* which causes an ugly manner of motion, as, e.g. one finds with camels and asses.

- Following are the eight karmas related to eight *pratyeka prakrtis*:

    - o *Paraghata nama karma*– It gives superiority over others. It endows the capability of injuring or vanquishing others; on the other hand, it prevents one from being injured or overcome by others.
    - o *Ucchvasa nama karma* – It bestows the capability of breathing.

- o *Atapa nama karma* – It causes the body of a being not in itself hot to emit a warm splendour.
- o *Uddyota nama karma*– It causes the transformation body of the gods and ascetics, as well as moon, stars, precious stones, herbs and shining insects to emit a cold lustre.
- o *Agurulaghu nama karma*– It makes a being neither heavy nor light, i.e., causes it to possess neither absolute weight nor absolute lack of it.
- o *Tirthankara nama karma*– It procures the position of a ford-maker of the Jain religion.
- o *Nirmana nama karma* – It causes the formation of the body, i.e., it causes the members of a being to be in their right place.
- o *Upaghata nama karma* – It causes self annihilation. It produces that the parts of the body of a being (e.g.the uvula in the throat) cause its death.

- The ten karmas related to *trasa prakrtis* (positive karmas) are:

  - o *Trasa nama karma,* which gives a voluntarily movable body.
  - o *Badara nama karma,* which gives a gross body.
  - o *Paryapta nama karma,* which causes the complete development of the organs (karana) and capacities (labdhi) of nourishment, of the body, of the senses, of breathing, of speech, and of thought.
  - o *Pratyeka nama karma,* which causes the being to possess an individual body.
  - o *Sthira nama karma,* which causes the teeth, bones, etc., to be firm.
  - o *Subha nama karma,* which causes the parts of the body above the navel to be beautiful.

- *Subhaga nama karma,* which causes some one to whom is not under an obligation to be sympathetic to one.
- *Susvara nama karma,* which bestows a voice which is melodious.
- *Adeya nama karma,* which causes that some one is suggestive, so that his speech meets with approbation and belief.
- *Yasahkirti nama karma,* which grants honour and glory.

• The ten karmas related to *sthavara prakrtis* (opposite of *trasa prakrtis*) are:

- *Sthavara nama karma,* which, causes a body (of plants and elementary beings) that cannot be moved voluntarily.
- *Suksma nama karma* gives (to elementary beings) a subtle body, imperceptible to our senses.
- *Aparyapta nama karma* causes that the organs or faculties of a being do not attain full development, but remain undeveloped.
- *Sadharana nama karma* gives (to plants etc.) a body in common with others of their species.
- *Asthira nama karma* causes that ears, brows, tongue, etc. are flexible.
- *Asubha nama karma* causes at all parts of the body, below the navel are considered to be ugly, so that somebody who is touched by the foot feels this to be unpleasaant.
- *Durbhaga nama karma* makes the jiva unsympathetic.
- *Duhsvara nama karma* makes the voice ill sounding.
- *Anadeya nama karma* makes the jiva unsuggestive.

- o *Ayasahkirti nama karma* causes dishonor and shame.

Gotra Karma

The gotra karma or the status determining karma destines the rank occupied by a person through his birth. They are of two types:

- *uccair gotra-karma* bestows high family surroundings.
- *nicair gotra-karma* bestows low family surroundings.

Vedaniya Karma

The *vedaniya karma* or feeling producing karmas are of two types:

- *sata vedaniya-karma* which causes a feeling of pleasure, created, e.g. by licking something sweet,
- *asata vedaniya-karma* which causes the feeling of pain, created, e.g. if one is hurt by a sword.

With gods and men the sata vedaniya is predominant, although, also with the former at the time of the downfall from the celestial world, and with the latter through cold and heat, death and accident, pain can be produced. Animals and infernal beings experience chiefly the asata vedaniya, although, also, at the birth of a Jina or on a similar occasion, they can experience a feeling of pleasure.

MOKSA (JAINISM)

Moksa (liberation) or **Mokkha** (Prakrit) means liberation, salvation or emancipation of soul. It is a blissful state of existence of a soul, completely free from the karmic bondage, free from samsara, the cycle of birth and death. A liberated soul is said to have attained its true and pristine nature of infinite bliss, infinite knowledge and infinite perception. Such a soul is called siddha or paramatman and considered as supreme soul or God. In Jainism, it is the highest and the noblest objective that a soul should strive to achieve. It fact, it is the only objective that a person should have; other objectives are contrary to the true nature of soul. With right faith, knowledge and efforts all souls can attain this state. That is why, Jainism is also known as moksamârga or the "path to liberation".

The Concept

The concept of moksa, presupposes an existence of infinite eternal souls, who alone are doer, enjoyer and responsible for their action. Thus, all souls are entangled in the mundane worldly activities, bound to karmas since beginningless time and transmigrating and reincarnating from one existence to another. According to Jainism, all souls can bring an end to this repeated cycle of births and deaths and attain liberation, that is moksa.

Description in Jain Texts

Samas Suttas contains the following description of Nirvâsa -

- Where there is neither pain nor pleasure, neither suffering nor obstacle, neither birth nor death, there is emancipation.(617)
- Where there are neither sense organs, nor surprise, nor sleep, nor thirst, nor hunger, there is emancipation.(618)
- Where there is neither Karma, nor quasi-Karma nor the worry, nor any type of thinking which is technically called Artta, Raudra, Dharma and Sukla, there is Nirvâsa. (619)

Uttaradhyana Sutra provides an account of Gautama explaining the meaning of moksa to Kesi, a disciple of Parsva.

There is a safe place in view of all, but difficult of approach, where there is no old age nor death, no pain nor disease. It is what is called Nirvâna, or freedom from pain, or perfection, which is in view of all; it is the safe, happy, and quiet place which the great sages reach. That is the eternal place, in view of all, but difficult of approach. Those sages who reach it are free from sorrows, they have put an end to the stream of existence. (81-4)

Bhavyata

However, from the point of view of potentiality of moksa, Jain texts bifurcates the souls in two categories–bhavya and abhavya. Bhavya souls are those souls who have faith in mokssa and hence will make some efforts to achieve liberation. This potentiality or quality is called bhavyata. However, bhavyata itself does not guarantee moksa, as the soul needs to expend necessary efforts to attain it. On the other hand abhavya souls are those souls who cannot attain liberation as they do not have faith in moksa and hence never make any efforts to attain it.

The Concept of Individuality

Jainism upholds the concept of individuality of souls, even after liberation. There are infinite living beings who have attained moksa and infinite living who have not attained moksa, The soul continues to maintain distinct individuality even after moksa. Hence, there are infinite siddhas or liberated beings existing in eternal infinite bliss.

Siddhasila

According to Jain cosmology, Siddhasila is the place where all the siddhas i.e. the liberated beings reside. It is at the apex of the universe.

Human Birth

Moksa or liberation can be attained only in the human birth. Even the demi-gods and heavenly beings have to reincarnate as humans and practice right faith, knowledge and conduct to achieve liberation. According to Jainism, human birth is quite rare and invaluable and hence one should make wise choices.

Milestones Towards Moksa

A soul is bound by the karmas since beginningless time. The first step to achieve moksa is to inculcate Samyaktva or rational faith or perception.

Samyaktva

According to Jainism, Samyak darsana (Rational Perception), Samyak Jnana (Rational Knowledge) and Samyak Caritra (Rational Conduct) collectively also known as Ratnatraya or the three Jewels of Jainism constitute true Dharma. According to Umasvati, Samyak Darsana, Jnana Caritra together constitutes moksamarga or the path to liberation.

Samyak Darsana or rational perception is the rational faith in the true nature of every substances of the universe.

Samyak Jnana or rational knowledge is the right knowledge of true and relevant knowledge of the reality, the tattvas. It incorporates the two principles of Anekantvada or non-absolutism and Syadvada or relativity of truth. Right knowledge must be free from three main defects: doubt, delusion, and indefiniteness

Samyak Caritra or rational conduct is the natural conduct of a (soul) living being. It consists in following austerities, engaging in right activities and observance of vows, carefulness and controls. Once a soul secures samyaktva, moksa is assured within a few lifetimes.

Kevala Jnana

Kevala Jñâna, the highest form of transcendental knowledge that a samyakdristi soul can attain, also means "absolute knowledge", "Enlightement" and "Omniscience" . Kevala is the state of isolation of the jîva from the ajîva attained through ascetic practices which burn off one's karmic residues, releasing one from bondage to the cycle of death and rebirth. Kevala Jñâna, thus means infinite knowledge of self and non-self, attained by a soul after annihilation of the all ghâtiyâ karmas. Such is person who has attained Kevala Jñâna is called a Kevali. He is also known as Jina (the victor) or Arhat (the worthy one) and worshipped as a god by the Jains. The soul who has reached this stage achieves moksa at the end of his life span, after annihilation of the aghâtiyâ karmas.

Nirvâsa

Nirvâsa means final release from the karmic bondage. When an enlightened human, such as, an Arhat or a Tirthankara extinguishes his remaining aghatiya karmas and thus ends his worldly existence, it is called nirvâna. Technically, the death of an Arhat is called nirvâna of Arhat, as he has ended his wordly existence and attained liberation. Moksa, that is to say, liberation follows nirvâna. However, the terms *moksa* and *nirvana* are often used interchangeably in the Jain texts. An Arhat becomes a siddha, the liberated one, after attaining nirvana.

NIRVANA (JAINISM)

Nirvâsa (**Nivvâsa**) in Jainism means final release from the karmic bondage. When an enlightened human, such as, an Arhat or a Tirthankara extinguishes his remaining aghatiya karmas and thus ends his worldly existence, it is called nirvâsa. Technically, the death of an Arhat is called nirvâsa of Arhat, as he has ended his wordly existence and attained liberation. Moksa, that is to say, liberation follows nirvâsa. An Arhat becomes a siddha, the liberated one, after attaining nirvana.

However, the word nirvâsa is often used to mean moksa, as well. Hence nirvâsa means:

1. Death of an Arhat, who becomes liberated thereafter, and
2. Moksa

Description of Nirvâsa of a Tirthankara in Jain Texts

Kalpasutra gives an elaborate account of Mahavira's nirvâna.

> "The aghatiya Karma's of venerable Ascetic Mahavira got exhausted, when in this Avasarpini era the greater part of the Duhshamasushama period had elapsed and only three years and eight and a half months were left. Mahavira had recited the fifty-five lectures which detail the results of Karma, and the thirty-six unasked questions (the Uttaradhyana Sutra). The moon was in conjunction with the asterism Svati, at the time of early morning, in the town of Papa, and in king Hastipala's office of the writers, (Mahivira) single and alone, sitting in the Samparyahka posture, left his body and attained nirvana, freed from all pains." (147)
>
> In the fourth month of that rainy season, in the seventh fortnight, in the dark (fortnight) of Karttika, on its fifteenth day, in the last night, in the town of Papa, in king Hastipala's office of the writers, the Venerable Ascetic Mahavira died, went off, cut asunder the ties of birth, old age, and death; became a Siddha, a Buddha, a Mukta, a maker of the end (to all misery), finally liberated, freed from all pains. (123)
>
> That night in which the Venerable Ascetic Mahavira died, freed from all pains, was lighted up by many descending and ascending gods. (125)

In that night in which the Venerable Ascetic Mahavira, died, freed from all pains, the eighteen confederate kings of Kasi and Kosala, the nine Mallakis and nine Licchavis, on the day of new moon, instituted an illuminations on the Poshadha, which was a fasting day; for they said: 'Since the light of intelligence is gone, let us make an illumination of material matter!'(128)"

DHARMA (JAINISM)

Jain texts assign a wide range of meaning to the word Dharma or Dhamma. It is often translated as "religion" and as such, Jainism is called as *Jain Dharma* by its adherents.

The word Dharma encompasses the following meanings n Jainism:

1. The true nature of a thing
2. Rationality of perception, knowledge and conduct
3. Ten virtues like forgiveness, etc. also called ten forms of Dharma
4. Ahimsa – protection to all living beings
5. Two paths – of the monks and the laity
6. Dharma as a dravya (substance or a reality) (the principle of motion)

The Nature of a Substance

According to Jainism, Universe and its constituents are uncreated and everlasting. These constituents behave according to the natural laws and their nature without interference from external entities. Dharma or true religion according to Jainism is *vatthu sahâvo dhammo* translated as "the intrinsic nature of a substance is its true dharma." *Kârtikeyânupreksâ* (478) explains it as: "Dharma is nothing but the real nature of an object. Just as the nature of fire is to burn and the nature of water is to produce a cooling effect, in the same manner, the essential nature of the soul is to seek self-realization and spiritual elevation."

Samyaktva - Rationality of Perception, Knowledge and Conduct

According to Jainism, *Samyak darsana* (Rational Perception), *Samyak jnana* (Rational Knowledge) and *Samyak caritra* (Rational Conduct) collectively also known as *Ratnatraya* or the "Three Jewels of Jainism" constitute true Dharma. According to Umasvati, Samyak Darsana, Jnana Caritra together constitutes moksamarga or the path to liberation.

Samyak Darsana or rational perception is the rational faith in the true nature of every substances of the universe. **Samyak Jnana** or rational knowledge is the right knowledge of true and relevant knowledge of the reality, the tattvas. It incorporates the two principles of Anekantvada or non-absolutism and Syadvada or relativity of truth. Right knowledge must be free from three main defects: doubt, delusion, and indefiniteness. **Samyak Caritra** or rational conduct is the natural conduct of a (soul) living being. It consists in following austerities, engaging in right activities and observance of vows, carefulness and controls.

Ten Virtues as Dharma

The following ten virtues constitute true Dharma -

1. Supreme forgiveness
2. Supreme humility
3. Supreme straightforwardness
4. Supreme truthfulness
5. Supreme purity
6. Supreme self-restraint
7. Supreme penance
8. Supreme renunciation
9. Supreme non-possessiveness
10. Supreme celibacy

Ahimsa as Dharma

According to Jain texts, Ahimsa is the greatest Dharma and there is no religion equal to the religion of non-violence.

Two Fold Path of Ascetics and Laypersons

Dharma is the twofold path of *Sravakadharma* i.e. the path for laypersons and *Sramanadharma* i.e the path of the ascetics or mendicants. Sravakadharma is the religious path for the virtuous householders, where charity and worship are the primary duties. The dharma of a householders consists of observance of twelve vows i.e. five minor vows and seven disciplinary vows. Sramanadharma is the religious path of the virtuous ascetics, where mediatation and study of scriptures is their primary duty. The religion of monks consists of five *Mahavratas* or great vows. They are endowed with right faith, right knowledge and right conduct and engaged in complete self-restraint and penances.

Dharma-Tattva and Dharmastikaya

Dharma is one of the six substances constituting the universe. These substances are – Dharma (medium of motion), Adharma (medium of rest), Akasa (space), kala (time), Pudgala (matter) and Jiva (soul). Since Dharma as a substance extends and pervades entire universe, it is also known as Dharmastikaya. It helps the matter and souls in movement. It itself is not motion, but is a medium of motion. Adharma is opposite of Dharma i.e. it assists the substances like soul and matter to rest.

TATTVA

Jain metaphysics is based on seven (sometimes nine, with subcategories) truths or fundamental principles also known as ***tattva*** or ***navatattva,*** which are an attempt to explain the nature and solution to the human predicament. The first two are the two ontological categories of the soul *jîva* and the non-soul *ajîva,* namely the axiom that they exist. The third truth is that through the interaction, called *yoga,* between the two substances, soul and non-soul, karmic matter flows into the soul (*âsrava*), clings to it, becomes converted into karma and the fourth truth acts as a factor of bondage (*bandha*), restricting the manifestation of the consciousness intrinsic to it. The fifth truth states that a stoppage (*sasvara*) of new karma is possible through asceticism through practice of right conduct, faith and knowledge. An intensification of asceticism burns up the existing karma – this sixth truth is expressed by the word *nirjarâ*. The final truth is that when the soul is freed from the influence of karma, it reaches the goal of Jaina teaching, which is liberation or *moksa*. Some authors add two additional categories: the meritorious and demeritorious acts related to karma (*pusya* and *pâpa*). These nine categories of cardinal truth, called *navatattva,* form the basis of entire Jain metaphysics. The knowledge of these reals is essential for the liberation of the soul.

Jîva

Jainism believes that the souls (*jîva*) exist as a reality, having a separate existence from the body that houses it. *Jîva* is characterised by *cetana* (consciousness) and *upayoga* (knowledge and perception). Though the soul experiences both birth and death, it is neither really destroyed nor created. Decay and origin refer respectively to the disappearing of one state of soul and appearance of another state', these being merely the modes of the soul.

Ajîva

Ajîva are the five non-living substances that make up the universe along with the *jîva*. They are:

- **Pudgala** (Matter) –Matter is classified as solid, liquid, gaseous, energy, fine Karmic materials and extra-fine matter or ultimate particles. Paramânu or ultimate particles are considered the basic building block of all matter. One of the qualities of the *Paramânu* and *Pudgala* is that of permanence and indestructibility. It combines and changes its modes but its basic qualities remain the same. According to Jainism, it cannot be created nor destroyed.

- **Dharma-tattva** (Medium of Motion) and **Adharma-tattva** (Medium of rest) – They are also known as *Dharmâstikâya* and *Adharmâstikâya.* They are unique to Jain thought depicting the principles of motion and rest. They are said to pervade the entire universe. *Dharma-tattva* and *adharma-tattva* are by themselves not motion or rest but mediate motion and rest in other bodies. Without *dharmâstikâya* motion is not possible and without *adharmâstikâya* rest is not possible in the universe.
- **Âkâúa** (Space) – Space is a substance that accommodates souls, matter, the principle of motion, the principle of rest, and time. It is all-pervading, infinite and made of infinite space-points.
- *Kâla* (Time) – Time is a real entity according to Jainism and all activities, changes or modifications can be achieved only through time. In Jainism, the time is likened to a wheel with twelve spokes divided into descending and ascending halves with six stages, each of immense duration estimated at billions of *sagaropama* or ocean years. According to Jains, sorrow increases at each progressive descending stage and happiness and bliss increase in each progressive ascending stage.

Âsrava

The *âsrava* is the influx of karmas. It occurs when the karmic particles are attracted to the soul on account of vibrations created by activities of mind, speech and body..

Tattvârthasûtra , 6:1–2 states: "The activities of body, speech and mind is called *yoga*. This three-fold action results in *âsrava* or influx of karma."

Bandha

The karmas have effect only when they are bound to the consciousness. This binding of the karma to the consciousness is called *bandha*. However, the *yoga* or the activities alone do not produce bondage. Out of the many causes of bondage, passion is considered as the main cause of bondage. The karmas are literally bound on account of the stickiness of the soul due to existence of various passions or mental dispositions.

Pâpa and Punya

In many texts *punya* or spiritual merit and *papa* or spiritual demerit are counted among the fundamental reals. But in *Tattvârthasûtra* the number of *tattvas* is seven because both *punya* and *papa* are included in *âsrava* or *bandha*. Both *punya* and *papa* are of two types – *dravya* type (physical type) and a *bhava* type (mental type).

SASVARA

Sasvara is stoppage of karma. The first step to emancipation or the realization of the self is to see that all channels through which karma has been flowing into the soul have been stopped, so that no additional karma can accumulate. This is referred to as the stoppage of the inflow of karma (*sasvara*). There are two kinds of *sasvara*: that which is concerned with mental life (*bhava-sasvara*), and that which refers to the removal of karmic particles (*dravya-sasvara*). This stoppage is possible by self-control and freedom from attachment. The practice of vows, carefulness, self-control, observance of ten kinds of dharma, meditation, and the removal of the various obstacles, such as hunger, thirst, and passion stops the inflow of karma and protect the soul from the impurities of fresh karma.

Nirjarâ

Nirjarâ is the shedding or destruction of karmas that has already accumulated. *Nirjarâ* is of two types: the psychic aspect of the removal of karma (*bhâva-nirjarâ*) and destruction of the particles of karma (*dravya-nirjarâ*). Karma may exhaust itself in its natural course when its fruits are completely exhausted. In this, no effort is required. The remaining karma has to be removed by means of penance (*avipaka-nirjarâ*). The soul is like a mirror which looks dim when the dust of karma is deposited on its surface. When karma is removed by destruction, the soul shines in its pure and transcendent form. It then attains the goal of *moksa.*

Moksa

Moksa means liberation, salvation or emancipation of soul. It is a blissful state of existence of a soul, completely free from the karmic bondage, free from samsara, the cycle of birth and death. A liberated soul is said to have attained its true and pristine nature of infinite bliss, infinite knowledge and infinite perception. Such a soul is called *siddha* or *paramatman* and considered as supreme soul or God. In Jainism, it is the highest and the noblest objective that a soul should strive to achieve. It fact, it is the only objective that a person should have; other objectives are contrary to the true nature of soul. With right faith, knowledge and efforts all souls can attain this state. That is why, Jainism is also known as moksamârga or the "path to liberation".

Samsara

In Jainism, **Sassâra** is the worldly life characterized by continuous rebirths and reincarnations in various realms of existence. Sassâra is described as mundane existence, full of suffering and misery and hence is considered undesirable and worth renunciation. The Sassâra is without any beginning and the soul finds itself in bondage with its karma since the beginningless time. Moksa is the only liberation from sassâra.

Samsara and Reincarnation

Jain texts describe sassâra as an never-ending cycle of re-birth and death. Uttarâdhyayana Sûtra describes sassâra as thus :

> "The universe is peopled by manifold creatures, who are, in this sassâra, born in different families and castes for having done various actions. Sometimes they go to the world of the gods, sometimes to the hells, sometimes they become Asuras in accordance with their actions. Sometimes they become Kshattriyas, or Kandâlas and Bukkasas, or worms and moths, or (insects called) Kunthu and ants. Thus living beings of sinful actions, who are born again and again in ever-recurring births, are not disgusted with the Samsâra, but they are like warriors (never tired of the battle of life)."

Mahavira's view of Samsara

Samsâra is described as a place of suffering and misery. Uttarâdhyayana Sûtra, which is said to contain Mahavira's last words, contains the following description of sassâra :

> *"All men who are ignorant of the Truth are subject to pain; in the endless Samsâra they suffer in many ways. Therefore a wise man, who considers well the ways that lead to bondage and birth, should himself search for the truth, and be kind towards all creatures."*

> *"By what acts can I escape a sorrowful lot in this unstable ineternal sassâra, which is full of misery?"*

> *"Thus the soul which suffers for its carelessness, is driven about in the sassâra by its good and bad Karman; Gautama, be careful all the while."*

"Birth is misery, old age is misery, and so are disease and death, and ah, nothing but misery is the samsâra, in which men suffer distress."

Samsara as a Place of Suffering and Misery

It is described as *bhavsagara* – an ocean of rebirths, that has to be crossed to reach the shores i.e. the Moksa. This can be achieved by enlightened perception, knowledge and conduct.

"A soul endowed with the **Three Jewels** constitutes an excellent ford. One can cross the ocean of transmigratory cycle (sassâra) with the aid of the divine boat of Three Jewels (of Right faith, Knowledge and conduct)."

The Tirthankaras have crossed the ocean called sassâra and reached Moksa and have shown us the path. That is why they have been described as Tirthankaras or ford-makers. Âcâranga Sûtra describes the way the Tirthankaras cross the Ocean of sassâra:

"The great heroes (i.e. the Tirthakaras) who for a long time walked in the former years, the worthy ones bore the troubles (mentioned above); endowed with perfect knowledge they had lean arms and very little flesh and blood. He who discontinues (to sin) and is enlightened, is said to have crossed (the sassâra), to be liberated, and to have ceased (to act)."

Sûtrakrtanga describes the Samsara in this way :

"The Samsâra which is compared to the boundless flood of water, know it to be impassable and of very long duration on account of repeated births. Men therein, seduced by their senses and by women, are born again and again both (as movable and immovable beings)."

Division of Souls

The basic classification of the souls in Jainism is on the basis of the freedom from sassâra i.e – liberated souls or siddhas and unliberated souls i.e. sassâric souls. Humans, plants, animals, hellish beings and demi-gods are all part of sassâra. . Âcâranga Sûtra classifies the living being of sassâra in this way :

> "There are beings called the animate, viz. those who are produced *1.* from eggs (birds), *2.* from a fetus (as elephants), *3.* from a fetus with an enveloping membrane (as cows, buffaloes), *4.* from fluids (as worms) *5.* from sweat (as bugs, lice), *6.* by coagulation (as locusts, ants), *7.* from sprouts (as butterflies, wagtails), *8.* by regeneration (men, gods, hell"beings). This is called the *Sassâra*".

7
Causes of Karma

The karmic process in Jainism is based on seven truths or fundamental principles (*tattva*) of Jainism which explain the human predicament. Out that the seven, the four—influx (âsrava), bondage (*bandha*), stoppage (*sasvara*) and release (*nirjarâ*)—pertain to the karmic process. Karma gets bound to the soul on account of two processes:

- *âsrava* – Influx of karmas, and
- *bandha* – bondage or sticking of karmas to consciousness

Influx of Karma

The *âsrava,* that is, the influx of karmic occurs when the karmic particles are attracted to the soul on account of vibrations created by activities of mind, speech and body. *Tattvârthasûtra* , 6:1–2 states: "The activities of body, speech and mind is called *yoga.* This three-fold action results in *âsrava* or influx of karma." The karmic inflow on account of *yoga* driven by passions and emotions cause a long term inflow of karma prolonging the cycle of reincarnations. On the other hand, the karmic inflows on account of actions that are not driven by passions and emotions have only a transient, short-lived karmic effect.

Causes of Influx

The karmas are attracted to the consciousness by combination of the following factors pertaining to action—

instrumentality, process , modality and motivation Thus, the karmas are attracted and bound on account of combination any element of the following four factors:

- the instrumentality of the actions, that is, either through:
  - body – physical action,
  - speech – verbal action, or
  - mind – mental action
- the process of action which consists of:
  - decision or plan to act,
  - making preparations for the act, like, collecting necessary materials, or
  - actually beginning of the action
- the modality of action, that consists of:
  - the act carried out by self, or
  - instigating someone else to carry out the act, or
  - giving approval or endorsing the act.
- the motivation for action. This includes any of the following negative emotions that motivates the action:
  - Anger
  - Greed
  - Pride
  - Manipulation or deceit

With a combination of any of the elements of the above four factors, there are 108 ways with which the karmas can be attracted to the soul. Even a silent assent or endorsements of acts of violence done by someone else far away, have karmic consequences for the soul. Hence, the scriptures advice carefulness in actions, awareness of the world, and purity in thoughts as a means to avoid the karmas.

Bondage of Karmas

The karmas have effect only when they are bound to the consciousness. This binding of the karma to the consciousness is called *bandha*. However, the *yoga* or the activities alone do not produce bondage. Out of the many causes of bondage, passion is considered as the main cause of bondage. The karmas are literally bound on account of the stickiness of the soul due to existence of various passions or mental dispositions. The passions like anger, pride, deceit and greed are called sticky (*kasayas*) because they act like glue in making karmic particles stick to the soul resulting in *bandha*. Hence the ancient Jain texts talk of subduing these negative emotions:

When he wishes that which is good for him, he should get rid of the four fault—anger, pride, deceit and greed—which increase the evil. Anger and pride when not suppressed, and deceit and greed when arising: all these four black passions water the roots of re-birth.

—*Daúavaikâlika sûtra, 8:36–39*

Causes of Bondage

According to *Tattvârthasûtra*, the causes of karmic bondage—in the order they are required to be eliminate by a soul for spiritual progress—are:

- *Mithyâtva* (Irrationality and a deluded world view) - The deluded world view is the misunderstanding as to how this world really functions on account of one-sided perspectives, perverse viewpoints, irrational scepticism, pointless generalisations and ignorance.

- *Avirati* (non-restraint or a vowless life) – The second cause of bondage, *avirati* is the inability to refrain voluntarily from the evil actions, that harms oneself and others. The state of *avirati* can only be overcome by observing the minor vows of a layman.
- *Pramâda* (carelessness and laxity of conduct) – This third cause of bondage consists of absentmindedness, lack of enthusiasm towards acquiring merit and spiritual growth, and improper actions of mind, body and speech without any regard to oneself or others.
- *Kasâya* (passions or negative emotions) – The four passions—anger, pride, deceit and greed—are the primary reason for the attachment of the karmas to the soul. They keep the soul immersed in the darkness of delusion leading to deluded conduct and unending cycles of reincarnations.
- *Yoga* (activities of mind, speech and body) – The threefold activities of mind, body and speech attract and bind the karmas when such actions are influenced by passions.

Each cause presupposes the existence of the next cause, but the next cause does not necessarily pre-suppose the existence of the previous cause. A soul is able to advances on the spiritual ladder called *gunasthâna,* only when it is able to eliminate the above causes of bondage one by one. Duration and intensity of the karmic bond are determined by *"Kasâya"* and type and quantity of the karmas bound depends on *yoga.*

Causes of Different Types of Karmas

Chapter VI of *Tattvârthasûtra* provides a detailed description of various causes for various types of karmas. According to Jain texts, there are eight main types of karma—*jñânavârana* (Knowledge obscuring karma), *darúanâvarana* (perception obscuring karma) *mohanîya* (deluding karma), *antarâya* (obstacles creating karma), *vedanîya* (feeling producing karma), *nâma* (body determining karma), *âyu* (life span determining karma) and "gotra" (status determining karma).

Causes of Knowledge Obscuring and Perception Obscuring Karmas

Jñânavârasa and *darúanâvarasa* karma are knowledge obscuring and perception obscuring. They are caused by:

1. harbouring a feeling of jealousy towards knowledge or perception, towards a possessor of it and towards a means of it.
2. Wilful concealment of knowledge or perception
3. Ungenerosity as to knowledge
4. Obstruction of knowledge or perception to others
5. Denial of receipt of knowledge
6. False accusation or misrepresentation

Causes of Feeling Producing Karma

Vedanîya, feeling producing karmas can be of two types: *sâtâvedanîya* i.e. pleasant and *asâtâvedanîya* i.e. unpleasant feeling producing karmas.

Causes of Asâtâvedanîya Karma

Asâtâvedanîya karma is bound on account of causing to other or oneself the following:

1. External or an internal pain
2. To feel troubled and worried on having been deprived of the company of a well wisher
3. Experience of acute distress or heart burning on account of insult or insulting others

4. To enjoy or wallow in misery, to weep and wail
5. Injurying self or others
6. Lamenting on recalling the merits of a departed one

Causes of Sâtâvedanîya Karma

Sâtâvedanîya karma is bound on account of causing to other or oneself the following:

1. Harbouring a feeling of compassion towards all the living
2. Leading a religious life i.e. practice of minor vows or anuvrata by householder and mahavrata by monks and ascetics
3. Donation and charity with humility
4. Self restraint or proper attentiveness towards disciplined life even if it is tinged with some attachment
5. Forbearance and forgiveness
6. Inculcating purity by suppressing the tendency towards greed and the like defilements

Causes of Deluding Karmas

Mohanîya karmas produce a delusion in a soul i.e. the soul is not able to distinguish between right and wrong. They are of two subtypes—*Darúana-mohanîya* (Perception delusion) and *câritra-mohanîya* (conduct deluding) karmas.

Causes of Daroeana-Mohanîya

1. Speaking ill of the omniscient and holders of true knowledge
2. Speaking ill of the scripture i.e. a jealous intellect leveling false charges against the scripture (e.g. Saying

that this scripture is useless because it is composed in Prakrit which is a language of the illiterate alternatively, because it is composed in a complication ridden language of the pedant or that it contains a futile and bothersome description of the various vows, regulations, expiations etc.)

3. Speaking ill of the religious order or levelling false charges against the religious order composed of four divisions viz. monks, nuns, laymen, laywomen (e.g. saying that these monks unnecessarily take the trouble of observing vows, regulations etc., since monkhood is in fact an impossibility nor is it conducive to a wholesome result, or saying about the laymen that they undertake no cultured performances like bath, donation etc., nor do they lead a life of purity.)
4. Speaking ill of the religion
5. Speaking ill of the deities or denigrating them

Causes of Câritra-Mohanîya Karmas

1. To produce a *kasaya* (passions) in oneself or in others and to undertake unworthwhile acts under the influence of a *kasaya*
2. To ridicule the true religion, to make fun of a poor or helpless person, to develop the habit of frivolous joking
3. Indulging in various recreations evincing disinclination towards the proper moral restrains like vows and regulations
4. To cause worry to others, to disturb someone in one's rest and to keep the company of petty persons
5. To maintain a sorrowful demeanour and to arouse a feeling of sorrow in others

6. To feel afraid and to frighten others
7. To despise a beneficial act and a beneficial general conduct
8. A habit for cheating and finding fault with others
9. To nourish mental impressions of various sexual feelings

The Causes of Lifespan Determining Karmas

The *âyu* karmas are the life span determining karmas and they determine the next destiny or reincarnation of a soul. Accordingly, as per the next reincarnations lifespan determined, a soul takes birth in either hell, heaven, animal kingdom or as a human.

Causes of the Narakayus Karma or Birth in Hells

Following reasons result in birth in naraka or hells:

1. Killing or causing pain with intense passion
2. Excessive attachment to things and worldly pleasure with constantly indulging in cruel and violent acts.
3. Vowless and unrestrained life

Causes of the Tiryagayus Karma or Birth as Animals

Following actions conducted with deceit lead to births animals, plants or microbes:

1. Preaching religion to introduce sheer falsity
2. Propagate religion with a selfish motive,
3. To keep one's life devoid of disciplined conduct
4. Vowless and unrestrained life

Causes of Manusyayus Karma or Birth as Human

1. To reduce the tendency to inflict injury and that to accumulate possession.

2. To exhibit softness and simplicity.
3. Vowless and unrestrained life

Causes of the Devayus Karma or Birth in Heavens

1. Having a disciplined and restrained life yet accompanied by some attachment
2. partial practice of vows like non violence, etc.
3. Refraining from evil acts but out of compulsion from external factors or for imitating others
4. Undergoing childish penances like fasting and austerities without understanding

Practicing vows and austerities normally leads to destructon of karmas and of attainment of *moksa* or liberation, but in above cases leads to merit and birth in heavens as demi gods for a long but finite period of time

Causes of Body Determining Karma

The *nâma* karmas or body determining karmas are of two types— *asubha* and *subha nama* karmas i.e. auspicious and inauspicious karmas. Their causes are:

1. Crooked and misleading actions (pertaining to mind, speech and body) causes inflow of inauspicious *nâma* karma
2. The opposite of the above—straightforwardness and genuine behaviour—causes inflow of auspicious *nâma* karma.
3. Sixteen dispositions that cause re-birth as a *Tîrthankara* on account of Tîrthankara–nâma-karma: (1) Purity of worldview, (2) humility, (3) non violation of vows and abstinences, (4) persistent cultivation of knowledge, (5) ever present fear of worldly existence,

(6) charity and renunciation as per one's capacity, (7) penance as per one's capacity, (8) ensuring harmony and peace in the religious order particularly the order of monks, (9) offering services to the competent and deserving persons, (10) devotion towards Siddhas and Tîrthankaras, (11) devotion towards the preceptor, (12) devotion towards learned monks, (13) devotion towards scriptures, (14) regard for compulsory duties, (15) to cultivate and honour the path of *moksa,* (16) feeling of unattached affection towards the co religionists.

Causes of Status Determining

The *gotra* karma or status determining karma is of two types:

1. *Nicagotra* karma: Praising oneself, defaming others, hiding others' merits and finding fault in others are the causes of low status or low class.

2. *Uccagotra* karma: Praising others, displaying one owns shortcomings, ignoring ones own merit along with humility and modesty causes the inflow of high status determining karma.

Causes of Obstructing Karma

The causes of inflow of obstructing or *antarâya* karma are — causing obstruction to others or intending to place or placing obstacles before others in their act of beneficence, gain, satisfaction, comfort and power.

●●

8
Jain Rituals and Festivals

Jain rituals and festivals play a prominent part in Jainism. Rituals can take place daily or more often, while festivals occur on designated days of the year.

Everyday Rituals

Pious Jains incorporate a number of rituals into their daily life. Spreading the grain for the birds in the morning, and filtering or boiling the water for the next few hours' use are ritual acts of charity and non-violence.

Some people dismiss the ritual acts as superstition. Others recognize that while the Jain idols have no miraculous powers, daily rituals help the worshipper towards a reverent state of mind.

Samayika

Samayika is the practice of equanimity, translating to meditation. It is a ritual act undertaken early in the morning and perhaps also at noon and night. It lasts for forty-eight minutes (Two Ghadis) and usually involves not only quiet recollection but also usually the repetition of routine prayers. The ritual is chanting and praying about the good things

Pratikramana

Pratikramana is performed in the morning for the repentance of violence committed during the night, and in the evening for the violence during the day and additionally on certain days of the year. During this, the Jain expresses remorse for the harm caused, or wrong doing, or the duties left undone.

Worship of Jain Idols

Worship before the Jain idols, bowing to the idols, and lighting a lamp in front of the idols is an ideal way to start the day for many Jains. More elaborate forms of worship (puja), as described, is a regular daily ritual usually done in the temple. The worshipper enters the temple with the words 'Namo Jinanam' 'I bow to the Jina', and repeats three times, 'Nisihii' (to relinquish thoughts about worldly affairs). The simpler surroundings of the household shrine can also provide a suitable setting. The members of some sects of Jainism don't believe in worship of the Jina image. They believe in meditation and silent prayers. Worship, or puja, can take many forms.

1. The ritual bathing of the image (Snatra Puja) is symbolic to the bathing of the newborn Tirthankara by the gods (celestial beings). A simple symbolic act is to touch one's forehead with the liquid used to bath the idol. Bathing the idol also takes place during the Panch Kalyanak Puja, a ritual to commemorate the five great events of the Tirthankara's life, namely conception, birth, renunciation, omniscience and moksa.

2. Antaraya Karma Puja comprises a series of prayers to remove those karmas which obstruct the spiritual uplifting power of the soul. A lengthy temple ritual which can take three days to complete is the

3. Arihanta Puja, paying respect to the arihants.

4. There is a ritual of prayer focused on the siddhachakra, a lotus-shaped disc bearing representations of the arhat, the liberated soul, religious teacher, religious leader and the monk (the

five praiseworthy beings), as well as the four qualities namely perception, knowledge, conduct and austerity to uplift the soul.

Festivals of Jaina

Paryusana Parva

The Paryusana Parva is the most important festival for the Jains. This is the eight-day period during which many Jains fast and carry out the religious activities. This period falls in the months of Shravana and Bhadra (August or September). During the rainy season in India Jain monks stop walking from one town to another and settle in a fixed location with the purpose of reducing the injury to the living things now springing to life. Often a township invites respected monks to stay in its vicinity during the rainy season (sometimes with a beautifully written manuscript invitation) and the people receive them with great pomp and rituals. A course of lectures or sermons by a monk or other respected person is a regular feature of the Paryusana Parva. The word Paryusana is derived from two words meaning (gada) 'a year' and 'a coming back'. It is a period of repentance for the acts of the previous year and of austerities to help shed the accumulated karmas. It should be remembered that the austerity is not just to shed karmas, but to control the desire for sensual pleasures as a part of the spiritual training to prevent the accumulation of the new karmas. During this period some people fast for all eight days, some for the lesser periods (a minimum of three days is suggested in the scriptures), but it is considered obligatory to fast on the last day of the Paryusana Parva. Fasting usually involves complete abstinence from any sort of food or drink, but some people do take boiled water during the daytime. There are regular ceremonies in the temple and discourses of Kalpa Sutra (one of the sacred books) in the Upashraya during this time. Kalpa Sutra contains the detailed account of Mahavira's life, is read to the congregation. On the third day of the Paryusana Parva the Kalpa Sutra receives a very special reverence and may be carried in the procession. On the fifth day, at a special ceremony, the auspicious dreams of Mahavira's mother, queen Trishala, are demonstrated. Listening to the Kalpa Sutra, taking active steps to prevent the animal killing, asking and offering forgiveness to all living beings, visiting the neighborhood temples, etc., are some of the important activities during this time. The final day of Paryusana is the most important of all. On this day those who have observed the fasts are specially honored. This is also the day when Jains ask for forgiveness from the family, friends and foes alike for any acts they might have committed towards them in the previous year. Therefore this annual occasion of repentance and forgiveness is very important. Shortly after Paryusana it is the custom to organize a Swami Vastyalaya-dinner when all the Jains get together and renew their friendship with each other regardless of their socio-economical status.

Mahavir Jayanti

Mahavira was born most probably in the year 599 B.C. and the exact date is given in the scriptures as the thirteenth day of the bright half of the Hindu calendar month of Chaitra. In the solar calendar this will fall in March or April. The festival to commemorate this, known as Mahavira Jayanti, is an occasion for great celebration. Jains gather together to hear Mahavira's message expounded, so that they can follow his teachings and example. The dreams of his mother before his birth may be dramatically presented and the circumstances of his birth, as narrated in the scriptures, explained to the assembled people. The idol of Mahavira is ceremonially bathed and rocked in a cradle. In many places the processions take place through the streets with the image having the place of honor, and in some regions in India this is a general public holiday.

Diwali

Diwali or Deepawali is the most important festival in India. For the Jains, it is the second most after the Paryusana Parva. For Jains Diwali marks the anniversary of Mahavir's moksha. Mahavir attained moksha on this day in 527 B.C. (and also of the achievement of total knowledge, omniscience, by his chief follower, Gautama Indrabhuti). The festival falls on the last day of the Hindu calendar month of Ashvina, the end of the year as per Indian calendar (in October or November), The celebration starts in the early morning of the previous day, for it was then that Mahavira commenced his last sermon which lasted till late in the night of Diwali. It is narrated that the eighteen kings of northern India who were in his audience decided that the light of their master's knowledge would be kept alive symbolically by lighting of the lamps. Hence it is called Dipawali, (dipa means lamp), or Diwali.

New Year

The New Year begins the next day of Diwali and is the occasion for joyful gatherings of Jains, with everybody wishing each other a Happy New Year.

Gyana Panchami (Knowledge day)

The fifth day of the New Year is known as Gyana Panchami, the day of knowledge, when the scriptures, which impart knowledge to the people, are worshipped with devotion.

Paush Dashami

This day is famous as the birthday of 23rd JainTirthankar lourd Parshvanath. On the 10th day of Posh month of Hindu calendar, hundreds and thousands of Jain men and women perform the tapasya of 3 Upavas-attham (continuous fasting for 3 days) and by means of recitation and meditation they try to attain spiritual welfare. A grand fair takes place in

Sankheswar which is a sacred place for Jains. Thousands of people gather here and perform the austerity of 'Attham'.

Varshi Tapa / Akshay Tritiya Tapa

Those noble people who perform the austerity of **Varshi tapa** complete the austerity on this day by taking sugar-cane juice in the cool shadow of Shatrunjay. First Jain Tirthankar Rishabhdev performed the Parana (completion of an austerity) on this day after fasting for 13 months and 13 days continuously. This day is considered to be very auspicious for making a pilgrimage to Shatrunjay (Palitana). This falls on the 3rd day of the bright fortnight of Vaishakh month of Hindu calendar.

Maun-Agiyaras

It in November/December when a day of complete silence and fasting is kept and meditation is directed towards the five holy beings, monk, teacher, religious leader, arhat and siddha. This day is regarded as the anniversary of the birth of many of the Tiirthankaras.

Navapad Oli

The serious Jain layman fast, more or less completely, and undertake other religious practices on many auspicious days throughout the year. As many as ten days in a given month are observed for the fasts by the pious Jains (though others may observe a lesser number). The first day of the three seasons in the Indian year is also of special sanctity. Twice a year, falling in March/April and September/October, the nine-day Oli period of semi-fasting is observed when Jains take only one meal a day, of very plain food.

PANCH-KALYANAK PRATISHTHA

Panch-kalyanak Pratishtha (installation with five auspicious events) is a traditional Jain ceremony that consecrates one or more Jain Tirthankara pratimas.

The five kalyanakas are the five major events associated with a tirthankara.

1. Garbh (conception)
2. Janma (birth)
3. Tapa (austerities)
4. Gyan (omniscience)
5. Moksha (liberation)

After the pratishtha the statue represents the Tirthankara, and becomes a worshippable object.

A pratishtha must be authorised by an acknowledged leader of the sangha, an Acharya or a Bhattaraka, or a representative (pratishthacharya), who can recite the sacred suri-mantra to mark the final step in the installation ceremony. The Shvetambara sect requires a ceremony called anjana-shalaka. Once an idol is fully installed, it must be worshipped daily.

The Bhattaraka Devendrakeerti of Humbaj is the only Bhattaraka who has participated in the installations in overseas countries including USA, Canada and Australia.

In Bundelkhand region, a panch-kalyanak pratishtha is accompanied by a gaj rath (chariot drawan by elephants) procession.

PRATIKRAMANA

Pratikraman (literally Sanskrit "introspection"), is a process of repentance of sins (prayaschit) during which Jains repent for their wrongdoings during their daily life, and remind themselves to refrain from doing so again. Devout Jains often do Pratikraman at least twice a day.

There are five types of Pratikraman:

1. Devasi
2. Rayi

3. Pakhi
4. Chaumasi
5. Samvatsari

Devasi Pratikraman is performed daily in the evening, Raysi Pratikraman is performed in the early morning, Pakhi Pratikraman is done once every fifteen days. Chaumasi Pratikraman is done once in four months on purnima (full moon day) of Kartik, Falgun and Asha°h months of lunar calendar year for the sins committed during that period. Samvatsari Pratikraman is done once per year on the last day of paryushana mahaparv for the sins committed during the whole year.

Samvatsari Pratikraman includes all six things a Jain must do:

1. Samayik - maintain equanimity
2. Chauvisanttho - honor the Tirthankars
3. Vandana - honor all sadhus and sadhvis
4. Pratikraman - repent wrongdoings
5. Kayotsarg - meditation and prayer
6. Pratyakhan - take vows to keep self-control

The soul, in its pure form, has infinite perception, infinite knowledge,infinite vigor, and is non-attached. These attributes are not seen in a worldly soul because it is soiled with karmas. By following religious principles principals and activities, we overcome our karmas and uplift our souls to liberation. There are various kinds of religious activities, sometimes called rituals, and among them Pratikraman is the most important ritual. During pratikraman we repent for our non-meritorious activities on a daily basis. We realize our mistakes and ask for forgiveness which helps us to minimize the intensity of the karmaic bondage. Pratikraman is a combination of six avshyakas.

●●

9
Jain Meditation

Jain meditation is called Samayika. The word Samayika means being in the moment of continuous real-time. This act of being conscious of the continual renewal of the universe in general and one's own renewal of the individual living being (*Jiva*) in particular is the critical first step in the journey towards identification with one's true nature, called the Atman. It is also a method by which one can develop an attitude of harmony and respect towards other humans and Mother Nature.

One begins by achieving a balance in time. By being fully aware, alert and conscious of the constantly moving present, one will experience their true nature, Atman.

The 24 Jain Tirthankaras are always seen in meditative posture.

Samayika gains a special significance during Paryushana.

Postures

The Samayika is done to practice meditation generally by sitting in the Kayotsarga (khadgasana) , Padmasana or Paryankasana postures. Although other postures have been used by yogis and others, the 24 Jain Tirthankaras are always seen in one of these two postures. The image to the right shows Jain monks in Samayika. Jains visit their temples and are seen sitting in this posture in one-on-one Samayika sessions in front of Tirthankar statues, for example, a Jain temple in Blairstown, NJ USA. Also included is an image of the Jain temple in Mt. Abu Rajastan, India.

Samayika word comes from Prakrit language. The aim of Samayika is to transcend our daily experiences as the "constantly changing" human beings, called Jiva, and allow identification with the "changeless" reality in us, called the Atman. Is it possible to identify with the "changelessness" in us when constant change and renewal in and around us dominate our attention and energies? Samayika addresses this question. One begins in Samayika by achieving a balance in time. If the present fine moment of time could be defined as the moving line between the past and the future, Samayika happens by being fully aware, alert and conscious in that moving timeline when one experiences one's true nature, Atman, which is considered common to all living beings. The Samayika is derived from the word samay - meaning time - in the Prakrit language. The Samayika takes on special significance during special 8-day period practiced by the Jains called Paryushana. Also see Jainism for more.

Preksha Meditation

Acharya Mahaprajna, The Tenth Head of Jain Svetambara Terapanth sect formulated Preksha Meditation in 1970s. He practiced various meditation techniques for nearly 30 years and developed this well organised meditation system and presented it in scientific light. Preksha Meditation is the combination of knowledge from ancient religious books, modern science and experience. Acharya Mahaprajna made a deep research on Agam - Jain holy scriptures, ancient scriptures, medical science, Yoga science, Naturopathy, Ayurveda, modern Physics, etc. while developing this meditation system.

Preksha meditation is the practice of purifying the emotions and conscious (*chitta*) and realizing the own self. It helps in leading a peaceful life and is a system of mediation for attitudinal change, behavioral modification and integrated development of personality.

The word preksha means 'to perceive carefully and profoundly'. In *preksha*, perception always means experience bereft of the duality of like and dislike, pleasure and pain. Impartiality and equanimity are synonymous with *Preksha*. *Preksha* is impartial perception, where there is neither the emotion of attachment nor aversion, neither pleasure or displeasure. Both these states of emotion are closely and carefully perceived but not experienced. And because both are perceived from close quarters, it is not difficult to reject both of them and assume a neutral position. Thus equanimity is essentially associated with preksha.

It aims at reaching and purify the deeper levels of existence. Regular practice strengthens the immune system, builds up stamina to resist against ageing, pollution, chemical toxins, viruses, diseases.

Important elements in the system are *Kayotsarg* - Full awareness with complete relaxation, Perception of the breath, body, the psychic centres, psychic colors (*lesya* meditation), contemplation processes, Yoga and Pranayaam, Mantra.

Important disciplines in the system are - Synchrony of mental and physical actions or simply present mindedness or complete awareness of one's actions, disciplining the reacting attitude, friendliness, diet, silence, spiritual vigilance.

One commences the practice of this technique with the perception of the body. Body contains the soul. Therefore, one must pierce the wall of the container to reach the content (the soul). Again, breathing is a part of the body and essence of life. To breath is to live; and so breath is naturally qualified to be the first object of perception, while the body itself would become the next one. The vibrations, sensations and other physiological events are worthy of attention. Conscious mind becomes sharpened to perceive these internal realities in due course, and then it will be able to focus itself on the minutest and the most subtle occurrences within the body. The direct perception of emotions, urges and other psychological events will then be possible. And ultimately the envelope of *karmic* matter, contaminating the consciousness could be clearly recognised.

The meditation training camps are organised on a regular basis. Major training centers in India are in Ladnun, Rajasthan, Delhi, Ahemedabad. Centers are also present in many countries like the US, UK, Russia, Germany, Ukraine, Australia, Singapore, Netherland, etc.

Existing and Historical Meditation Techniques in Jainism

According to the some commonly practiced *yoga* systems, high concentration is reached by meditating in an easy (preferably lotus) posture in seclusion and staring without blinking at the rising sun, a point on the wall, or the tip of the nose, and as long as one can keep the mind away from the outer world, this strengthens concentration. *Garuda* is the name Jainism gives to the yoga of self-control and control of mind, body and speech, so that even earth, water, fire and air can come under one's control. *Œiva* is in Jainism control over the passions and the acquisition of such self-control that under all circumstances equanimity is maintained.

Prânayâma – breathing exercises – are performed to strengthen the flows of life energy. Through this, the elements of the constitution – earth, water, fire and air – are also strengthened. At the same time the five *chakras* are controlled. *Prânayâma* also helps to stabilize one's thinking and leads to unhampered direct experience of the events around us.

Next one practices *pratyâhâra*. Pratyâhâra means that one directs the senses away from the enjoyment of sensual and mental objects. The senses are part of the nervous system, and their task is to send data to the brain through which the mind as well as the soul is provided with information. The mind tends to enjoy this at the cost of the soul as well as the body. *Pratyâhâra* is obtained by focusing the mind on one point for the purpose of receiving impulses: on the eyes, ears, tip of the nose, the brow, the navel, the head, the heart or the palate.

Contemplation is an important wing in Jain meditation. The practitioner meditates or reflects deeply on subtle facts or philosophical aspects. The first type is *Agnya vichâya,* in which one meditates deeply on the seven elementary facts - life and non-life, the inflow, bondage, stoppage and removal of *karmas,* and the final accomplishment of liberation. The second is *Apaya vichâya,* in which incorrect insights and behaviour in which "sleeping souls" indulge, are reflected upon. The third is *Vipaka vichâya dharma dhyâna,* in which one reflects on the eight causes or basic types of *karma.* The fourth is *Sansathan vichâya dharma dhyâna,* when one thinks about the vastness of the universe and the loneliness of the soul, which has had to face the results of its own causes all alone.

Practitioner can apply a number of meditation techniques known as *pindâstha-dhyâna, padâstha-dhyâna, rûpâstha-dhyâna, rûpâtita-dhyâna, savîrya-dhyâna,* etc.

In *pindâstha-dhyâna* one imagines oneself sitting all alone in the middle of a vast ocean of milk on a lotus flower, meditating on the soul. There are no living beings around whatsoever. The lotus is identical to *Jambûdvîpa,* with Mount *Meru* as its stalk. Next the meditator imagines a 16-petalled lotus at the level of his navel, and on each petal are printed the (Sanskrit) letters "arham" and also an inverted lotus of 8 petals at the location of his heart. Suddenly the lotus on which one is seated flares up at the navel and flames gradually rise up to the inverted lotus, burning its petals with a rising golden flame which not only burns his or her body, but also the inverted lotus at the heart. The flames rise further up to the throat whirling in the shape of a swastika and then reach the head, burning it entirely, while taking the form of a three-sided pyramid of golden flames above the head, piercing the skull sharp en straight up. The whole physical body is charred, and everything turns into glowing ashes. Thus the *pinda* or body is burnt off and the pure soul survives. Then suddenly a strong wind blows off all the ashes; and one imagines that a heavy rain shower washes all the ashes away, and the pure soul remains seated on the lotus. That pure Soul has infinite virtues, it is Myself. Why should I get polluted at all? One tries to remain in his purest nature. This is called *pindâstha dhyâna,* in which one ponders the reality of feeling and experiencing.

In *padâstha dhyâna* one focuses on some mantras, words or themes. Couple of important mantra are, OM - it signifies remembrance of the five classes of spiritual beings (the embodied and non-embodied Jinas, the ascetics, the monks and the nuns), pronouncing the word "Arham" makes one feel "I myself am the omniscient soul" and one tries to improve one's character accordingly. One may also pronounce the holy name of an *arhat* and concentrate on the universal richness of the soul.

In *rûpâstha dhyâna* one reflects on the embodiments of arhats, the svayambhuva (the self-begotten), the omniscients and other miraculous people and their attributes, such as three umbrellas and whiskers – as seen in many icons – unconcerned about one's own body, but almighty and benevolent to all living beings, destroyer of attachment, enmity, etc. Thus the meditator as a human being concentrates his or her attention on the virtues of the omniscients to acquire the same virtues for himself.

Rûpâtita dhyâna is a meditation in which one focuses on bodiless objects such as the liberated souls or *siddhas,* which stand individually and collectively for the infinite qualities that such souls have earned. That omniscient, potent, omnipresent, liberated and untainted soul is called a *nirañjâna,* and this stage can be achieved by right vision, right knowledge and right conduct only. Right vision, right knowledge and right conduct begin the fourth stage of the 14-fold path.

The ultimate aim of such yoga and meditation is to pave the way for the spiritual elevation and salvation of the soul. Some yogis develop their own methods for meditation.

The *kayotsarg* method is found to be very useful by many Jains. It means full awareness with complete relaxation. The practitioner takes a comfortable posture either lying down or sitting or standing and breathes calmly. Then auto suggests each and every part and entity of the body to be relaxed and feel the same. Once the body is completely relaxed, the practitioner forgets about the body and tries to identify the Self. Then one practices of complete awareness of the self without any hindrance.

Lord Mahavira and Meditation

Meditation was an integral part of Lord Mahavira's life. Lord Mahavira had meditated in different ways:

- Meditation by fixing the gaze for hours on an oblique wall and also for acquiring high levels of magnetism in the eyes.
- Adoption of various steady postures in meditation. He meditated on various spaces in the universe, the higher *loka* - upper, in the downward direction - lower *loka* and in the transverse direction - the transverse *loka*, making them objects for meditation.
- Meditating mostly in standing posture.
- Practiced *Kayotsarga* for full awareness and deep relaxation.
- Meditating in the open without clothes and shelter.
- Being ceaselessly conscious at every moment of the day and night. Total vigilance in the sixth step, and Samadhi, the seventh step of the meditative path.

- Practicing meditation, both with the support of an object and without any support of any object.
- Usage of different objects for his meditation sessions. He would change the targets of his attention.

Objects on which he had meditated:

- The *Karmas* moving upward, downward and in a transverse direction.
- Bondage, the cause of bondage and its consequences.
- Salvation, its cause and its bliss.
- The head, the navel and the big toe.
- Matter, its characteristic and modes (its changing conditions).
- The origin, permanence and transitory nature of Matter.
- The gross world and the cosmos.
- Subtle objects like the molecular structure.
- The soul, by intuition.
- Practice of contemplations (*Bhawanas*) during practice of meditation. The main subjects were: Loneliness, transitoriness and absence of protection, etc.
- Concentration on the body for a long stretch of time; he could change it on the mental and vocal level. He could change his meditations from matter to mode and from word to silence

GURU VANDANA

Guru Vandana means "Reverence for the Teacher" – it is the thanksgiving from a student to a teacher, expressing his or her gratitude. The Guru Vandana programme provides a platform for students to honor their teachers for imparting knowledge and wisdom to them.

The concept of Guru is as old as humanity itself. Primarily, the word Guru means a 'teacher' and as such it is a universal concept based on the idea of transmitting knowledge from a person, who knows something, to an ignorant student or disciple. In an extended view, a Guru can also be a priest, a rabbi, a master, a school teacher, even a father or a mother. Guru does not mean a teacher imparting formal training but a person who contributes to the overall development and learning of an individual.

Guru transforms his disciple through his presence and spiritual knowledge. According to RamaKrishna Prarahamsa Spiritual knowledge can not be attained completely by reading books. But for obtaining complete spiritual enlightenment Guru's presence is a must. Only when there is a strong bond between Guru and Shishya spiritual enlightenment might takes place.

Origins of Guru Shishya Parampara

Thus our great sanathana darma tradition has been enriched by the GURU-SISHYA relationship. Lord Rama's greatness lay in His relationship with His most loyal disciple HANUMAN who taught the essence of Ramanamamritim. Lord Krishna gave us the Bhagavad Gita, thanks to his devoted and most trusted disciple Arjuna. Saint Ramakrishna Paramahamsa gave to the world Swami Vivekananda who in turn gave to the world the Ramakrishna Mission, embodying the soul of India. Saint Thyagaraja, an avatar of Sage Valmiki, composed hundreds of soulful Krithis in praise of God. Two Krithis, in particular, refer to the GURU'S role in guiding the seeker on the right path. Guru leka in 'Gowrimanohari' raga is a Krithi in which the Saint of Thiruvaiyar sings how one who is trapped in the jungle of desire, can come out of it with help of the right Guru. Saint Thyagaraja says however learned and good a person might be, life would be meaningless without the guidance of a Satguru. In another Krithi, Sri Naradamuni Gururaya ganti in Bhairavi raga, Thyagaraja explains how Satguru Smaranam helps one in getting rid of ignorance.

In Modern Times

American Hindu Education Foundation (HEF) had conducted the programme in Houston in which over 30 teachers and a principal were honored by students. Children from Houston Balagokulams area picked up their favorite teachers. Acharya Premchand Sridhar of Arya Samaj Houston presided over the programme. The programme started with Sridhar lighting the lamp and it was followed by cultural programmes and with the explanation of Hindu Concept of Gurus. After the felicitation of teachers Veda Vrinda group chanted the section of the Taittariya Upanishad known as the Vedic Commencement Address. Columbus chapter of HEF is planning to conduct similar programme in October 2008.

Guruvandana is also performed by disciples to spiritual masters. During Guru.Vandana programme GuruGita is recited by disciple to honor his guru. GuruGita forms section of Skanda Purana. In Bangalore Guruvandana was offered to Sankaracharya of Kanchi Kamakoti Peetam, Sri Jayendra Saraswathi. Despite rains lots of people gathered in Malleshwaram to felicitate their Spiritual Guru. In ISskon temples Guruvandana is performed for spiritual Guru Srila Prabhupada throughout the year.

In Other Religions

Apart from Hinduism Guru-Shishya concept is followed in other religions like Jain, Sikh, Buddhism. In fact the word Sikh has origins from Sanskrit 'shishya'. Jains celebrate Guru Vandana as part of their rituals.

●●

10
Jain Philosophy

Jain philosophy (Jain darsana) deals extensively with the problems of metaphysics, reality, cosmology, ontology, epistemology and divinity. Jainism is essentially a transtheistic religion of ancient India. It is a continuation of the ancient Œramana tradition which co-existed with the Vedic tradition since ancient times. The distinguishing features of Jain philosophy are its belief on independent existence of soul and matter, denial of creative and omnipotent God, potency of karma, eternal and uncreated universe, a strong emphasis on non-violence, accent on relativity and multiple facets of truth, and morality and ethics based on liberation of soul. Jain philosophy attempts to explain the rationale of being and existence, the nature of the Universe and its constituents, the nature of bondage and the means to achieve liberation. It has often been described as an ascetic movement for its strong emphasis on self-control, austerities and renunciation. It has also been called a model of philosophical liberalism for its insistence that truth is relative and multifaceted and for its willingness to accommodate all possible view-points of the rival philosophies. Jainism strongly upholds the individualistic nature of soul and personal responsibility for one's decisions; and that self-reliance and individual efforts alone are responsible for one's liberation.

Throughout its history, the Jain philosophy remained unified and single, although as a religion, Jainism was divided into various sects and traditions. The contribution of Jain philosophy in developing the Indian philosophy has been significant. Jain philosophical concepts like Ahimsa, Karma, Moksa, Samsara and like have been assimilated into the philosophies of other Indian religions like Hinduism and Buddhism in various forms. While Jainism traces its philosophy from teachings of Mahavira and other Tirthankaras, various Jain philosophers from Kundakunda and Umasvati in ancient times to Yaœovijaya in recent times have contributed greatly in developing and refining the Jain and Indian philosophical concepts.

Jain Cosmology

Jain cosmology denies the existence of a supreme being responsible for creation and operation of universe. According to Jainism, the universe and its constituents are eternal and uncreated.

Jain Conception of the Universe

According to Jainism, this *loka* or Universe is an uncreated entity, existing since infinity, immutable in nature, beginningless and endless. Jain texts describe the shape of the Universe as similar to a man standing with legs apart and arm resting on his waist. The Universe according to Jainism is narrow at top and broad at middle and once again becomes broad at the bottom. Mahâpurâna of Âcârya Jinasena is famous for this quote -

> "Some foolish men declare that the creator made the world. The doctrine that the world was created is ill advised and should be rejected.
>
> If god created the world, where was he before the creation? If you say he was transcendent then and needed no support, where is he now?
>
> How could god have made this world without any raw material? If you say that he made this first, and then the world, you are faced with an endless regression."

The Constituents of Reality

This Universe is made up of what Jains call the six *dravyas* or substances which are the basic constituents of reality and are classified as follows:

- ***Jîva* - The living substances** Jains believe that souls (*Jîva*) exist as a reality, having a separate existence from the body that houses it. *Jîva* is characterised by *cetana* (consciousness) and *upayoga* (knowledge and perception). Though the soul experiences both birth and death, it is neither really destroyed nor created. Decay and origin refer respectively to the disappearing of one state of soul and appearance of another state, these being merely the modes of the soul.

- ***Ajîva* - Non-Living Substances**
  - o ***Pudgala* - Matter** - Matter is classified as solid, liquid, gaseous, energy, fine Karmic materials and extra-fine matter or ultimate particles. Paramânu or ultimate particles are considered the basic building block of all matter. One of the qualities of the *Paramânu* and *Pudgala* is that of permanence and indestructibility. It combines and changes its modes but its basic qualities remain the same. According to Jainism, it cannot be created nor destroyed.
  - o ***Dharma-tattva* - Medium of Motion** and ***Adharma-tattva* - Medium of Rest** - Also known as *Dharmâstikâya* and *Adharmâstikâya*, they are unique to Jain thought depicting the principles of motion and rest. They are said to pervade the entire universe. *Dharma-tattva* and *Adharma-tattva* are by themselves not motion or rest but mediate motion and rest in other bodies. Without *dharmâstikâya* motion is not possible and without *adharmâstikâya* rest is not possible in the universe.

- *Âkâúa* - **Space** - Space is a substance that accommodates souls, matter, the principle of motion, the principle of rest, and time. It is all-pervading, infinite and made of infinite space-points.

- *Kâla* - **Time** - Time is a real entity according to Jainism and all activities, changes or modifications can be achieved only through time. In Jainism, the time is likened to a wheel with twelve spokes divided into descending and ascending halves with six stages, each of immense duration estimated at billions of sagaropama or ocean years. According to Jains, sorrow increases at each progressive descending stage and happiness and bliss increase in each progressive ascending stage.

These are the uncreated existing constituents of the Universe which impart the necessary dynamics to the Universe by interacting with each other. These constituents behave according to the natural laws and their nature without interference from external entities. *Dharma* or true religion according to Jainism is *vatthu sahâvo dhammo* translated as "the intrinsic nature of a substance is its true religion."

Ontology and Metaphysics

Jain ontology postulates existence of principle of sentient or consciousness called as *Jiva* or soul characterized by knowledge and perception. There are infinite independent souls categorized into: liberated and non-liberated. Infinite knowledge, perception and bliss are the intrinsic qualities of a soul. These qualities are fully enjoyed unhindered by liberated souls, but obscured by karmas in the case of non-liberated souls resulting in karmic bondage. This bondage further results in a continuous co-habitation of the soul with the body. Thus, an embodied non-liberated soul is found in four realms of existence - heavens, hells, humans and animal world – in a never-ending cycle of births and deaths also known as *samsâra*. The soul is in bondage since beginningless time; however, it is possible to achieve liberation through rational perception, rational knowledge and rational conduct. Harry Oldmeadow notes that Jain ontology is both realist and dualist metaphysics. It is realist in the sense that knowledge of ultimate reality does not exclude the reality of the existing world; the enlightened worldview includes the knowledge of particulars and the world continues to be real even after the liberation. It is dualist in that the two prime categories of substance,soul and matter, are mutually exclusive.

According to Jainism, the soul is the master of its own destiny. One of the qualities of the soul is complete lordship of its own destiny. The soul alone chooses its actions and soul alone reaps its consequences. No god, prophet or angel can interfere in the actions or the destiny of the soul. Furthermore, it is the soul alone who makes the necessary efforts to achieve liberation without any divine grace. Amongst the twelve contemplations *(anupreksâs)* of Jains, one of them is the loneliness of one's soul and nature of the Universe and transmigration. Hence only by cleansing our soul by our own actions can we help ourselves.

Jain metaphysics is based on seven (sometimes nine, with subcategories) truths or fundamental principles also known as *tattva*, which are an attempt to explain the nature and solution to the human predicament. The first two are the two ontological categories of the soul and the non-soul, namely the axiom that they exist. The third truth is that through the interaction, called *yoga*, between the two substances, soul and non-soul, karmic matter flows into the soul *âsrava*, clings to it, becomes converted into karma and the fourth truth acts as a factor of bondage *bandha*, restricting the manifestation of the consciousness intrinsic to it. The fifth truth states that a stoppage (*samvara*) of new karma is possible through asceticism through practice of right conduct, faith and knowledge. An intensification of asceticism burns up the existing karma – this sixth truth is expressed by the word nirjarâ. The final truth is that when the soul is freed from the influence of karma, it reaches the goal of Jaina teaching, which is liberation or *moksa*. Some authors add two additional categories: the meritorious and demeritorious acts related to karma *(punya and pâpa)*. These nine categories of cardinal truth, called *navatattva*, form the basis of entire Jain metaphysics.

Epistemology and Logic

Jainism made its own unique contribution to this mainstream development of philosophy by occupying itself with the basic epistemological issues, namely, with those concerning the nature of knowledge, how knowledge is derived, and in what way knowledge can be said to be reliable. Knowledge for the Jains takes place in the soul, which, without the limiting factor of karma, is omniscient. Humans have partial knowledge – the object of knowledge is known partially and the means of knowledge do not operate to their full capacity. According to *Tattvârthasûtra*, the knowledge of the basic Jaina truths can be obtained through:

- **Pramâsa** - means or instruments of knowledge which can yield a comprehensive knowledge of an object, and

- **Naya** - particular standpoints, yielding partial knowledge.

Pramâsa are of five kinds:

- *mati* or "sensory knowledge",
- *Sruta* or "scriptural knowledge",
- *avadhi* or "clairvoyance",
- *manahparyaya* or "telepathy", and
- *kevala" or "omniscience"*

The first two are described as being indirect means of knowledge *(paroksa)*, with the others furnishing direct knowledge *(pratyaksa)*, by which it is meant that the object is known directly by the soul.

As per Jainism, the truth or the reality is perceived differently from different points of view, and that no single point of view is the complete truth. Jain doctrine states that, an object has infinite modes of existence and qualities and, as such, they cannot be completely perceived in all its aspects and manifestations, due to inherent limitations of the humans. Only the *Kevalins* - the omniscient beings - can comprehend the object in all its aspects and manifestations, and that all others are capable of knowing only a part of it. Consequently, no one view can claim to represent the absolute truth. In the process, the Jains came out with their doctrines of relativity used for logic and reasoning –

- ***Anekântavâda*** - the theory of relative pluralism or manifoldness;
- ***Syâdvâda*** – the theory of conditioned predication and;
- ***Nayavâda*** – The theory of partial standpoints.

These philosophical concepts have made most important contributions to the ancient Indian philosophy, especially in the areas of skepticism and relativity.

Morality and Ethics

The Jain morality and ethics are rooted in its metaphysics and its utility towards the soteriological objective of liberation. Jaina ethics evolved out of the rules for the ascetics which are encapsulated in the *mahavratas* or the five great vows :

- ***Ahimsa,*** non-violence
- ***Aparigraha,*** non-possession
- ***Asteya,*** non-stealing
- ***Satya,*** truth
- ***Brahmacarya,*** celibacy

The ethics are governed not only through the instrumentality of physical actions, but also through verbal action and thoughts. Thus, ahimsa has to be observed through mind, speech and body. The other rules of the ascetics and laity are derived from these five major vows. Jainism does not invoke the fear of God as a reason for moral behaviour. The observance of the moral code is not necessary simply because it is a commandment of a God or any other supreme being. Neither, is its observance necessary simply because it is conducive to general welfare of the state or the community. While it is true that in Jainism, the moral and religious injunctions were laid down as law by *Arhats* who have achieved perfection through their supreme moral efforts, their adherence is just not to please a God, but because the life of the Arhats has demonstrated that such commandments were conductive to *Arhat's* own welfare, helping him to reach spiritual victory. Just as *Arhats* achieved *moksa* or liberation by observing the moral code, so can anyone, who follows this path.

Karma: Law of Causation

Karma in Jainism conveys a totally different meaning as commonly understood in the Hindu philosophy and western civilization. It is not the so called inaccessible mystic force that controls the fate of living beings in some inexplicable way. It does not mean "deed", "work", nor invisible, mystical force (adrsta), but a complexes of very fine matter, imperceptible to the senses, which interacts with the soul and causes great changes in it. The karma, then, is something material (*karmapaudgalam*), which produces in the soul certain conditions, even as a medical pill which, when introduced into the body, produces therein manifold effects. According to Robert Zydendos, karma in Jainism can be considered a kind of system of laws, but natural rather than moral laws. In Jainism, actions that carry moral significance are considered to cause certain consequences in just the same way as, for instance, physical actions that do not carry any special moral significance. When one holds an apple in one's hand and then let go of the apple, the apple will fall: this is only natural. There is no judge, and no moral judgment involved, since this is a mechanical consequence of the physical action.

Hence in accordance with the natural karmic laws, consequences occur when one utters a lie, steals something, commits acts of senseless violence or leads the life of a debauchee. Rather than assume that moral rewards and retribution are the work of a divine judge, the Jains believe that there is an innate moral order to the cosmos, self-regulating through the workings of karma. Morality and ethics are important not because of the personal whim of a fictional god, but because a life that is led in agreement with moral and ethical principles is beneficial: it leads to a decrease and finally to the total loss of karma, which means: to ever increasing happiness.

The karmas can be said to represent a sum total of all unfulfilled desires of a soul. They enable the soul to experience the various themes of the lives that it desires to experience. They ultimately mature when the necessary supportive conditions required for maturity are fulfilled. Hence a soul may transmigrate from one life form to another for countless of years, taking with it the karmas that it has earned, until it finds conditions that bring about the fruits. Hence whatever suffering or pleasure that a soul may be experiencing now is on account of choices that it has made in past.

The following quote in *Bhagavatî Ârâdhanâ* (1616) sums up the predominance of karmas in Jain doctrine:-

> "There is nothing mightier in the world than karma;
>
> karma tramples down all powers, as an elephant a clump of lotuses."

The Nature of Divinity and God

The undercurrent of non-creationism and absence of omnipotent God and divine grace runs strongly in all the philosophical dimensions of Jainism, including its cosmology, karma, moksa and its moral code of conduct. Jainism shows how a religious and virtuous life is possible without the idea of a creator god to whom one can turn to. Models for ethical life in Jainism are provided by the biographies of the twenty-four Jinas, the conquerors of the passions, of whom Mahâvîra was the last. They are worshipped as divine beings, as their lives serve as a guiding principle and an emulation of their virtues can lead one to the same goal of liberation that they achieved. According to Jainism, gods, that are worthy of worship and emulation, can be categorized into :

- ***Tîrthankara***, the ford makers
- ***Arihants*** or ordinary Kevalin, and
- ***Siddha***, the liberated beings

Jainism considers, demi-gods and goddesses who dwell in heavens owing to meritorious deeds in their past lives, as unliberated beings who are subject to further re-incarnations. Worship of such gods is considered as *mithyâtva* or wrong belief leading to bondage of karmas. However, many Jains are known to worship such gods for material gains.

Soteriology : The Path to Moksha

Jainism is essentially a soteriological path where all the practices and beliefs are geared towards attainment of the ultimate objective- liberation of the soul. Jainism is also known as moksamârga – the path to liberation. Moksa is a blissful state of existence of a soul, completely free from the karmic bondage, free from samsara, the cycle of birth and death. A liberated soul is said to have attained its true and pristine nature of infinite bliss, infinite knowledge and infinite perception. Such a soul is called siddha or paramatman and considered as supreme soul or God. In Jainism, it is the highest and the noblest objective that a soul should strive to achieve. It fact, it is the only objective that a person should have; other objectives are contrary to the true nature of soul. With right faith, knowledge and efforts all souls can attain this state.

Contributions to Indian Philosophy

Jainism had a major influence in developing a system of philosophy and ethics that had a major impact on all aspects of Indian culture in all ages : from Upanishads to Mahatma Gandhi. The scholarly research and evidences have shown that philosophical concepts that are considered typically Indian – Karma, Ahimsa, Moksa, reincarnation and like - either have their origins in the sramana school of thought or were propagated and developed by the Jaina teachers. These concepts were later assimilated in Hinduism and other religions, often in a different form and sometimes having a different meaning. The sramanic ideal of mendicancy and renunciation, that the worldly life was full of suffering and that emancipation required giving up of desires and withdrawal into a lonely and contemplative life, was in stark contrast with the brahmanical ideal of an active and ritually punctuated life based on sacrifices, household duties and chants to deities. Sramanas developed and laid emphasis on Ahimsa, Karma, moksa and renunciation. Early Upanishad thinkers like Yajnavalkya were acquainted with the sramanic thinking and tried to incorporate these ideals into the vedic thought implying a disparagement of the vedic ritualism and recognising the mendicancy as an ideal.

Schools and Traditions

Jain philosophy arose from the Sramana philosophy. In its 2,500 years post-Mahavira history, Jain philosophy remained, more or less, fundamentally the same as preached by Mahavira, who preached essentially the same religion as the previous Tirthankaras. However, he modified the four vows of Parsva by adding a fifth vow of celibacy. Jain texts like Uttaradhyana Sutra speak of parallel existence the order of Parsva which was ultimately merged into Mahaviras order. Harry Oldmeadow notes that the Jain philosophy remained fairly standard through out history and the later elaborations only sought to further elucidate preexisting doctrine and avoided changing the ontological status of any of the components. For a few centuries after Mahavira, the Jain religion remained united. The schisms into Úvetâmbara and Digambara traditions arose mainly on account of differences in question of practice of nudity amongst monks and liberation of women. Apart from these minor differences in practices, there are no major philosophical differences between the different sects of Jainism. Tattvârthasûtra which encapsulates the major philosophical doctrine of Jainism is accepted by all traditions of Jainism. This coherence in philosophical doctrine and consistency across different schools has led many scholars like Jaini to remark that in the course of history of Jainism no heretical movements like Mahayana, tantric or bhakti movement developed outside mainstream Jainism. Thus, we have many traditions within the Jainism, but basically the same philosophy that is at the core of all the sects and sub-sects.

Earlier Traditions

As per the tradition, Jain Sangh was divided into two major sects, a few centuries after the nirvana of Mahavira :

- Úvetâmbara – Svetambaras believe that women can attain liberation and that nudity is optional. Úvetâmbara scriptures support both *acelakatva,* nudity in monks and *sacelakatva,* the wearing of white clothes by ascetics. They also hold that Jain canon were not lost.

- Digambara - Digambaras hold that nudity is necessary for liberation and only men can attain the final stage of non-attachment to the body by remaining nude. They also hold that the canonical literature was eventually lost.

The now defunct, Yapaniya sect followed Digambara nudity and eating from the hands while standing up; along with several Úvetâmbara beliefs and texts. They are now believed to have been absorbed in the Digambara community during the medieval period.

Medieval Traditions

The period of 16th to 18th century was a period of reforms in Jainism. The later schools arose against certain practices and belief that were perceived as corrupting and not sanctioned by scriptures. The following schools arose during this period :

- Sthanakvasi – Sthanakvasi arising from Svetambara tradition rejected idol worship as not sanctioned by scriptures.
- Terapanthi (Digambara) – Digambara Terapantha movement arose in protest against the institution of Bhattarakas (Jain priestly class), usage of flowers and offerings in Jain temples, and worship of minor gods.
- Terapanthi (Úvetâmbara) – Terapanthi, also a non-iconic sect, arose from Sthanakvasi on account of differences in religious practices and beliefs.

Recent Developments

Dissatisfaction with the monkhood and its related emphasis on austerities saw rising of two new sects within Jainism in 20th Century. These were essentially led by laity rather than ascetics and soon became a major force to be reckoned with. The non-sectarian cult of Srimad Rajcandra, who was one of the major influences on Mahatma Gandhi is now one of the most popular cults amongst the Jains. Another cult founded by Kanjisvami laying stress on determinism and "knowledge of self" has gained a large following among Jains.

Jain Philosophers

Jains hold the Jain doctrine to be eternal and based on universal principles. In the current time cycle, they trace the origins of its philosophy to Rsabha, the first Tîrthankara. However, the tradition holds that the ancient Jain texts and Purvas which documented the Jain doctrine were lost and hence, historically, the Jain philosophy can be traced from Mahâvîras teachings. Post Mahâvîra many intellectual giants amongst the Jain ascetics contributed and gave a concrete form to the Jain philosophy within the paramaters set by Mahavira. Following is the partial list of Jain philosophers and their contributions:

- **Kundakunda** (1st—2nd Century CE) - exponent of Jain mysticism and Jain nayas dealing with the nature of the soul and its contamination by matter, author of *Pañcâstikâyasâra* (Essence of the Five Existents), the *Pravacanasâra* (Essence of the Scripture), the *Samayasâra* (Essence of the Doctrine), *Niyamasâra* (Essence of Discipline), *Atthapâhuda* (Eight Gifts), *Dasabhatti* (Ten Worships) and *Bârasa Anuvekkhâ* (Twelve Contemplations).

- **Samantabhadra** (2nd Century CE) - first Jain writer to write on *nyâya,* (Apta-Mimâmsâ), which has had the largest number of commentaries written on it by later Jain logicians. He also composed the *Ratnakaranda Srâvakâcâra* and the *Svayambhu Stotra.*

- **Umâsvâti** or **Umasvami** (2nd Century CE) - author of first Jain work in Sanskrit, Tattvârthasûtra, expounding the Jain philosophy in a most systematized form acceptable to all sects of Jainism.

- **Siddhasena Divâkara** (5th Century CE) - Jain logician and author of important works in Sanskrit and Prakrit, such as, *Nyâyâvatâra* (on Logic) and *Sanmatisûtra* (dealing with the seven Jaina standpoints, knowledge and the objects of knowledge).
- **Akalanka** (5th Century CE) - key Jain logician, whose works such as *Laghiyastraya, Pramânasangraha, Nyâyaviniscaya-vivarana, Siddhiviniscaya-vivarana, Astasati, Tattvârtharâjavârtika,* et al. are seen as landmarks in Indian logic. The impact of Akalanka may be surmised by the fact that Jain *Nyâya* is also known as *Akalanka Nyâya.*
- **Pujyapada** (6th Century CE) - Jain philosopher, grammarian, Sanskritist. Composed *Samadhitantra, Ishtopadesha* and the *Sarvarthasiddhi,* a definitive commentary on the *Tattvârthasûtra* and *Jainendra Vyakarana,* the first work on Sanskrit grammar by a Jain monk.
- **Manikyanandi** (6th Century CE) - Jain logician, composed the *Parikshamaukham,* a masterpiece in the *karika* style of the Classical Nyaya school.
- **Jinabhadra** (6-7th Century) – author of *Avasyaksutra* (Jain tenets) *Visesanavati* and *Visesavasyakabhasya* (Commentary on Jain essentials) He is said to have followed Siddhasena and compiled discussion and refutation on various views on Jaina doctrine.
- **Mallavadin** (8th Century) – author of *Nayacakra* and *Dvadasaranayacakra* (Encyclopedia of Philosophy) which discusses all the school of Indian Philosophy.. Mallavadin was known as a *vadin* i.e. a logician and he is said to have defeated many Buddhist monks on the issues of philosophy.

- **Haribhadra** (8th Century CE) - Jain thinker, author, philosopher, satirist and great proponent of anekântavâda and classical yoga, as a soteriological system of meditation in the Jain context. His works include *sasdarœanasamuccaya, Yogabindu* and *Dhurtakhyana*. he pioneered the *Dvatrimshatika* genre of writing in Jainism, where various religious subjects were covered in 32 succinct Sanskrit verses..

- **Prabhacandra** (8th-9th Century CE) - Jain philosopher, composed a 106-Sutra Tattvarthasutra and exhaustive commentaries on two key works on Jain Nyaya, *Prameyakamalamartanda*, based on Manikyanandi's *Parikshamukham* and *Nyayakumudacandra* on Akalanka's *Laghiyastraya*.

- **Abhayadeva** (1057 CE to 1135CE) - author of *Vadamahrnava* (Ocean of Discussions) which is a 2,500 verse *tika* (Commentary) of *Sanmartika* and considered a great treatise on logic.

- **Hemacandra** (1089–1172 CE) - Jain thinker, author, historian, grammarian and logician. His works include *Yogaúâstra* and *Trishashthishalakapurushacaritra* and the *Siddhahemavyakarana*. He also authored an incomplete work on Jain Nyâya, titled *Pramâna-Mimâmsâ*.

- **Vadideva** (11th Century) – He was a senior contemporary of Hemacandra and is said to have authored *Paramananayatattavalokalankara* and its voluminous commentary *syadvadaratnakara* that establishes the supremacy of doctrine of syadvada.

- **Vidyanandi** (11th Century CE) - Jain philosopher, composed the brilliant commentary on Acarya Umasvami's Tattvarthasutra, known as *Tattvarthashlokavartika*.

- **Yaoeovijaya** (1624–88 CE) – Jain logician and considered one of the last intellectual giants to contribute to Jain philosophy. He specialised in *Navya-Nyâya* and wrote Vrttis (commentaries) on most of the earlier *Jain Nyâya* works by Samantabhadra, Akalanka, Manikyanandi, Vidyânandi, Prabhâcandra and others in the then-prevalent *Navya-Nyâya* style. Yaœovijaya has to his credit a prolific literary output – more than 100 books in Sanskrit, Prakrit, Gujarati and Rajashtani. He is also famous for *Jnanasara* (essence of knowledge) and *Adhayatmasara* (essence of spirituality).

In recent times, Aacharya Mahapragya, Pt. Sukhlal and Dr. Mahendrakumar Nyayacarya have made important contributions to Jain Philosophy.

SHRAMANA

A **shramana** is a wandering monk in certain ascetic traditions of ancient India, including Jainism, Buddhism, and Âjîvika religion (now extinct). Famous úramasa include religious leaders Mahavira and Gautama Buddha.

Traditionally, a œramasa is one who renounces the world and leads an ascetic life of austerity for the purpose of spiritual development and liberation. Typically œramasas assert that human beings are responsible for their own deeds and reap the fruits of those deeds, for good or ill. Liberation, therefore, may be achieved by anybody irrespective of caste, creed, color or culture, in contrast to certain historical caste-based traditions, providing the necessary effort is made. The cycle of rebirth, *sassâra,* to which every individual is subject, is viewed as the cause and substratum of misery. The goal of every person is to evolve a way to escape from the cycle of rebirth. Sramanic traditions dispense with the rites and rituals of formal religion as factors in emancipation, emphasizing instead the paramount importance of ascetic endeavor and personal conduct.

The Sanskrit word *œramasa* is derived from the Sanskrit verbal root *œram* "to exert effort, labour or to perform austerity". "Oeramasa" thus means "one who strives" in Sanskrit.

One of the earliest uses of the word is in Taittiriya Aranyaka (2-7-1) with the meaning of 'performer of austerities'. A traditional Sanskrit definition is *úramati tapasyatîti úramasas* ("a œramasa is he who exerts himself and performs religious austerities").

Buddhist commentaries associate the word's etymology with the quieting (*samita*) of evil (*pâpa*) as in the following phrase from the Dhammapada, verse 265: *samitattâ pâpânaK ssamasos ti pavuccati* ("someone who has pacified evil is called *samasa*").

Various forms of the word became known throughout Central and East Asia, largely through the spread of Buddhism in that area. According to a still disputed etymology, the word *shaman*, used by the Tungus people for their religious practitioners, may be borrowed from a local variant of the word œramasa.

Sramasa Movement

Several Sramasa movements are known to have existed before the 6th century BCE dating back to Indus valley civilization, where they peaked during the times of Mahavira and Buddha. Oeramasas adopted a path alternate to the Vedic rituals to achieve liberation, while renouncing household life. They typically engage in three types of activities: austerities, meditation, and associated theories (or views). As spiritual authorities, at times Sramasa were at variance with traditional Brahmin authority, and they often recruited members from

Brahmin communities themselves, such as Cânakya and Úâriputra.

Mahâvîra, the 24th *Jina,* and Gautama Buddha were leaders of their Sramasa orders. According to Jain literature and the Buddhist Pali Canon, there were also some other œramasa leaders at that time. Thus, in the Mahâparinibbâna Sutta (DN 16), a Sramasa named Subhadda mentions:

> *"those ascetics, samasa and Brahmins who have orders and followings, who are teachers, well-known and famous as founders of schools, and popularly regarded as saints, like Pûrasa Kassapa, Makkhali Gosâla, Ajita Kesakambalî, Pakudha Kaccâyana, Sañjaya Belasshaputta and the Nigassha Nâtaputta...".*

Nigassha Nâtaputta (Pâli; Skt.: Nirgrantha Jñâtaputra) refers to Mahâvîra. In regard to the above other teachers identified in the Pali Canon, Jain literature mentions Pûrasa Kassapa, Makkhali Gosâla and Sañjaya Belammhaputta. (The Pali Canon is the only source for Ajita Kesakambalî and Pakudha Kaccâyana.)

Gautama Buddha regarded extreme austerities and self-mortification as useless or unnecessary in ataining enlightenment, recommending instead a "middle way" between the extremes of hedonism and self-mortification. Devadatta, a cousin of Gautama, caused a split in the Buddhist *sasgha* by demanding more rigorous practices. Followers of Mahâvîra continued to practice fasting and other austerities.

The oeramana idea of wandering began to change early in Buddhism. The *bhiksu* started living in monasteries (Pali, Skt. *vihâra*), at first during the rainy seasons, but eventually permanently. In medieval Jainism also, the tradition of wandering waned, but it got revived in the 19th century. Similar changes have regularly occurred in Buddhism.

Sramasa Philosophy

Indian philosophy is a confluence of Sramasic and Vedic streams that co-exist and influence each other. Sramasas held a pessimistic world view of samsara as full of suffering (or dukkha). They practiced Ahimsa and rigorous ascetism. They believed in Karma and Moksa and viewed re-birth as undesirable.

Vedics, on the contrary, hold an optimistic world view of the richness of worldly life. They believe in the efficacy of rituals and sacrifices, performed by a privileged group of people, who could improve their life by pleasing certain Gods. The Sramanic ideal of mendicancy and renunciation, that the worldly life is full of suffering and that emancipation requires abandoning desires and withdrawal into a solitary contemplative life, is in stark contrast with the Brahminical ideal of an active and ritually punctuated life. Traditional Vedic belief holds that a man is born with an obligation to study the Vedas, to procreate and rear male offspring and to perform sacrifices. Only in later life may he meditate on the mysteries of life. The idea of devoting one's whole life to mendicancy seems to disparage the whole process of Vedic social life and obligations. Because the Sramanas rejected the Vedas, Brahmins labelled their philosophy as "nastika darsana" (heterodox philosophy).

Beliefs and concepts of Sramana philosophies:-

- Denial of creator and omnipotent Gods
- Rejection of the Vedas as revealed texts
- Affirmation of Karma and rebirth, Samsara and transmigration of Soul (Later these practices were accepted in Brahminic religion Hinduism
- Affirmation of the attainment of moksa through Ahimsa, renunciation and austerities
- Denial of the efficacy of sacrifices and rituals for purification.

- Rejection of the caste system

Ultimately, the sramana philosophical concepts like ahimsa, karma, re-incarnation, renunciation, samsara and moksa were accepted and incorporated by the brahmans in their beliefs and practices, eg. by abandoning the sacrifice of animals.. According to Gavin Flood, concepts like karmas and reincarnation entered mainstream brahaminical thought from the sramana or the renounciant traditions. According to D. R. Bhandarkar, the Ahimsa dharma of the sramanas made an impression on the followers of Brahamanism and their law books and practices.

Following are the two main schools of Sramana Philosophy that have continued since ancient times in India:

Jain Philosophy

Jainism derives its philosophy from the teachings and lives of the twenty-four Tirthankaras (ford-makers or enligtened teachers), of whom Mahavira was the last. Jain Acaryas - Umasvati (Umasvami), Kundakunda, Haribhadra, Yaœovijaya Gasi and others further developed and reorganized Jain philosophy in its present form. The distinguishing features of Jain philosophy are its belief in the independent existence of soul and matter, predominance of karma, the denial of a creative and omnipotent God, belief in an eternal and uncreated universe, a strong emphasis on non-violence, an accent on relativity and multiple facets of truth, and morality and ethics based on liberation of the soul. The Jain philosophy of Anekantavada and Syadvada, which posits that the truth or reality is perceived differently from different points of view, and that no single point of view is the complete truth, have made very important contributions to ancient Indian philosophy, especially in the areas of skepticism and relativity.

Buddhist Philosophy

Buddhist philosophy is a system of beliefs based on the teachings of Siddhartha Gautama, an Indian prince later known as the Buddha. Buddhism is a non-theistic philosophy, one whose tenets are not especially concerned with the existence or nonexistence of a God or gods and which denies the existence of a creator god. The question of God is largely irrelevant in Hinayana Buddhism, though most sects of Mahayana Buddhism, notably Tibetan Buddhism and most of East Asian Buddhism (in the Shurangama Mantra and Great Compassion Mantra) do regularly practice with a number of gods (as Dharmapalas and Wrathful Deities, Four Heavenly Kings, and Five Wisdom Kings) drawn from both the Mahayana Sutras and Buddhist Tantras sometimes combined with local indigenous belief systems. The Buddha criticised all concepts of metaphysical being and non-being. A major distinguishing feature of its philosophy is the rejection (anatman) of a permanent, self-existent soul (atman).

Usage of "Sramasa" in Jain Texts

In Jainism the monks and ascetics are known as Oeramasas , while the Jain laymen are called as Sravakas. The religion or code of conduct of the monks is known as Sramasa Dharma. Jain canons like Âcâranga Sûtra and other later texts contain a multitude of references to Sramanas with one of the verse defining a good Sramana :

> "Disregarding (all calamities) he lives together with clever monks, insensitive to pain and pleasure, not hurting the movable and immovable (beings), not killing, bearing all: so is described the great sage, a good Sramana."

- Âcâranga Sûtra. 1097

The chapter on renunciation contains references to vow of non-possession by the Sramanas :

> "I shall become a Sramana who owns no house, no property, no sons, no cattle, who eats what others give

him; I shall commit no sinful action; Master, I renounce to accept anything that has not been given.' Having taken such vows, (a mendicant) should not, on entering a village or scot-free town, take himself, or induce others to take, or allow others to take, what has not been given."

-Âcâranga Sûtra, 799

Acaranga Sutra speaks of three names of Mahavira the twenty fourth Tirthankara , one of which was a Sramana :

"The Venerable ascetic Mahavira belonged to the *Kasyapa gotra*. His three names have thus been recorded by tradition: by his parents he was called **Vardhamana**, because he is devoid of love and hate; (he is called) **Sramana** (i.e. ascetic), because he sustains dreadful dangers and fears, the noble nakedness, and the miseries of the world; the name Venerable Ascetic **Mahavira** has been given to him by the gods."

- Âcâranga Sûtra 954

Another Jain canon, Sûtrakrtanga describes Sramana as an ascetic who has taken Mahavratas or five great vows:

"He is a Sramana for this reason that he is not hampered by any obstacles, that he is free from desires, (abstaining from) property, killing, telling lies, and sexual intercourse; (and from) wrath, pride, deceit, greed, love, and hate: thus giving up every passion that involves him in sin, (such as) killing of beings. (Such a man) deserves the name of a Sramana, who subdues (moreover) his senses, is well qualified (for his task), and abandons his body."

- Sûtrakrtanga, Book 1: 16.3

In one of the disputations with other heretical teachers, prince Ardraka, who became a disciple of Mahavira, tells Makkhali Gosala the qualities of Sramanas :

> "He who (teaches) the great vows (of monks) and the five small vows (of the laity 3), the five Âsravas and the stoppage of the Âsravas, and control, who avoids Karman in this blessed life of Sramanas, him I call a Sramana."
>
> - **Sûtrakrtanga, Book 2: 6.6**

Sramasa in Western Literature

Various references to "Sramanas", with the name more or less distorted, have been handed down in Western literature about India.

Nicolaus of Damascus (c.10 CE)

Nicolaus of Damascus is famous for his account of an embassy sent by an Indian king "named Pandion (Pandyan kingdom?) or, according to others, Porus" to Caesar Augustus around 13 CE. He met with the embassy at Antioch. The embassy was bearing a diplomatic letter in Greek, and one of its members was a "Sarmano" who burnt himself alive in Athens to demonstrate his faith. The event made a sensation and was quoted by Strabo and Dio Cassius.

Clement of Alexandria (150-211)

Clement of Alexandria makes several mentions of the Sramanas, both in the context of the Bactrians and the Indians:

> "Thus philosophy, a thing of the highest utility, flourished in antiquity among the barbarians, shedding its light over the nations. And afterwards it came to Greece. First in its ranks were the prophets of the Egyptians; and the Chaldeans among the Assyrians; and the Druids among the Gauls; and the **Samanaeans** among the Bactrians; and the philosophers of the Celts;

and the Magi of the Persians, who foretold the Saviour's birth, and came into the land of Judaea guided by a star. The Indian gymnosophists are also in the number, and the other barbarian philosophers. And of these there are two classes, some of them called **Sarmanae**, and Brahmanae." Clement of Alexandria, "Exhortation to the Heathen"

To Clement of Alexandria, "Bactrians" apparently means "Oriental Greek", as in a passage of the Stromata:

> "It was after many successive periods of years that men worshipped images of human shape, this practice being introduced by Artaxerxes, the son of Darius, and father of Ochus, who first set up the image of Aphroditė Anaitis at Babylon and Susa; and Ecbatana set the example of worshipping it to the Persians; the Bactrians, to Damascus and Sardis." The Stromata, or Miscellanies, Book I, Clement of Alexandria.

Porphyry (233-305)

Porphyry extensively describes the habits of the Sramanas (whom he calls Samanaeans) in his "On Abstinence from Animal Food" Book IV . He says his information was obtained from "the Babylonian Bardesanes, who lived in the times of our fathers, and was familiar with those Indians who, together with Damadamis, were sent to Caesar":

> "For the polity of the Indians being distributed into many parts, there is one tribe among them of men divinely wise, whom the Greeks are accustomed to call Gymnosophists. But of these there are two sects, over one of which the Brahmins preside, but over the other the **Samanaeans**. The race of the Brahmins, however, receive divine wisdom of this kind by succession, in the same manner as the priesthood. But the Samanaeans are elected, and consist of those who wish to possess divine

knowledge." Porphyry, "On abstinence from animal food," Book IV.

"All the Brahmins originate from one stock; for all of them are derived from one father and one mother. But the Samanaeans are not the offspring of one family, being, as we have said, collected from every nation of Indians..." Porphyry, "On abstinence from animal food," Book IV.

On entering the order:

"The Samanaeans are, as we have said, elected. When, however, any one is desirous of being enrolled in their order, he proceeds to the rulers of the city; but abandons the city or village that he inhabited, and the wealth and all the other property that he possessed. Having likewise the superfluities of his body cut off, he receives a garment, and departs to the Samanaeans, but does not return either to his wife or children, if he happens to have any, nor does he pay any attention to them, or think that they at all pertain to him. And, with respect to his children indeed, the king provides what is necessary for them, and the relatives provide for the wife. And such is the life of the Samanaeans. But they live out of the city, and spend the whole day in conversation pertaining to divinity. They have also houses and temples, built by the king". Porphyry, "On abstinence from animal food," Book IV.

On life and death:

"They are so disposed with respect to death, that they unwillingly endure the whole time of the present life, as a certain servitude to nature, and therefore they hasten to liberate their souls from the bodies [with which they are connected]. Hence, frequently, when they are seen to be well, and are neither oppressed, nor driven to desperation by any evil, they depart from life." Porphyry, "On abstinence from animal food", Book IV.

Sramasa in Contemporary Western Culture

German novelist Hermann Hesse, long interested in Eastern, especially Indian, spirituality, wrote *Siddhartha,* in which the main character becomes a Samana upon leaving his home (where he was a Brahmin).

●●

11
Buddhism, Jainism and Other Religion

Buddhism and Jainism are the two branches of the Shramana tradition that still exist today. Jainism has been largely confined to India, while Buddhism eventually all but died out in India, and has flourished in countries outside of India. However the two traditions share notable similarities.

Buddhism separates itself from the Jain tradition by teaching an alternative to "extreme asceticism". Buddhist scriptures record that during Prince Siddhartha's ascetic life (before the great enlightenment) he undertook many fasts, penances and austerities, the descriptions of which are elsewhere found only in the Jain tradition (for example, the penance by five fires, plucking of hair, and the consumption of food using only one's cupped hands). Ultimately, Buddha abandoned reliance upon these methods on his discovery of the Middle Way (Majjhima-Magga in Pali; Madhyamaka in Sanskrit). However, it is interesting to note that even under the Jain tradition, there exists a non-extreme pathway, which is the path of the laymen with minor vows. Some Buddhist teachings, principles, and terms used in Buddhism are identical to those of Jainism, but they may hold different or variant meanings for each.

Although both Buddhists and Jains had nuns orders, Buddhist Pali texts record Buddha saying that a woman has the ability to obtain Nirvana in the Buddha Dhamma and

Vinaya. Jain traditions differ on the issue of female enlightenment, with the Digambara sect stating that women are capable of spiritual progress but must be reborn male in order to attain final spiritual liberation; and the Shvetambara sect maintaining that liberation (Moksha) is attainable by both males and females. The issue of female enlightenment is, however, an academic one in the Jain context since in the current universal age of corruption, Moksha is nearly impossible for any soul to attain.

While the Jain Sadhu and Sadhvi are referred to as the Sramans and Sramanis, the Shravak and Shravika are the lay men and women (Grihastha), respectively, who have not abandoned worldly affairs, i.e., not having obtained "Diksha", but are still following the religious guidelines, in the given constraints. There are separate norms that have been prescribed for the Shravak and Shravika under the Jain tradition.

Whether or not it was an influence of Jain culture and philosophy in ancient Bihar that gave rise to Buddhism is unclear, but there are some striking similarities between the two traditions, and Buddhism may have adopted many of its ideas and traditions from pre-existing ones held by the Jains. The Buddha Nirvana calendar (with a zero point in 544 BCE) may actually be significantly older than the Kaliyuga calendar. And so, quite possibly, is the Mahavira Nirvana calendar of the Jains (with a zero point in 527 BCE).

Mahâvîra and Buddha were contemporaries. The Pali Canon does not record that the two teachers ever met, though instances of Mahavira's disciples questioning Gautama Buddha are to be found in various suttas. The Buddhists have always maintained that by the time Buddha and Mahavira were alive, Jainism was already an entrenched faith and culture in the region. Buddhist scriptures record philosophical dialogues between the wandering seeker Siddartha Gautama (who was to become the Buddha) and **Udaka Ramaputta**, and the first of several teachers that young Siddartha Gautama studied with before his enlightenment. Buddhist scriptures attest that some of the first Buddhists were in fact Jains (*Nirgranthas* as they were then called, meaning "the unbonded ones") who "converted", but were encouraged by Buddha to maintain their Jain identity and practises such as giving alms to Jain monks and nuns.

Buddhists recorded that Mahavira preached the "fourfold restraint" of the Nirgrantha tradition—a clear reference to the teachings of Mahavira's predecessor Lord Parshva (877-777 BCE), traditionally the 23rd Tirthankara of Jainism—who propounded the four vows of Ahinsa (Ahimsa), Satya (truth), Aparigraha (non-possessiveness), and Asteya (non-stealing), which may have been the template for the Five Precepts of Buddhism. Additionally, the Buddhist *Anguttara Nikaya* scripture quotes the independent philosopher Purana Kashyapa (the sixth century BCE founder of a now extinct order) as listing the Nirgranthas as one of the six major classifications of humanity. The Pali texts mention the Buddha referring to the liberation of Mahavira (referred to as Niggantha Nataputta) at Pava.

Similarities and Differences in Jain and Buddhist Terminology

The common terms in Buddhism and Jainism:

- Shramana
- Samsara
- Nirvana: (the definition is somewhat different in the two traditions)
- Arhat/arhant: the term is used somewhat similarly.
- Dhamma/dharma
- sangha

- Jina
- Buddha(all Jain Jinas/Tirthankars are also called Buddha)
- samyaksambuddha/sayamsammbuddha :attaining enlightenment without a teacher(guru)
- pratyekbuddha :getting the feeling of dispassion or deattachment by seeing an object
- Acharya (chief of the orders)
- Sutra/sutta (scriptures)
- Indra/Shamkra (chief of the gods)

The Terms that are used with Different Meanings:

- Pudgala
- Siddha
- Karma

Common Symbols:

- Pratima idol in meditation posture, foot prints
- Stupa
- The dharma-chakra
- The swastika
- The tri-rathna
- The ashta-mangalas
- Minor devas

Vegetarianism is required for both monks and laity in Jainism. In Buddhism, the monks in China, Japan, Korea and Vietnam are vegetarian; however strict vegetarianism is not required. By monastic tradition, a monk should eat whatever is placed in his bowl when begging food. The exceptions to not eat given meat were if the monk knew an animal was killed especially for him or he heard the animal being killed.

Buddhist writings reflect that Jains had followers by the time Buddha lived. Suggesting close correlations between the teachings of the Jains and Buddha, the *Majjhima Nikaya* relates dialogues between Buddha and several members of the *Nigantha* (Jain) community, sometimes resulting in the latter's acceptance of Buddha as a teacher.

In many instances, both philosophies continue to share similar Prakrit terminology for important themes even though meaning may differ a bit, for example the term nirvana where its meaning is same in both the traditions but the state of nirvana described is somewhat different.The teachings may differ significantly in the interpretation .This method of teaching adopted by the Buddha points to the pragmatic aspect of Buddha's style of teaching wherein the Buddha uses words and terms that are familiar to the audience instead of introducing new and complex technical jargon. In this way, Buddhism sought to appeal to a broad audience.

> Jains consider Jainism to be an ancient religion and school of thought that predates Buddhism since they have records of other Jinas. Buddhism too can claim great antiquity as it records several Buddhas predating Sakyamuni Buddha in the "Buddhavamsa". Sakyamuni also clearly states that he is following the "tradition of the Buddhas",
>
> "But it is the custom of my Buddha lineage. Several thousands of Buddhas have gone by seeking alms"

The names of previous Buddhas mentioned Buddhist scriptures has striking similarities with the names of Tirthankars or Jain Arhants,which arises many unanswered questions of both religions being one and the same previously which latter resulted in the division.

Both Buddha and Mahavira might have built upon the pre-existing meditative teachings in north-eastern India at that time, which also explains some of the similarities in terminology.

The last Tirthankara Mahâvîra (599 - 527 BC) was possibly a senior contemporary of the Buddha whose philosophy, sometimes described as dynamism or vitalism, was a blend of the earlier Jain teacher Pârúvanâtha's (877-777 BC) order and the reforms instituted by Mahavira himself. Debates between Buddhists and Jains are recorded in Jain texts, and dialogues between Jains and the Buddha are included in Buddhist texts. (See also the "Origins" section, above.).

Indian Buddhist tradition categorized all non-buddhist schools of thought as "Pasanda" (*pasanda* means to throw a noose or *pasha* – stemming from the doctrine that schools labelled as *Pasanda* foster views perceived as wrong because they are seen as having a tendency towards binding and ensnaring rather than freeing the mind). The difference between the schools of thought are outlined in the Samaññaphala Sutta of the Digha Nikaya.

ISLAM AND JAINISM

Islam and Jainism came in close contact with each other following the Islamic conquest from Central Asia and Persia in the seventh to the twelfth centuries, when much of north and central India came under the rule of the Delhi Sultanate, and later the Mughal empire.

The Miyana Rajputs, many of whom were Jains (as per their last name) adopted Islam at the time of Allauddin Khilji (Kumar Suresh Singh, Rajendra Behari Lal, Anthropological Survey of India, P. 9390, *Gujarat*).

Muslim Invaders and Jain Institutions

The first mosque built in Delhi, the "Quwwat al-Islam" (near Qutb Minar) was built after the Jain temples built previously during the Tomar rule were sold to the Muslims.

27 Jain and Hindu temples were demolished to build this mosque also known as "might of Islam". The remains of the temple were used for to provide the building material for the mosque. Similarly the Jami Masjid at Cambay was build on ruins of Jain temples.

Jainism in the Delhi Sultanate

Jinaprabha Suri (d.1333) writes in his "Vividhatirthakalpa" ("Guide to Various Pilgrimage Places") of his relationship with Sultan Muhammad bin Tughluq (r.1325-1351). In two chapters that discuss his relationship with the Sultan (one of which was actually written by his disciple), Jinaprabha travels to Delhi to recover an image that had been taken from a temple. After impressing the Sultan with his poetic flair and his thorough knowledge of the various religious and philosophical schools in India, the Sultan awards him with some blankets and other gifts, which Jinaprabha reluctantly accepts. In the second chapter, Jinaprabha is called back to Delhi to settle some religious matters for the Sultan. He is greeted warmly by the Sultan and even introduced to the Sultan's mother. One of his chief ministers is ordered to wipe the mud from Jinaprabha's feet. After getting the image back from the Sultan's treasury, Jinaprabha is paraded around the town on an elephant as a display of his pre-eminence in debate. He accompanies the Sultan on his military campaigns and upon his return is awarded a quarter of town in Tughluqabad for the Jain community, including a hall for Jinaprabha to teach in. Amid great fanfare and celebration the Jain community is declared by our author as prosperous and "just as when the Hindus ruled and times were not so bad, the glorious Jinaprabhasuri taught all those who come to him, even those of other faiths, and all rush to serve him." Jinaprabha also secured edicts (firmans) to allow Jains to go on pilgrimage unharmed and untaxed.

Under the leadership of Jinaprabhasuri and the Kharatara Gaccha, the Jains would remain an economically powerful and culturally vibrant community. While temples were desecrated, Jinaprabha speaks of these incidents as due to the power of the Dark Age (Kali Yuga), in which such things are going to happen. He also speaks of these desecrations as opportunities to earn "endless merit" by restoring temples, which laymen did with gusto.

Jainism in the Mughal Period

Some Jain customs and characters that influenced the Mughal court of Akbar have been documented. Akbar honored Hiravijaya Suri, the leader of the Shvetambara Tapa Gachchha. They persuaded the emperor to forbid the slaughter of animals for six months in Gujarat and abolish the confiscation of property of deceased persons, the Sujija Tax (Jazia) and a Sulka (possibly a tax on pilgrims) and free caged birds and prisoners. Akbar is said to have given up hunting and quit meat-eating forever as it had become repulsive. Akbar also declared "Amari Ghosana" banning the killing of animals during Jain festival of Paryushana and Mahavir Jayanti. He rolled back the Jazia tax from Jain pilgrim places like Palitana. These farmans were also issued in 1592, 1594 and 1598. Jain monks gained the respect of the Mughal emperors Jahangir and Shah Jahan. Akbar banned animal slaughter near important Jain sites during the Paryushana festival.

JAINISM AND SIKHISM

Both **Jainism and Sikhism** have originated in South Asia and are Eastern philosophical faiths. Jainism, like Sikhism, rejected the authority of the Vedas and created independent textual traditions based on the words and examples of their early teachers, eventually evolving entirely new ways for interacting with the lay community.

Jainism is the oldest living Shramana tradition in India. In its current form, the Jain tradition is traced to Vardhamana

Mahavira (The Great Hero; ca. 599-527 B.C.), the twenty-fourth and last of the Tirthankaras (Sanskrit for fordmakers). Mahavira was born to a ruling family in the town of Vaishali, located in the modern state of Bihar. The first Tirthankara was Lord Rishabha, who lived long before Mahavira. That makes Jainism one of the oldest religions.

Next to the Baha'i Faith, Sikhism is the youngest of the world's major monotheistic religions. Sikhism was established in 15th century in the state of Punjab in North India. Guru Nanak, although born into a Hindu household in 1469 in the Punjab region, he challenged the existing practices and is considered the founder of the new faith. The Guru loved to travel and observe concepts and ideas regarding spiritual practices of various faiths. At the heart of his message was a philosophy of universal love, devotion to God. By the time he had left this world he had founded a new religion of "disciples" (shiksha or sikh) that followed his example.

Lineage of Teachers

The 24th Tirthankara of the Jain community was Vardhamana, the last in a series of 24 who lived in East India. Jains have 24 Tirthankaras, the Sikhs have 10 Gurus with the final Sovereign Authority of living Guru conferred upon Guru Granth Sahib by the tenth Master, Guru Gobind Singh.

Mutual Cooperation

Noted author Khushwant Singh notes that many eminent Jains admired the Sikh Gurus and came to their help in difficult times. When the ninth Sikh Guru, Tegh Bahadur, was on his preaching mission in east India, he and his family were invited by Salis Rai Johri to stay in his haveli in Patna. In his hukamnamas sent from Assam, the Guru Sahib referred to Patna as guru-ka-ghar, meaning, home of the Guru. Salis Rai donated half of his haveli to build a gurdwara, Janam Sthaan, because Guru Gobind Singh was born there. On the other half, he built a Svetambara Jain Temple — both have a common wall. Diwan Todar Mal was an Oswal Jain who rose to become the diwan in the court of Nawab Wazir Khan of Sirhind. When the Nawab had Guru Gobind Singh's two younger sons put to death, Todar Mal conveyed the sad news to their grand mother — who died of shock — and had the three bodies cremated. He had built Gurdwara Jyoti Sarup on the site of the cremation at Fatehgarh Sahib. A large hall of this gurdwara honours the builder by being named after him — Diwan Todar Mal Jain Yadagiri Hall.

Practices and Differences

Diwali

Diwali is celebrated by both. Although Sikhs celebrate the day as Bandhi Chhor Diwas, the homecoming to Amritsar of the sixth Sikh Guru, Guru HarGobind Sahib from Gwalior. The release of 52 Rajas from the fort of Gwalior is attributed to this Guru.

For Jains, Diwali is the celebrarion of the 24th Thirthankar, Mahavir, reaching Nirvana or Moksha on this day at Pavapuri on Oct. 15, 527 BC, on Chaturdashi of Karti.

Ahimsa and Vegetarianism

The Jains are strictly vegetarian. Sikhs are not vegetarian. There are, however,some group/sects/cults of Sikhism (Akhand Kirtani Jatha, Guru Nanak Nishkam Sewak Jatha, Namdhari's, Damdami Taksal etc) who encourage vegetarianism. The majority of Sikhs believe, eating meat is left up to the individual's conscience in Sikhism, as it will not affect spirituality.Khushwant Singh also notes that most Sikhs are meat-eaters and decry vegetarians as daal khorey (lentil-eaters). The food served in the Sikh temples (Gurudwaras) is invariably vegetarian in order to accommodate all sections of society.

Ahimsa for the Jains is a code of practice to always be kind and compassionate and prevent hurt to oneself and others. Sikhs reject Ahimsa. There are occasional references to Jainism in the Guru Granth Sahib and other Sikh texts.

Asceticism

Sikhism rejects asceticism - The Gurus lived as householders. On asceticism Guru Nanak stated :

> Asceticism doesn't lie in ascetic robes, or in walking staff, nor in the ashes. Asceticism doesn't lie in the earring, nor in the shaven head, nor blowing a conch. Asceticism lies in remaining pure amidst impurities. Asceticism doesn't lie in mere words; He is an ascetic who treats everyone alike. Asceticism doesn't lie in visiting burial places, It lies not in wandering about, nor in bathing at places of pilgrimage. Asceticism is to remain pure amidst impurities. (Suhi)

Jains have an organised ascetic order of monks and nuns. The lay people are householders.

Other Practices

A Sikh is bound to the Truth at all times and practices god Consciousness through Nam Simran and selfless service (Sewa). Jains too place high regard in prayers and meditation.

Sikhs reject the caste system and promote social and gender equality as the soul is the same for both men and women. All are equal in the eyes of God. God is accessible without priests or a middle person. Sikhs and Jains, like Hindus, are expected to be tolerant of all faiths and do not believe that any one path has a monopoly on the Truth.

There are many paths to seek out the Love of God and incur Divine Grace. In fact to call another's path inferior is sign of ignorance and intolerance. Both, personal devotion and communal prayers are a part of Sikh's way of life.

Concept of God

Jains do not believe in the concept of a Godhead responsible for the manifestation of the Creation. They believe the universe is eternal, without beginning or end, and that all happens in an autonomous fashion with no necessity of a co-ordinator/God.

Sikhism is a monotheistic religion, believing in the singular power of the Formless Creator God, Ik Onkaar, without a parallel. In the Guru Granth Sahib, God is called by all the Hindu names and as Allah as well.

Customs

During the 18th century, there were a number of attempts to prepare an accurate portrayal of Sikh customs. Sikh scholars and theologians started in 1931 to prepare the Reht Maryada – the Sikh code of conduct and conventions. This has successfully achieved a high level of uniformity in the religious and social practices of Sikhism throughout the world. It contains 27 articles. Article 1 defines who is a Sikh:

Any human being who faithfully believes in:

- One Immortal Being,
- Ten Gurus, from Guru Nanak Dev to Guru Gobind Singh,
- The Guru Granth Sahib,
- The utterances and teachings of the ten Gurus and the baptism bequeathed by the tenth Guru, and who does not owe allegiance to any other religion, is a Sikh.

Fasting is an accepted practice for the Jains. A Sikh will eat to partially satisfy the hunger at all times.

Where the Guru Granth Sahib is present, that place becomes a Gurdwara. The focal point of worship in a

Gurdwara (the gateway to God) is the eternal teachings of Guru Granth Sahib the Shabad (Word) Guru.

Jains exhibit the statues of their Tirathankars in their temples. Special shrines in residences or in public temples include images of the Tirthankaras, who are not worshiped but remembered and revered; other shrines house images of deities who are more properly invoked to intercede with worldly problems. Daily rituals may include meditation and bathing; bathing the images; offering food, flowers, and lighted lamps for the images; and reciting mantras in Ardhamagadhi, an ancient language of northeast India related to Sanskrit.

Jainism express non violence in thought, word and action. Sikhism seeks peace; when all other means have been exhausted then they find it justifiable to draw the sword against oppression and injustice. Jains believe a peaceful way can always be found, perhaps sometimes after tremendous effort. War or violence against humans or animals is never justified.

Karma and Salvation

Both Jains and Sikhs believe in the Karma Theory and re-incarnation of the soul. Salvation for a Sikh is attained through the Divine Grace and Will of Waheguru (God) and through good deeds in one's life and the selfless service of Sewa and charity. Jains too believe in personal effort and aims and do not depend on a heavenly being for assistance. Both believe in the conquest of the mind through control of the passions through the five senses as the path to ending the cycle of sufferance of birth and death.

●●

12

Christianity and Islam

The historical interaction between **Christianity and Islam**, in the field of comparative religion, connects fundamental ideas in Islam with similar ones in Christianity. Islam and Christianity share their origins in the Abrahamic tradition, as does Judaism. Islam accepts many aspects of Christianity as part of its faith - sometimes with differences in interpretation - but rejects other aspects.

Islamic Views on Jesus

Islam teaches that Jesus (Isa) was one of the most important prophets, but Muslims do not believe that he was the Son of God, nor that he is divine or part of a triune God as Christians believe. According to Muslims, Jesus was a human prophet who brought to mankind a closer relationship with God and each other. Muslims believe that Jesus was miraculously born of the Virgin Mary, but disagree on the nature of Jesus' paternity in relation to the conception. Muslims believe the creation of Jesus was like the creation of Adam, they were both created by God without human fathers, but neither are seen as being the "sons of God" in the literal sense.

Islam and Christianity differ in their fundamental views in regard to the crucifixion and resurrection. Christians believe that Jesus was condemned to death by the Sanhedrin and the Roman prefect Pontius Pilate, physically crucified and resurrected. Muslims believe that Jesus was condemned to crucifixion and then miraculously saved:

> "That they rejected Faith; that they uttered against Mary a grave false charge; That they said in boast, "We killed Jesus the son of Mary, the Messenger of Allah";- but they killed him not, nor crucified him, but so it was made to appear to them, and those who differ therein are full of doubts, with no certain knowledge, but only conjecture to follow, for of a surety they killed him not:- Nay, Allah raised him up unto Himself; and Allah is Exalted in Power, Wise"

Other Christian terms are also present in Islam, although their meanings are not always the same. These include the Second Coming, Antichrist and The Beast.

As Abrahamic Religions

Christianity, Islam and Judaism are known as Abrahamic religions because of their common origin through Abraham. Muslims consider Ishmael, the firstborn son of Abraham, to be the "Father of the Arabs" and Abraham's second son, Isaac, is called "Father of the Hebrews". The story of Abraham and his sons is told in the Book of Genesis.

Ishmael is considered to be the ancestor of the Islamic prophet Muhammad.

Muslims commonly refer to Christians and Jews as "People of the Book" (called dhimmi in post-classical period), people who follow the same general teachings in relation to the worship of the One God as known by Abraham.

The Catechism of the Catholic Church, the official doctrine document released by the Roman Catholic church, has this to say regarding Muslims:

> "The Church's relationship with the Muslims: The plan of salvation also includes those who acknowledge the Creator, in the first place amongst whom are the Muslims; these profess to hold the faith of Abraham, and together

with us they adore the one, merciful God, mankind's judge on the last day (apocalypse)." (CCC 841).

Similarities between the Bible and the Qur'an

The Qur'an contains many references to people and events that are mentioned in the Bible; that Jesus was given the *Injil* (Greek *evangel,* or *Gospel*) from the Abrahamic God (*Allah* in Arabic). Traditionally, Muslims have believed that parts of these teachings were eventually lost or distorted to produce what is now the Hebrew Bible and the Christian New Testament.

Christians, with exception, generally agree that the Pentateuch (*Torah*) is the original work of Moses but has been modified in translation, tranliteration or transcription to include more recent names of places and similar insubstantial alterations. Jesus relies on specifc statements in the Pentateuch and claims them as authored by Moses, which gives credence to the claim that Moses was at least the originator of the substance of the Pentateuch if indeed he did not write the currently accepted text word-for-word.

In stark contrast to the Muslim position Christians do not credit all the Psalms to David, indeed a common view is that only half of the psalms were created by David:

> "While almost half of the psalms are credited to David, at least one was written 500 years after his birth. A number of poets and writers contributed, and about a third of the psalms are completely anonymous."

The Bible on Islam

The Bible was written hundreds of years before Muhammad was born. Some Muslims have claimed that the Paraclete (comforter, helper) referred to in the Gospel of John is a prophecy of the coming of Mohammed. Islam teaches that the Bible was originally the inspired word of God but that it became corrupted over the centuries.

Some Christians point to Pauline Bible verses such as the following when criticising Mohammed's claim to be a prophet:

> But even if we or an angel from heaven should preach a gospel other than the one we preached to you, let him be eternally condemned! As we have already said, so now I say again: If anybody is preaching to you a gospel other than what you accepted, let him be eternally condemned! (Galatians 1:8)

Another verse in the Christian New Testament that points out major rift between Christianity and Islam is:

> Who is false but he who says that Jesus is not the Christ? He is the Antichrist who has no belief in the Father or the Son.

Islamic Scholars point out that there were many issues between Paul and other early Christians, such as James, the Brother of Jesus.

Early Christian Writers

John of Damascus

In 746 John of Damascus (sometimes St. John of Damascus) wrote the *Fount of Knowledge* part two of which is entitled *Heresies in Epitome: How They Began and Whence They Drew Their Origin.* In this work St.John makes extensive reference to Muhammad's Koran and, in St. Johns's opinion, its failure to live up to even the most basic scrutiny. The work is not exclusively concerned with the *Ishamaelites* (a name for the Muslims as they claimed to have descended from Ishmael) but all heresy. The *Fount of Knowledge* references several suras directly often with apparent incredulity.

> "From that time to the present a false prophet named Mohammed has appeared in their midst. This man, after

having chanced upon the Old and New Testaments and likewise, it seems, having conversed with an Arian monk, devised his own heresy. Then, having insinuated himself into the good graces of the people by a show of seeming piety, he gave out that a certain book had been sent down to him from heaven. He had set down some ridiculous compositions in this book of his and he gave it to them as an object of veneration."

"There are many other extraordinary and quite ridiculous things in this book which he boasts was sent down to him from God. But when we ask: 'And who is there to testify that God gave him the book? And which of the prophets foretold that such a prophet would rise up?'—they are at a loss. And we remark that Moses received the Law on Mount Sinai, with God appearing in the sight of all the people in cloud, and fire, and darkness, and storm. And we say that all the Prophets from Moses on down foretold the coming of Christ and how Christ God (and incarnate Son of God) was to come and to be crucified and die and rise again, and how He was to be the judge of the living and dead. Then, when we say: 'How is it that this prophet of yours did not come in the same way, with others bearing witness to him? And how is it that God did not in your presence present this man with the book to which you refer, even as He gave the Law to Moses, with the people looking on and the mountain smoking, so that you, too, might have certainty?'—they answer that God does as He pleases. 'This,' we say, 'We know, but we are asking how the book came down to your prophet.' Then they reply that the book came down to him while he was asleep."

Theophanes The Confessor

Theophanes Confessor (died c.822) wrote a series of chronicles (284 onwards and 602-813 AD) based initially on those of the better known George Syncellus. Theophanes reports about *Mouamed* thus:

> At the beginning of his advent the misguided Jews thought he was the Messiah But when they saw him eating camel meat, they realized that he was not the one they thought him to be, those wretched men taught him illicit things directed against us, Christians, and remained with him.

Whenever he came to Palestine he consorted with Jews and Christians and sought from them certain scriptural matters. He was also afflicted with epilepsy. When his wife became aware of this, she was greatly distressed, inasmuch as she, a noblewoman, had married a man such as he, who was not only poor, but also an epileptic. He tried deceitfully to placate her by saying, 'I keep seeing a vision of a certain angel called Gabriel, and being unable to bear his sight, I faint and fall down.'

Nicetas

In the work "A history of Christian-Muslim relations" Hugh Goddard mentions both John of Damascus and Theophanes and goes on to consider the relevance of Nicetas of Byzantium who formulated replies to letters on behalf of Emperor Michael III (842-867). Goddard sums up Nicetas view:

> In short, Muhammad was an ignorant charlatan who succeeded by imposture in seducing the ignorant barbarian Arabs into accepting a gross, blaspheming, idolatrous, demoniac religion, which is full of futile errors, intellectual enormities, doctrinal errors and moral aberrations.

Goddard further notes that in Nicetas we can see in his work a knowledge of the whole Koran including an extensive knowledge of suras 2-18. Nicetas account from behind the

Byzantine frontier apparently set a strong precedent for later writing both in tone and points of argument.

The Qur'an on Christianity

The following sura mention Christians and/or Christianity:

> "And do not dispute with the followers of the Book except by what is best, except those of them who act unjustly, and say: We believe in that which has been revealed to us and revealed to you, and our Allah and your Allah is One, and to Him do we submit."

> "And if you are in doubt as to that which We have revealed to Our servant, then produce a chapter like it and call on your witnesses besides Allah if you are truthful."

> "And believe in what I have revealed, verifying that which is with you, and be not the first to deny it, neither take a mean price in exchange for My communications; and Me, Me alone should you fear. And do not mix up the truth with the falsehood, nor hide the truth while you know (it)."

> "Surely those who believe, and those who are Jews, and the Christians, and the Sabians, whoever believes in Allah and the Last day and does good, they shall have their reward from their Lord, and there is no fear for them, nor shall they grieve."

> V.2:89 "And when there came to them (the Jews), a Book (this Qur'ân) from Allâh confirming what is with them [the Taurât (Torah) and the Injeel (Gospel)], although aforetime they had invoked Allâh in order to gain victory over those who disbelieved, then when there came to them that which they had recognised, they disbelieved in it. So let the Curse of Allâh be on disbelievers."

V.2:97 "Say : 'Whoever is an enemy to Jibrael (Gabriel)(let him die in his fury), for indeed he has brought it (this Qur'ân) down to your heart by Allâh's Permission, confirming what came before it [i.e. the Taurât (Torah) and the Injeel (Gospel)] and guidance and glad tidings for the believers.'"

V.2:105 "Neither those who disbelieve among the people of the Scripture (Jews and Christians) nor *Al-Mushrikûn* (the idolaters, polytheists, disbelievers in the Oneness of Allâh, pagans, etc.) like that there should be sent down unto you any good from your Lord. But Allâh chooses for His Mercy whom He wills. And Allâh is the Owner of Great Bounty."

V.2:109 "Many of the people of the Scripture (Jews and Christians) wish that if they could turn you away as disbelievers after you have believed, out of envy from their ownselves, even after the truth has become manifest unto them. But forgive and overlook, till Allâh brings His Command. Verily Allâh is Able to do all things."

V.2:111 "And they say, 'None shall enter Paradise unless he be a Jew or a Christian.' These are their own desires. Say 'Produce your proof if you are truthful.'"

V.2:113 "The Jews said that the Christians follow nothing (i.e. are not on the right religion); and the Christians said that the Jews follow nothing (i.e. are not on the right religion); though they both recite the Scripture. Like unto their word, said (the pagans) who know not. Allâh will judge between them on the Day of the Resurrection about that wherein they have been differing."

V.2:116 "And they (Christians) say: Allâh has begotten a son (children or offspring). Glory be to Him (Exalted be He above all that they associate with Him). Nay, to

Him belongs all that is in the heavens and on earth, and all surrender with obedience (in worship) to Him."

V.2:120 "Never will the Jews nor the Christians be pleased with you till you follow their religion. Say: 'Verily, the Guidance of Allâh (i.e. Islamic Monotheism) that is the (only) Guidance. And if you were to follow their (Jews and Christians) desires after what you have received of Knowledge (i.e. the Qur'ân), then you would have against Allâh neither any *Walî* (protector or guardian) nor any helper."

V.2:135 "And they say, 'Be Jews or Christians, then you will be guided.' Say, 'Nay (we follow) only the religion of Ibrâhîm (Abraham), *Hanîfa* [Islamic Monotheism, i.e. to worship none but Allâh (Alone)], and he was not of *Al-Mushrikûn* (those who worshiped others along with Allâh – see V.2:105).'"

V.2:139 "Say, 'Dispute you with us about Allâh while He is our Lord and your Lord? And we are to be rewarded for our deeds and you for your deeds. And we are sincere to Him [in worship and obedience (i.e. we worship Him Alone and none else, and we obey His Orders)].'"

V.2:140 "Or say you that Ibrâhîm (Abraham), Ismâ'îl (Ishmael), Ishâq (Isaac), Ya'qûb (Jacob) and *Al-Asbât* [the offspring of the twelve sons of Ya'qûb (Jacob)] were Jews or Christians? Say, 'Do you know better or does Allâh (know better...that they all were Muslims)? And who is more unjust than he who conceals the testimony he has from Allâh? And Allâh is not unaware of what you do.'"

V.2:144 "Verily! We have seen the turning of your face towards the heaven. Surely, We shall turn you to a *Qiblah* (prayer direction) that shall please you, so turn your face in the direction of *Al-Masjid-Al-Harâm* (at Makkah). And wheresoever you people are, turn your faces (in prayer) in that direction. Certainly, the people who were given the Scripture (i.e. Jews and the Christians) know well that, that (your turning towards the direction of the *Ka'bah* at Makkah in prayers) is the truth from their Lord. And Allâh is not unaware of what they do."

V.2:145 "And even if you were to bring to the people of the Scripture (Jews and Christians) all the *Ayât* (proofs, evidences, verses, lessons, signs, revelations, etc.) they would not follow your *Qiblah* (prayer direction), nor are you going to follow their *Qiblah* (prayer direction). And they will not follow each other's *Qiblah* (prayer direction). Verily, if you follow their desires after that which you have received of knowledge (from Allâh), then indeed you will be one of the *Zâlimûn* (polytheists, wrong-doers)."

V.2:253 "Those Messengers! We preferred some of them to others; to some of them Allâh spoke (directly); others He raised to degrees (of honour); and to 'Îsâ (Jesus), the son of Maryam (Mary), We gave clear proofs and evidences, and supported him with *Rûh-ul-Qudus* [Jibrael (Gabriel)]. If Allâh had willed, succeeding generations would not have fought against each other, after clear Verses of Allâh had come to them, but they differed – some of them believed and others disbelieved. If Allâh had willed, they would not have fought against one another, but Allâh does what He likes."

"...now that a Book confirming their own has come to them from God, they deny it...they reply: 'We believe in what was revealed to us.' But they deny what has since been revealed, although it is truth...Say: 'Whoever is an enemy of Gabriel' (who has by God's grace revealed to you [Muhammad] the Koran as a guide...confirming previous scriptures)..will surely find that God is the enemy of the unbelievers.'...And now that an apostle has come to them from God confirming their own Scriptures, some of those to whom the Scriptures were given cast off the Book of God behind their backs...The unbelievers among the People of the Book, and the pagans, resent that any blessings should have been sent down to you from your Lord. " (Surah 2:88-, 98-, 103)

"Believers, do not make friends with any but your own people...They desire nothing but your ruin....You believe in the entire Book...When they meet you they say: 'We, too, are believers.' But when alone, they bite their finger-tips with rage." (Surah 3:118, 119)

"To those that declare: 'God has commanded us to believe no apostle unless he brings down fire to consume an offering,' say: 'Other apostles before me [Muhammad] have come to you with veritable signs and worked the miracle you asked for...If they reject you [Muhammad], other apostles have been rejected before you..." (Surah 3:183-)

"The Jews and Christians say: 'We are the children of God and His loved ones.' Say: 'Why then does He punish you for your sins?" (Surah 5:18)

"The God will say: 'Jesus, son of Mary, did you ever say to mankind 'Worship me and my mother as gods besides God?' 'Glory to You, 'he will answer, 'how could I ever say that to which I have no right?" (Surah 5:114-)

"O you who believe! the idolaters are nothing but unclean, so they shall not approach the Sacred Mosque after this year; and if you fear poverty then Allah will enrich you out of His grace if He please; surely Allah is Knowing Wise. Fight those who do not believe in Allah, nor in the latter day, nor do they prohibit what Allah and His Messenger have prohibited, nor follow the religion of truth, out of those who have been given the Book, until they pay the tax in acknowledgment of superiority and they are in a state of subjection. And the Jews say: Uzair is the son of Allah; and the Christians say: The Messiah is the son of Allah; these are the words of their mouths; they imitate the saying of those who disbelieved before; may Allah destroy them; how they are turned away! They have taken their doctors of law and their monks for lords besides Allah, and (also) the Messiah son of Marium and they were enjoined that they should serve one Allah only, there is no god but He; far from His glory be what they set up (with Him). They desire to put out the light of Allah with their mouths, and Allah will not consent save to perfect His light, though the unbelievers are averse. He it is Who sent His Messenger with guidance and the religion of truth, that He might cause it to prevail over all religions, though the polytheists may be averse."

"And say: (All) praise is due to Allah, Who has not taken a son and Who has not a partner in the kingdom, and Who has not a helper to save Him from disgrace; and proclaim His greatness magnifying (Him)."

"'How shall I bear a child,' she [Mary] answered, 'when I am a virgin...?' 'Such is the will of the Lord,' he replied. 'That is no difficult thing for Him...God forbid that He [God[Himself should beget a son!...Those who say: 'The Lord of Mercy has begotten a son,' preach a monstrous falsehood..." (Surah 19:12-, 29-, 88)

Artistic Influences

Islamic influences on Christian art show multi-faceted contributions of Islamic art and culture in the achievements of Christian art. Most Christian arts have received such influence, from religious architecture to religious painting.

Islam and Protestantism

Islam and Protestantism entered into contact during the 16th century, at a time when Protestant movements in northern Europe coincided with the expansion of the Ottoman Empire in southern Europe. As both were in conflict with the Catholic Holy Roman Empire, numerous exchanges occurred, exploring religious similarities and the possibility of trade and military alliances. Relations became more conflictual in the early modern and modern periods, although recent attempts have been made at rapprochement. In terms of comparative religion, there also interesting similarities such as textual criticism and iconoclasm, as well as differences, in both religious approaches.

Nostra Aetate

The question of Islam was not on the agenda when Nostra Aetate was first drafted, or even at the opening the Second Vatican Council. However, as in the case of the question of Judaism, several events again came together to prompt consideration of Islam.

By the time of the Second Session of the Council in 1963 reservations began to be raised by bishops of the Middle East about the inclusion of this question. The position was taken that either the question not be raised at all, or if it were raised then some mention of the Muslims be made. Melkite patriarch Maximos IV was among those pushing for this latter position.

Early in 1964 Cardinal Bea notified Cardinal Cicognani, President of the Council's Coordinating Commission, that the Council fathers wanted the Council to say something about the great monotheistic religions, and in particular about Islam. The subject, however, was deemed to be outside the competence of Bea's Secretariat for the Promotion of Christian Unity

Bea expressed willingness to "select some competent people and with them to draw up a draft" to be presented to the Coordinating Commission. At a meeting of the Coordinating Commission on 16-17 April Cicognani acknowledged that it would be necessary to speak of the Muslims."

The period between the first and second sessions saw the change of pontifiate to Pope Paul VI, who had been a member of the circle (the *Badaliya*) of the Islamologist Louis Massignon. Pope Paul VI chose to follow the path recommended by Maximos IV and he therefore established commissions to introduce what would become paragraphs on the Muslims in two different documents, one of them being Nostra Aetate, paragraph three, the other being Lumen Gentium, paragraph 16.

The text of the final draft bore traces of Massignon's influence. The reference to Mary, for example, resulted from the intervention of Mgr. Descuffi, the Latin archbishop of Smyrna with whom Massignon collaborated in reviving the cult of Mary at Smyrna. The commendation of Muslim prayer may reflect the influence of the Badaliya.

In Lumen Gentium, the Second Vatican Council also declares that the plan of salvation also includes Muslims, due to their professed monotheism.

●●

13
Legal Status of Jainism

Jainism is considered as a legally distinct religion in India. Many others consider it a reformist movement that is a part or sub-sect of Hinduism, historically and legally. The Supreme Court of India has made several pronouncement on the question, most recently observing that Jainism is "indisputably is not a part of Hindu Religion". The question is politically charged because the Jains if recognised as a religious minority would be eligible for a series of benefits granted to minority groups by the Constitution of India. Since India became a Republic in 1950, the Constitution has brought the various social contracts such as marriage and inheritance of all Jains fully under the purview of Hindu Laws, a status that remains unchanged today. . The Union of India does not accord Jains, Buddhists and Sikhs the status of a religious minority even as some States have passed judgments pronouncing such a status at the state level.

Most scholars have come to view Jainism an independent phenomenon having non-Vedic origins. J. L. Jaini sums up this view as follows :

> "As to Jainas being Hindu dissenters, and, therefore governable by Hindu law, we are not told this date of secession Jainism certainly has a longer history than is consistent with its being a creed of dissenters from Hinduism."

Dr. Prof. Padmanabh Jaini further states that Jainas themselves have no memory of a time when they fell within the Vedic fold. Any theory that attempts to link the two traditions, moreover fails to appreciate rather distinctive and very non-Vedic character of Jaina cosmology, soul theory, karmic doctrine and atheism.

History of Jain Demand for Minority Status

- The Jain demand for minority status is almost a century old, when in British India the Viceroy and Governor General of India, Lord Minto took a decision in principle of giving representation to important minorities in the Central Legislature. Seth Manek Chand Hirachand from Mumbai, an eminent Jain leader from Mumbai and the then Acting President of the Bharatvarshiya Digamber Jain Subha made an appeal in 1909 to the Governor General for the inclusion of the Jain community for representation in the Council. Seth Manek Chand's petition was transferred to the Government of Bombay and the Secretary to the Government of Bombay stated in his reply dated 15th oct.1909 as under.

  "I am directed to inform you that a number of seats have been reserved for representation of minorities by nomination and that in allotting them, the claim of the important Jain Community will receive full consideration. "

- In a Memorandum by the Representative of the Jain Community to the Constituent Assembly in March/ April 1947 a strong appeal was made for the inclusion of the Jain community as a minority religious community.

- In his speech on 3rd Sept.1949, Jawahar Lal Nehru said: No doubt India has a vast majority of Hindus, but they could not forget in fact there are also minorities Mustions, Christians, Parsis and Jains. If India were understood as Hindu Rashtra it meant that the minorities were not cent per cent citizens of the country:

- Jainism is mentioned as a religion along with Buddhism and Sikhism in explanation II of the Article 25 of the India Constitution relating to Fundamental Right to religions freedom. On this issue Jawahar Lal Nehru, the then prime Minister, in his letter dated 31.01.1950 assured a Jain Deputation that they need not have any misgivings on this clear constitutional position.

- The second stanza of Jana Gana Mana, Indian National Anthem clearly enunciates Jainism as a separate religious denomination in line with Hinduism, Islam and other religions.

Recommendation of National Minorities Commission

The National Minorities Commission arrived at their recommendation that the Jain community be declared as a minority religious community. It was in consideration of the following:

- the relevant constitutional provisions,

- various judicial pronouncements,

- the fundamental differences in philosophy and beliefs (theism vs.atheism principally) vis-a-vis Hinduism, and

- the substantial number of Jain population in the country.

It resolved to recommend to the Government of India that the Jains deserve to be recognised as a distinct religious minority, and that, therefore the Government of India may consider including them in the listing of "Minorities."

The Bal Patil Judgement

In 2005, the Supreme Court of India declined to issue a writ of Mandamus towards granting Jains the status of a religious minority throughout India. The Court however left it to the respective states to decide on the minority status of Jain religion.

In one of the observations of the Supreme Court, not forming part of the judgment, the Court said:

> "Thus, 'Hinduism' can be called a general religion and common faith of India whereas 'Jainism' is a special religion formed on the basis of quintessence of Hindu religion. Jainism places greater emphasis on non-violence ('Ahimsa') and compassion ('Karuna'). Their only difference from Hindus is that Jains do not believe in any creator like God but worship only the perfect human-being whom they called Tirthankar. Lord Mahavir was one in the generation of Thirthankars. The Tirathankars are embodiments of perfect human-beings who have achieved human excellence at mental and physical levels. In philosophical sense, Jainism is a reformist movement amongst Hindus like Brahamsamajis, Aryasamajis and Lingayats. The three main principles of Jainism are Ahimsa, Anekantvad and Aparigrah."

The Supreme Court also noted: " ... that the State Governments of Chhatisgarh, Maharashtra, Madhya Pradesh, Uttar Pradesh and Uttarakhand have already notified Jains as 'minority' in accordance with the provisions of the respective State Minority Commissions Act."

This cast a doubt on the independent standing of Jain religion. Scholars in the Jain tradition, as well as several groups amongst the Jain community protested, and emphasised that Jain religion stands as a religion in its own right. While Hinduism as a mode of living, and as a culture is to be found across various religions in India because of several common customs, traditions and practices, but as religions Hindu religion and Jain religion are distinct.

U.P. Basic Shiksha Parishad Judgment

In 2006, the Supreme Court opined that "Jain Religion is indisputably is not a part of Hindu Religion".

Illustrations noted by the Supreme Court

Jainism and Other Religions: Illustrations noted by Supreme Court of India in the U.P. Basic Shiksha Parishad Judgment (the para numbers refer to the paragraphs in the Judgment):

Jawaharlal Nehru

10.1 On September 3, 1949, while addressing a public meeting at Allahabad, the first Prime Minister of India, Shri Jawaharlal Nehru said:

> "No doubt India has a vast majority of Hindus, but they could not forget the fact that there were also minorities - Muslims, Parsis, Christians, Sikhs and Jains. If India was understood as a Hindu Rashtra, it meant that the minorities were not cent percent citizens of this country."

The said speech can be considered as a clarification on Article 25 of the Constitution of India.

10.2 On January 31, 1950, the PPS to the then Prime Minister of India sent a letter to the Jain Deputation on behalf of the then Prime Minister, which reads as under:

> "With reference to the deputation of certain representatives of the Jains, who met the Prime Minister on the 25 January, 1950, I am desired to say that there is no cause whatever for the Jains to have any apprehensions regarding the future of their religion and

community. Your deputation drew attention to Article 25, explanation II of the Constitution. This explanation only lays down a rule of construction for the limited purpose of the provision in the article and as you will notice, it mentions not only of Jains but also Buddhists and the Sikhs. It is clear therefore, there is no reason for thinking that Jains are considered as Hindus. It is true that Jains in some ways closely linked to Hindus and have many customs in common, but there can be no doubt that they are a distinct religious community and constitution does not in any way affect this well recognised position.

Yours faithfully,

Sd.

A.V. Pai

Principal Private Secretary to the Prime Minister"

10.5 Jawaharlal Nehru, in his book *Discovery of India*, mentioned as under:

"Buddhism and Jainism were certainly not Hinduism or even the Vedic Dharma. Yet they arose in India and were integral parts of Indian life, culture and philosophy. A Buddhist or Jain, in India, is a hundred per cent product of Indian thought and culture, yet neither is a Hindu by faith. It is, therefore, entirely misleading to refer to Indian culture as Hindu culture."

Dr. S. Radhakrishnan

10.3 Dr. S. Radhakrishnan, the former President of India, in his book "Indian Philosophy Vol I" mentioned as under:

"The Bhagawat Purana endorses the view that Rishbhadeva was the founder of Jainism. There is evidence to show that so far back as the first century B.C. there were people who were worshipping Rishabhadeva, the first Tirthankara. There is no doubt that Jainism prevailed even before Vardhamana Mahaveera or Parsvanatha. The Yajurveda mentions the names of three Tirthankaras-Rishab, Ajitnath & Aristanemi."

15. Dr. Radhakrishnan, who edited the 6th Volume of The Cultural Heritage of India, mentioned as under:

"The Jains claim a great antiquity for their religion. Their earliest prophet was Rishabhdeva. Who is mentioned even in the Vishnu and Bhagawat Puranas as belonging to a very remote past. In the earliest Brahmanic literature are found traces of the existence of a religious Order."

"Freedom of Religion Bill" Controversy in Gujarat

The **Freedom of Religion Bill** was a controversial bill passed by the Gujarat state assembly. The bill was passed in 2003. An amendment to the bill was passed on September 19, 2006 which banned the forced conversion from one religion to another. The Anti-Conversion Act passed earlier was not clear on what forced conversion meant and to whom should it apply. Under the amendment Bill, a person need not seek permission in case he/she is converting from one sect to another of the same religion. It clubbed Jainism and Buddhism as denominations of Hinduism, like Shia and Sunnis are of Islam or Catholicism and Protestantism of Christianity. The move evoked strong protests from the state's Jain, Buddhist and Christian communities. The National commission for minorities also criticised the Gujarat Assembly's decision to club Jainism and Buddhism with Hinduism terming it to be in contravention of its October 23, 1993, notification classifying Buddhists as a "minority community."

Ultimately on 31 July 2007, finding it not in conformity with the concept of freedom of religion as embodied in Article 25 (1) of the Constitution, Governor Nawal Kishore Sharma returned back the Gujarat Freedom of Religion (Amendment) Bill, 2006. The Governor held that Jainism and Buddhism are recognised as religions rather than denominations of Hinduism, something that the Amendment Bill sought to wrongly convey. A press release issued by Raj Bhawan, said "the proposed amendment would amount to withdrawing the protection against forceful or inappropriate religious conversions, particularly in case of Jains and Buddhists". The release cited large scale protests from different religious and social organisations, especially from the Jain and Christian communities, in indicating toward the unacceptability of the proposed amendment.

Chronological Order of various Court Judgments on Jainism as a Separate Religion

1. 1927 - As early as 1927 Madras High Court in Gateppa v. Eramma and others reported in AIR 1927 Madras 228 held that "Jainism as a distinct religion was flourishing several centuries before Christ". Jainism rejects the authority of the Vedas which form the bedrock of Hinduism and denies the efficacy of the various ceremonies which Hindus consider essential.

2. 1939 - In Hirachand Gangji v. Rowji Sojpal reported in AIR 1939 Bombay 377, it was observed that "Jainism prevailed in this country long before Brahmanism came into existence and held that field, and it is wrong to think that the Jains were originally Hindus and were subsequently converted into Jainism."

3. 1951 - A Division Bench of the Bombay High Court consisting of Chief Justice Chagla and Justice Gajendragadkar in respect of Bombay Harijan Temple

Entry Act, 1947 (C.A. 91 of 1951) held that Jains have an independent religious entity and are different from Hindus.

4. 1954 - In The Commissioner Hindu Religious Endowments, Madras v. Sri Lakshmindra Thirtha Swamiar of Sri Shirur Mutt reported in AIR 1954 SC 282 this Court observed that there are well known religions in India like Buddhism and Jainism which do not believe in God, in any Intelligent First Cause. The Court recognised that Jainism and Buddhism are equally two distinct religions professed in India in contrast with Vedic religion.

5. 1958 - In well known Kerala Education Bill's case, 1957 reported in AIR 1958 SC 956, this Court held that to claim the minority rights, the Community must be numerically a minority by reference to the entire population of the State or country where the law is applicable. In that way also, the Jain Community is eligible for the claim.

6. 1968 - In Commissioner of Wealth Tax, West Bengal v. Smt. Champa Kumari Singhi & Others reported in AIR 1968 Calcutta 74, a Division Bench of the Calcutta High Court observed that "Jains rejected the authority of the Vedas which forms the bedrock of Hinduism and denied the efficacy of various ceremonies which the Hindus consider essential. It will require too much of boldness to hold that the Jains, dissenters from Hinduism, are Hindus, even though they disown the authority of the Vedas".

7. 1976 - In Arya Samaj Education Trust, Delhi & Others v. The Director of Education, Delhi Administration, Delhi & Others reported in AIR 1976 Delhi 207, it was held as follows: "Not only the Constitution but also

the Hindu Code and the Census Reports have recognised Jains to belong to a separate religion." In the said judgment, the Court referred to the observations of various scholars in this behalf. The Court quoted Heinrich Zimmer in "Philosophies of India" wherein he stated that "Jainism denies the authority of the Vedas and the orthodox traditions of Hinduism. Therefore, it is reckoned as a heterodox Indian religion". The Court also quoted J. N. Farquhar in "Modern Religious Movements in India" wherein he stated that "Jainism has been a rival of Hinduism from the beginning". In the said judgment, in conclusion, the Court held that "for the purpose of Article 30(1), the Jains are a minority based on religion in the Union Territory of Delhi".

8. 1993 - In A.M. Jain College v. Government of Tamil Nadu (1993) 1 MLJ 140, the Court observed that it is also an admitted fact that the Jain community in Madras, Tamil Nadu is a religious and linguistic minority.

TAMIL JAIN

Tamil Jains or **Samanar** are Tamil people from the Indian state of Tamil Nadu who practice Jainism/Samanam. They are a micro community of around 85,000 in number (Around 0.13% of population of Tamil Nadu). Tamil Jains belong to the Jain Digambara sect, who speak Tamil in their homes. Jainism is called Samanam in Tamil and the practitioners of the religion are called Samanar. They are mostly scattered in Northern Tamil Nadu, mostly in the districts of Chennai, Villupuram, Kancheepuram, Vellore, Tiruvannamalai, Cuddalore and Thanjavur. Their mother tongue is Tamil. They are not to be confused with the other Jains who have settled in Tamilnadu in the past century, who speak Hindi, Marwari, Gujarati or other languages.

Not many people (even within Tamilnadu)in India know that Jains are indigenous Tamil population. Although there are a number of Jain families who have migrated from the North India that live in Tamilnadu (especially in and around Chennai), the indigenous Tamil Jains have lived here for thousands of years.

Samanars or Tamil Jains have a legacy that is more than 2,000 years old. Early Tamil Brahmi Jain inscription in Tamilnadu are dated back to 3rd century BCE. Many of the rich Tamil literature works were written by Samanars, such as Civaka Cintamani. Three of the Five great Epics (Aim-perum-Kaapiyangal) in Tamil literature is attributed to Samanars.

Origin of Jainism in Tamil Nadu

Some scholars feel that Jain philosophy must have entered South India same time in 3rd century. Literary sources and inscription have it the Shruthakevali Bhadrabahu came over to Shravanabelagola with a 12000 strong relinue of Jain sages when north India found it hard to negotiate with the 12 year long famine in the reign of Chandragupta Maurya. Even Chandragupta accompanied this constellation of sages. On reaching Shravanabelagola, Bhadrabahu felt his end approaching he decided stay back along with Chandragupta and he instructed the Jain saints to tour over the Chola and Pandiya domins. This information found in an inscription belonging to 6 Th or 7 Th centuries A.D, at Chandragiri (Shravanbelagula).

But according to some other scholars Jainism must have existed in south India well before the visit of Bhadrabhu and Chandragupta. This deduction based on the following particulars:

- o Bharabahu would not have a big retinue if had no idea of Janis living in the southern parts of Karnataka and Tamilnadu.

- The Buddhist composition 'Mahavamsa' composed during the reign of Dhatusena (461-479) describes the period between 5432 and 3012. It gives elaborate description of the capital of Anuradhapura while king Pandugabhaya was on throne. While giving a details list of building in the new capital, it says that a building called 'Giri' was constructed soly for Digambar Jain saints and that many Digambar sages lived there.
- Arahanthar Mandir existed on mount Udayagiri eve before Kharvela's time. Kharavela's inscription refers to this. Jainism had been the state religion for centuries in Kharavela's time. Andhra was then part of Kalinga. Hence it possible that Jainism entered Andhra at the time of Lord Mahaveera. It must have moved over to Tamil Nadu. The Pashanothkeerna inscription and idols in arcot substantiate this. Jainism might have proceeded further to south Tamil Nadu and crossed over to Srilanka between the 5th and 4th century B.C.
- Ammanan (a naked man) is also another significant term used in Tamil literature for a Nigantha.

So whether Samanam spread from further North to Tamilnadu remains unclear.

History

Exact origins of Jainism in ancient Tamil land is not clear. However Jains have been known to have existed and flourished in Tamil Nadu at least as early as 3rd century BCE. Tamil Jaina tradition however places their origins are much earlier. Ramayana, an Hindu literature mentions that Lord Rama paid homage to Jaina monks living in South India on his way to Sri Lanka. Some scholars believe that the author of the oldest extant work of literature in Tamil (3rd century BCE), Tholkappiyam, was a Jain.

According to Prof. George Hart, who holds the endowed Chair in Tamil Studies by University of California, Berkeley, has written that the legend of Tamil Sangam (literary assembly) was based on the Jain assembly (Sangham) at Madurai:

> "There was a permanent Jaina assembly called a Sagha established about 604 A.D. in Maturai.It seems likely that this assembly was the model upon which tradition fabricated the cangkam legend."

Jainism in the region started to decline around the 5th century CE with many Tamil kings embracing Hindu religions, especially Saivism. Moreover, since the Chalukyas embraced Jainism the Pallava and Pandya kings started to see Jainism as a foreign philosophy. With the advent of Bhakthi poetry which were much closer to the lifestyle of the Tamil people at that time, Tamil Jain literature (along with its Buddhist counterpart) started to seem distanced to Tamil.

Presence

Tamil Jain families are found in the Chennai, Thiruvallur, Kancheepuram, Villupuram, Cuddalore, Vellore, Thiruvannamalai and Thanjavur districts of Tamil Nadu. One can find Jain temples constructed in Dravidian style in these areas. In many of these temples daily worship takes place.

Religion, Sects, Titles, Castes or Lack thereof

Samanars are Tamil Jains who adhere to the Digamabara form of Jainism. They believe in Ahimsa, Satya and Asceticism. Unlike other religions, there is no **"God"** in Jainism. Instead Jains believe in "Jivan" the divine or pure soul. Although Mahavira is commonly attributed as the founder of Jainism, Jainism was present many centuries before Mahavira. Mahavira is the 24th or the last Tirthankara. Jainism complements and was a contemprory of Ajivika philosophy.

The Thirthankara (enlightened souls) are the guides, inspiration and model for the path to ascetic life and moksha. Although the philosophy of Jainism is non-theistic, more Jains worship the Thirthankaras, increasingly Amman, along with Ganesha and also other Hindu Gods. All Samanars are of the Digambara sect. Tamil Jains or Samanars use various titles such as Udayar in Gingee, Iyer in Kancheepuram, Mudaliars in Tanjavur and Chettiars in the Kumbakonam area. Another common title is Nainar. These are merely titles given to Samanars living in those regions and are not actual caste within Samanam. Samanam in Tamil denotes the Digamabara sect within the Jain religion and there is no sub-division under it. The Samanars today have ended up calling themselves with these titles and also as Nainars. Samanars are strict followers of Ahimsa (Non-Violence) and hence purely vegetarians. They consider it a grave sin to hurt or kill a living being for any reason. During the period of "Samanar Kazhuvetrum" akin to crucifixion (7th century AD), many Samanars had been killed and persecuted. The Samanar motto is **"Vaazhu Vaazha Vidu"**, translated as **"Live and Let Live"**.

Lifestyle

The occupation of the majority of the Tamil Jain families is agriculture. Many are teachers. A considerable number of them are settled in urban areas, they are employed in public and private sectors. A small population has settled overseas (US, Canada, UK, Australia and other places).

Identity

Tamil Jains are well assimilated in Tamil society without any outward differentiation. Their physical features are similar to any Tamilians (tamil people). Apart from certain religious adherences, practices and vegetarianism, their culture is similar to the rest of Tamil Nadu. However, they name their children by the names of Tirthankaras, characters of Jaina literature.

Some of the examples are Appandai nathan,Appandai Raj, Aadhi Doss, Athirajan, Parsuvanathan, Aadhiraj, Virushabadoss, Ajitha Doss, Srisanthinathan, Jeeva, Arugan, Aruga Dasan, Sambava Doss, Mahaveeran, Nabirajan, Neminathan, Appandai Rajan, Parsvanathan, Jeevagan, Dhanyakumaran, Sreyankumaran, Sripalan, Seevagan, Bharatha chakravarthi, Jinasenan, Vasavadhattan, Gandharvadhattan, Rajamathi, Padmavathi, Jinapriya, Kemasari, Vijayamathim, Chakraeshwari, Indirakumar etc. Increasingly they also name their children with other common Tamil names. Common pet names being Thambi, Kuzhandhai and Mani, with adjectives periya, nadu and chinna.

The names of Tamil Jains are similar to other Tamilians, but different from other jains around India who have Hindi or other language names.

Religious Head

Bhattaraka Swasti Shri Laxmisena Swamiji of Jina Kanchi Jain Mutt or madam at Mel-Sithamoor (near Tindivanam, Villupuram District) is the religious head of the community. He performs the Upadesam ceremony (similar to Baptism) for Jain children. In the past, this mutt had been the centre for religious study, guiding and helping the economic activities of its members, organising religious discourses, maintenance of temples and such activities. The mutt was able to achieve such multifarious operations with the help and contributions of its members. At present the mutt is also maintaining A Gousala (Cows & others).

The present finance position of the mutt is inadequate for even day-to-day maintenance. Planting of coconut and mango trees has been started to increase the revenue of the fund for the purpose of day-to-day maintenance of the mutt. The car ('Ther') in the mutt requires replacement of wooden wheels.

In additional to the above, a new mutt named Thirumalai Mutt located at Thirumalai near Polur, Tiruvannamalai district, has been functioning from 1999 with the name Dhavalakeerti Swamigal. Now in the mutt more than 100 students are studying from Primary to Higher Secondary school including Jain philosophy with free boarding and lodging. Maintenance of the above is done through contributions from donars.

There were other Samanar religious institutions which had been taken over by the Svetambaras due to the lack of Financial Capacity and interest of Samanars.

Fastings and Other Religious Practices

Full moon days, Chaturdasi (14th day of the fortnight), Ashtami (8th day of the fortnight) are days chosen for fasting and religious observations. Women take food only after reciting the name of a Thirthankara five times. People undertake such practices as a vow for certain period of time - sometimes even for years. On completion, Udhyapana festivals (special prayer services) are performed , religious books and memorabilia are distributed. People who take certain vows eat only after sunrise and before sunset.

Lifetime Ceremonies

Ezhankaapu - On the seventh day of its birth, a new born baby is adorned with bracelets.

Kaathu Kutthal - Ear piercing and adorning child with ear rings - This ceremony is mostly performed in either Aarpakkam temple or Thirunarangkondai i.e. Thirunarungkundram. (Appandai Nathar is name of the deity).

Other Ceremonies

Upadesam - Formal induction into religious practices and adherences is called Upadesam. This is done to both men and women - at around the age of 15 years. After Upadesam, one is supposed to follow religious practices with vigor and seriousness.

Marriage - Outwardly Jain marriages resemble Hindu marriages. However, mantras chanted are of Jaina orientation. There is no brahmin priest, instead there is a samanar temple priest who is called as "Koyil Vaadhiyar(Temple priest)" who conducts the ceremonies.

Pilgrimage - Most Jain people go on pilgrimage to major Jain temples in the North of India - Sammed Sikharji (Tamil: Sanmesagaram, Samaesigaram), Pavapuri, Champapuri, Ujjayantagiri. Also other places in the South India such as in Karanataka, Shravanabelagola (Tamil: Beligulam), Humbaj (Tamil: Ombujam), Simmanagadde and Ponnur Malai in Tamil Nadu.

Funeral rites - Dead are placed on a pyre and incinerated. Ashes are disbursed in water courses and ceremonies are performed on tenth or sixteenth day. Annual remembrance ceremonies similar to Hindu practice are not performed. But no festivities or functions are followed that year on the paternal side.

Festivals

Akshaya trithiyai - a festival in commemoration of the first Thirthankara Rishabadeva partaking food after many long years of penance.

Jinaratri - in commemoration of Shri Rishabadeva attaining moksha.

Mahavir Jayanti - festivity on the day of thirthankara Shri Mahaveera's birth.

Deepavali - in commemoration of Sri Mahavira attaining moksha.

Shruthapanchami - to worship agamas and scriptures

Avani Avittam - in commemoration of emperor Bharatha acknowledging true scholars by giving them the sacred thread.

Saraswati Pooja, Varsha Pirappu and Pongal are the other common festivals celebrated along with other Tamils. Also the festival of Karthikai Deepam at the onset of Kaarthikai month.

TULU JAINS

Tuluva Jains or **Jaina Bunts** are a small community of Tulu speaking people who adhere to Jainism and other philosophies associated with it.The community is mainly concentrated in Tulu Nadu region in the Indian states of Karnataka and Kerala. They were traditionally Feudal Lords,who rarely participated in warfare since they adhere to the philosophy of Ahimsa. For Warfare they were mostly dependent on their cousin Bunts.The Tulu Jains trace their lineage through the Nagavanshi order of Kshatriyas. Many erstwhile royalty in the tulu region like the Chowta dynasty were jains.

The Community Traces its origins to the Landlord Bunts who embraced Jain Traditions during the rule of the Hoysala Kingdom who propagated Jainism. In spite of accepting Jainism they follow almost all Hindu customs of the Bunts.In fact it is hard to distinguish between Tulu Jains And Bunts. Both communities are Matrilineal.Have great faith in the unique Hindu rituals of Bhuta Kola and Nagaradhane. Worship the same pantheon of Hindu gods and goddesses. The only difference between the two communities is that Tulu Jains believe in the teachings of Teerthankara and Bunts do not.

Traditions

- **Jain Traditions :** Tulu Jains are strictly vegetarian and do not consume anything after sunset.They also abstain from eating vegetables grown below the ground. They adhere to the principles of the Digambara sect of Jainism.The Ascetic Gummataraya Bahubali is greatly revered by the Tulu Jains. Statues in his honour have been erected by them at Dharmasthala and Karkala.Many magnificent Jain *Basadi* have been built by the Jains especially in Karkala

- **Aliya Katt:** The most unique feature of Tulu Jains is that they follow Matrilineal inheritance called Aliya Katt in Tulu. This is in sharp contrast to other jain communities. Jains attribute their matrilineality to Bhutala Pandya, a legendary king of unknown antiquity.

- **Bhuta Kola :** Along with Hindu gods and Jain tirthankaras,Tulu Jains worship spirit deities which are of both Puranic and local origins. They spirit deities are seen as protectors. Annual Ritual Dances called Bhuta Kola or Dharma Da Nema is performed in the honour of Them. A spirit deity called **Annappa Panjurli** who is widely revered in the Tulu region is associated with the jains and the Highly revered Dharmasthala Temple which is managed by a Tulu Jain Family called The **Pergades**, the members of which use the title of Heggade. The eldest male member of this family inherits the position of **Dharmadhikari** - the one who dispenses justice on behalf of Lord Manjunatha and Goddess Ammanavaru,the main deities of the temple. The succession to the post of Dharmadikari is according to the Tulu laws of Matrilineality called Aliya Santana Katt.

- **Nagaradhane :** Tulu Jains greatly revere the cobras. They are considered to be sacred creatures and embodiment of Hindu Serpent deities like Ananta, Vasuki, Takshaka etc. These Snake gods are worshipped in sacred groves called Naga Bana. Rituals of Nagaradhane are performed in honour of them.

Surnames

Jainism in South India predates any caste specific divisions. But Tulu Jains are all converts from the elite Community of Bunts. Heggade is one of most common Tulu Jain surnames Other surnames of Jains are *Alva, Ariga, Ajila, Arasa, Konde, Kottary, Pergade* etc which are also found among Bunts. Even Today marriage alliances between Tulu jains And Bunts is not uncommon. Jainism and Hinduism are in harmonious co-existence in the Tulu Nadu region. Because of their Affinity with the Bunts they are also referred to as *Jaina Bunt* In Karnataka, Jains formed 0.78% of the population according to 2001 census. However, majority of Jains in Karnataka today are migrants from North India. The natives Tulu Jains, are a minority even among this population. However, their exact numbers is largely unavailable. It is estimated they are less than 50000 in number.

Prominent Tulu Jains

- Abbakka Rani, Queen of Ullal, Anti European imperialist.
- Dharmadhikari Veerendra Heggade of Dharmasthala.

●●

Index